# PRESIDENTS OF THE U.S.A.

## DENYS COOK

**DAVID & CHARLES**

Newton Abbot  London  North Pomfret (Vt)

**British Library Cataloguing in Publication Data**

Cook, Denys
   Presidents of the USA.
   1. Presidents—United States—Biography.
   I. Title
   973'.099'2       E176.1

ISBN 0-7153-8067-2


Library of Congress Catalog Card Number 80-85497

Typeset by Typesetters (Birmingham) Ltd,
and printed in Great Britain
by Redwood Burn Ltd, Trowbridge and Esher
for David & Charles (Publishers) Limited
Brunel House Newton Abbot Devon


Published in the United States of America
by David & Charles Inc
North Pomfret Vermont 05053 USA

# CONTENTS

# INTRODUCTION

'The executive power shall be vested in a President of the United States' — so opens the momentous Article II of the Constitution of the United States drawn up at Philadelphia by the 'Founding Fathers' in 1787.

The Chief Executive, who was also to be Commander-in-Chief of the Army and Navy, 'and of the Militia of the several States', was to be over 35 and a natural-born citizen of the United States, resident therein for fourteen years. He was to be elected by a complex, indirect process, for four years at a time, and was to receive a moderate salary. He was to swear (or affirm) an oath and could only be removed 'on impeachment for, and conviction of, treason, bribery, or other high crimes and misdemeanours'.

His powers were defined, but to avoid an autocracy he was to be further restricted by a 'separation of powers' and a number of 'checks and balances'. There was to be a physical separation of powers: neither the president nor any member of the administration or cabinet (which, by implication, he was to have) could belong to the legislature or Congress. Bills passed in Congress required the president's assent before they could become laws; if he chose to exercise the power of veto with which he was provided, that, in turn, could be over-ridden by a two-thirds vote in Congress. His scope was further checked by the Senate, without whose 'advice and consent' he could neither make treaties nor key appointments. The judicial branch of government, the United States Supreme Court, could declare legislation to be 'unconstitutional'.

Thus the leaders of a rural and minor country sought to provide their new nation with a head of state who would carry out the will of Congress, 'take care that the laws be faithfully executed', and implement foreign policy. He was intended to be the high servant of the people, a chief magistrate, but not a ruler.

However, presidents managed to escape from the trammels of the office — and soon ceased to be mere chief executives because, whilst closely defined on paper, the office has in fact the elasticity of a rubber glove and everything depends upon the wearer. A president can keep within the narrow constitutional definitions of the office, or he can stretch the provisions enormously. The presidency is what each president is prepared to make of it. 'It's a plan, not a strait jacket,' said Harry S. Truman. 'A president,' said John F. Kennedy, 'must be prepared to exercise the fullest powers of his office — all that are specified and some that are not.' 'The president,' wrote Woodrow Wilson, 'is at liberty, both in law and conscience, to be as big a man as he can.'

The presidency began to be reformed as soon as it went into operation. Not only did George Washington establish precedents but one of the main intentions of the Founding Fathers went by the board. The president had been intended to be a character 'pre-eminent for ability and virtue' (John Adams) and above the hurly-burly of political life. This was thwarted by the advent of party politics and the ideal was realised only in George Washington himself.

The original method of electing the president was designed to combine the maximum of democratic shop-window-dressing with the minimum of popular involvement lest, by popular ballot, a personality should be chosen rather than an able and virtuous character. The electorate in each state (which each state was to determine for itself), was to choose Presidential Electors, who were to be entrusted with the final choice of a president in an Electoral College. With the growth of parties, however, presidential candidates emerged, each with an organised following. Consequently, Electors began to be chosen because they supported specified candidates. With the parallel rapid growth of the popular franchise in America, the Electors rapidly became what they have remained, mere puppets, and the presidential election became a popular election in fact if not in theory. Yet the cumbersome electoral machinery remains.

Every four years on the first Tuesday after the first Monday in November (a public holiday in many states), taverns, hotels and liquor stores are forbidden to sell drinks, and the American electorate goes to the polls to choose a new president, among others. (In 1980 Americans were electing 34 Senators, 435 members of the House of Representatives, plus a number of State Governors and state legislators, as well as countless other officials.) The turn-out is very low by European standards: in 1976, 57.4% voted; in 1932, 52.5%; in 1948 51%. These are typical figures in a country where the total percentage has not exceeded the low sixties in half a century. The explanation is partly that the American voters are called upon to vote very often — at federal, state, county and district level. They are also likely to regard 'local' elections as of far greater importance than the British whose local polling hovers around 40%.

Voters in a presidential election usually record their preference for either the Democratic Electors who will represent their state in the Electoral College or the Republican Electors (or possibly the Electors of one of the many minority parties — in 1932, for example, there were eight, including the Communist party and the Prohibition parties). These Electors have been chosen, state by state, to record, at an official meeting of the Electoral College, the will of the people.

The number of Electors in each state depends upon the size of the state's representation in Congress which, in turn, depends upon its population. Each state is entitled to $2 + x$ Electors, where 2 is its number of Senators (the same for every state irrespective of size), and $x$ is the number of Representatives to which it is entitled in the lower House of Congress in the ratio of one to about every 400,000 people. In 1980, for example, California's total was 45, New York's 41, Georgia's 12, Delaware's 3, whilst Texas had 26.

Following the popular election the rule is that 'the winner takes all' in a first-past-the-post system. If the Democrats win New York — a majority of one would suffice — they can claim the entire slate of 41 Electoral votes allocated to their state. On the first Monday after the second Wednesday in December following election day, the Electors meet in their respective state capitals and formally record their votes, without much drama, since everybody has known since early November who the next president is going to be. (The Electors, incidentally, are under a pledge — rarely violated — to vote for their party's nominee).

The sealed results are then sent to Washington where, on 6 January at high noon, Congress convenes. The vice-president of the United States formally opens the Electors' ballots and announces the result. The next president is whichever candidate has most Electoral votes. If no candidate has a majority, it becomes the constitutional duty of the House of Representatives, where each state has one vote, to choose from among the three leading candidates (as in 1800 and 1824). If no vice-presidential candidate receives a majority in the Electoral College, his election then passes to the Senate, where voting is on an individual basis (as in 1836).

To prevent the nation from reaching Inauguration Day without a president — the disputed election of 1876 was resolved only two days before — additional safeguards have been established by means of constitutional amendments and by Laws of Succession. If the 'president elect' were to die before Inauguration Day, he would be succeeded by the vice-president and, in the event of his death, an order of succession has been established.

This method of electing the president, which was devised in the eighteenth century, has had important, unforeseen consequences. For example, a candidate can poll more popular votes than his opponent (as in 1888), and still lose heavily in the Electoral College. In 1860, Stephen A. Douglas polled 29.4% of the popular vote and Abraham Lincoln 39.9%; Douglas won only 12 Electoral College votes, Lincoln, 180. The crucial issue is whether a candidate can win the states with the largest Electoral Votes — Lincoln won only 18 out of 33 states in 1860, yet Ford won more states than Carter in 1976 — and he can ignore the few votes from the small states. When Nixon became the first candidate to campaign in all 50 states in 1960 he probably contributed to his narrow defeat.

Yet the advantage of the Electoral College system is that it does produce a clear-cut result by the simple expedient of exaggerating even the narrowest popular vote margin (as in 1960), into a respectable Electoral College victory. This can be a valuable boost for a president whose party may have done badly in the parallel, and separate, Congressional elections, even to the extent of losing control over one or both Houses.

When the Chief Justice of the United States administers the oath to the successful candidate at noon on 20 January, this is the culmination of a process that goes back to the days when the candidate first began to be talked of as a presidential aspirant. In election year itself he will have tested his degree of popularity in many of the state 'primary' elections. (These were held in thirty-five states plus Washington DC and Puerto Rico in 1980.) As a result he will have built up a considerable delegate following for his party's national nominating convention held during the summer in one of America's major centres.

At these conventions, which have been described as democratic

10

folk-dances, the major parties choose their presidential candidates. Each state sends Representatives according to numbers agreed at the previous convention. Each delegation, chosen either in a state primary election or a state convention, vies with every other state, to make the most noise in a great jamboree of bands, banners, majorettes, streamers, balloons, hats, posters and slogans. Most delegates come pledged to a particular candidate, at least for the first ballot, and it is possible for a candidate to arrive with the nomination effectively sewn up, as Reagan did at Detroit in 1980; though in 1976 Ford did not become certain of the nomination until the alphabetical voting by states reached West Virginia.

The convention, which lasts four to five days, spends time initially listening to a 'key-note' speech and drafting the party 'platform' before it gets down to the serious business of the presidential nomination. Each state, alphabetically, makes its 'nomination' before the 'roll call' or ballot begins. A simple majority of delegates votes will suffice to secure the nomination and increasingly in recent times only one ballot (during prime viewing time) has been necessary — though in 1924 the Democrats required 103 ballots to choose their candidate.

The winner then makes his acceptance speech which, as in 1932 or 1960, can be memorable and important, before the vice president is formally adopted. It has become customary in the twentieth century for the presidential nominee to have complete control of the choice of his running-mate. He is selected to 'balance the ticket' where the candidate is weakest geographically and politically; and because he can be expected to help win votes in all regions and among all sections of the community during the three to four months of arduous campaigning.

In the absence of any strong third party candidate, the Democratic or Republican convention has, in effect, chosen the next president of the United States, and this goes some way towards providing an answer to a question which is asked, with a complacent air, on this side of the Atlantic. 'Europeans often ask,' wrote James Bryce in 1888, 'how it happens that this great office, the greatest in the world unless we except the Papacy, to which any man can rise by his own merits, is not more frequently filled by great and striking men.'

James Bryce devoted a chapter of his *American Commonwealth* (1888) to this problem. It is entitled, 'Why Great Men Are Not Chosen Presidents'. The method of selection, he believed, in a

11

nation as vast as the United States favours men who are neither too strong nor too positive. Brilliant men tend to make enemies and are not desirable and, unless the party is in a mood of self-destruction (like the Republicans in 1964), it will 'play safe'. Witness the choice of candidates in the 1840s and 1850s when political pygmies were chosen in preference to the *real* leaders of the period, men of the calibre of Henry Clay, John C. Calhoun and Daniel Webster. Some men might also make 'good' presidents but 'bad' candidates, and since it is essential that the party wins the White House and the power that goes with it, this can be another reason for preferring B to A. In addition, argued Bryce, an American president need not have brilliant intellectual gifts, or be a brilliant orator, or capable of devising comprehensive legislation. If he is eloquent, imaginative and profound he will be a better president, but those gifts are not necessary for him to discharge the duties of his post, four-fifths of which are of the same kind as those which devolve upon the manager of a railway company. These require the ability to choose good subordinates and to supervise them. Firmness, common sense and, above all, honesty, were the qualities for the presidency.

Bryce was describing a contemporary situation where America was of little account and there is clearly rather more to be said. First, the ablest people are not always attracted to politics. Certainly in nineteenth-century Europe there was a tradition of public service and of *noblesse oblige*, but in the United States, at that time, industrial development was more attractive than politics, which tended to be left to professionals who were sneered at as 'the politicians' and something of this tradition still remains. Also, national politics in the United States has always been riskier than in other democracies. Senators and Congressmen must be inhabitants of the states they represent, so that the chances of winning a seat are limited, and after an election rebuff a candidate must wait for up to six years before trying again. When it is remembered that Washington, unlike London, is not an attraction in itself; that it is not the financial, cultural or business centre of the nation; that an American politician can be hundreds, if not thousands, of miles from home, family and interests — making it virtually impossible to combine politics with certain careers — it is perhaps not surprising that there has been a dearth of pre-eminent men in politics at the national level.

However, is there any evidence that by some mysterious process of political alchemy the situation in Britain, for example, has been any different? The present writer estimates that between 1789 and 1945 the American and British systems have 'tied' in the number of great men who have also been great political figures. To set against Washington, Jefferson, Jackson, Lincoln, Theodore Roosevelt, Wilson and Franklin D. Roosevelt, Britain, in the same period, can only produce Pitt, Peel, Palmerston, Gladstone, Disraeli, Lloyd George and Winston S. Churchill. If few people have ever heard of Franklin Pierce, how many know of Viscount Goderich? The moral would seem to be that great men are rare in politics anyway: and/or that the method of selection does not bring them to the top, especially if they are strong and positive characters.

Nowhere in Europe is there a position to which the presidency can be compared, though Europeans insist on reading into the American situation their own system of parliaments and parties. The president resembles neither a king nor a prime minister: a sovereign is not a party leader, a prime minister is nothing else. An American president enjoys more authority, if less dignity, than a king. His powers are narrower than a prime minister's, but more secure, because they do not rest upon a parliamentary majority but run until the end of his term. He is not comparable to a French president who has a prime minister and a cabinet, dependent upon a Chamber, who can eclipse him. In short, as an English observer (Harold Laski) noted: 'The President of the United States is both more and less than a king; he is also both more and less than a prime minister. The more carefully his office is studied, the more does its unique character appear.'

The president, though a party leader, does not owe his position to the party which can command a majority in the legislature, as in Britain. Partly because of the staggered system of American elections, his party may not even control Congress throughout his term. The Republicans were in the White House from 1953–61 and from 1969–77; after 1955 they controlled neither House of Congress — and Nixon became the only president to face a Congress controlled by the opposition during both his terms. Even if there is initial control (as in 1953–5 for the Republicans), this can be lost at the next mid-term elections where, traditionally, there is an anti-Administration swing. Though the same party controls the executive and the legislature, this unity can be more apparent than real in such a vast nation where political labels can mean different things in different 'sections'; and where 'liberals' and 'conserva-

13

tives' can be light years apart and where, for instance, Southern Democrats and Northern Democrats have nothing in common.

All this means that a president must practice consensus politics if he is to achieve his aims. 'The President proposes, Congress disposes,' runs the adage and this is particularly true of domestic politics. During the twentieth century, for example, there have been only three relatively brief periods when an administration has overcome constitutional restraints to achieve legislative reform: during the first terms of Woodrow Wilson and Franklin D. Roosevelt and under Lyndon Baines Johnson from 1964–6.

A president can only make recommendations for legislation — which Congress may act upon or ignore. He can address them directly only through his annual 'State of the Union' message, when he outlines policies and makes suggestions. Otherwise, though relations with Congress and its leaders on both sides are vital, they are necessarily informal. In such discussions the president does have some very powerful weapons. He controls a vast amount of patronage — Jimmy Carter found that he had 75 important and some 2,000 less important government posts in his gift. Above all, since he is the only politician elected by the entire nation, he can take strength from the fact that his powers emanate directly from the people in any struggle with the legislature. When it comes to educating that same public opinion he enjoys an unrivalled platform — what Theodore Roosevelt termed a 'bully pulpit' — from which to get his ideas across. But the fact remains that no president can hope to persuade Congress to pass more than a fraction of the legislative programme that he would like to see voted into law.

Is it the case that the president can exercise greater authority in foreign policy? Has the White House become, in fact, a home for the uneasy co-existence of two presidents? Nixon once said: 'I've always thought that this country could run itself domestically without a president. All you need is a competent Cabinet to run the country at home. You need a president for foreign policy.' The Founding Fathers sought to impose careful limitations on a president's powers. He does not have a totally free hand. He cannot declare war and Congress holds the purse strings. He cannot make treaties without the approval of two thirds of the Senate. Yet he has come to play a greater role than the constitution-makers foresaw, as the period from Woodrow Wilson to Nixon demonstrates. He can, by means of messages to Congress and through the media, outline his policies. He can adopt hostile and hectoring tones in diplomatic conversations. He can sever diplomatic relations. Above all, by virtue of his constitutional position as Commander-in-Chief, he can move American forces into troubled areas and effectively involve the United States in undeclared wars. However, there are signs that, in the wake of Vietnam (and Watergate), some Congressional shackles are being relocked. Presidents are increasingly finding less freedom of initiative in the foreign, as in the domestic, sphere.

In the closing years of the twentieth century the essential paradox of the presidency is in fact becoming more and more apparent: namely, that the holder of what is proverbially the world's most powerful office can find it difficult to achieve what he wants to do, is pledged to do and is expected to do. By a strange irony of history he is coming to resemble increasingly the chief magistrate envisioned two centuries ago. Constrained, for example, by Congress, by pressure groups, the energy gap and America's declining global power, he is becoming ever less capable of giving an influential lead either at home or abroad. Failure to appreciate the narrow limits of presidential power, both in theory and in fact, can have very serious repercussions. It is all too easy to belittle a president's efforts and to regard him as incompetent. The thirty-ninth president, for example, whom it became fashionable to disparage, in fact fared no worse than many of his predecessors. He became, in part, the much publicised first victim of a new 'expectation gap'.

# GEORGE WASHINGTON

**Full name**  George Washington, 1732–99
**Born**  Wakefield, Westmoreland County, Virginia, 22 February 1732 (11 February 1731/2 Old Style), the eldest of the 6 children of his father's second marriage
**Parents**  Captain Augustine Washington (1694?–1743), farmer, planter, and his second wife, Mary Ball Washington (1708/9?–43). 4 sons, 2 daughters
**Family lineage**  English
**College**  None. In 1749 Washington received a licence, equivalent to a degree in engineering, from the College of William and Mary, Williamsburg, Virginia
**Married**  1759, Martha Dandridge Custis (1731–1802), widow, with two surviving children, of Colonel Daniel Parke Custis (died 1757), daughter of John Dandridge, planter. No children
**Occupation**  Surveyor, soldier, planter; Commanding General of the Continental Army, 1775–83; subsequently Lieutenant General and Commander-in-Chief of the United States Army, 1798–9
**Religious denomination**  Episcopalian
**Notable relationships**  Washington was descended from two English kings, Henry III and Edward I. Washington and Queen Elizabeth II were second cousins seven times removed. He was a third cousin twice removed of General Robert E. Lee, to whom his stepson's granddaughter, Mary Custis, was married in 1831. Washington and Sir Winston Churchill were eighth cousins six times removed
**Died**  From pneumonia, at Mount Vernon, Virginia, 14 December 1799, aged 67
**Buried**  Mount Vernon, Virginia

**Party**  None/Federalist **State represented** Virginia **Terms of office** 30 April 1789 to 4 March 1797 **Age on taking office 57 Presidential administrations** 1st and 2nd **Congresses** 1st, 2nd, 3rd, 4th

17

138 Presidential Electors from 10 states (North Carolina and Rhode Island had not yet ratified the Constitution; New York had not yet chosen its Electors), cast their ballots in New York, as follows:

George Washington 69 (the maximum possible; each Elector voted for two persons)

John Adams 34 (elected vice president)

10 other candidates shared 35 votes

*Note* The first Presidential Inauguration took place in New York on 30 April 1789.

## PRESIDENTIAL ELECTION 1792

264 Presidential Electors from 15 states cast their ballots as follows:

George Washington 132 (maximum possible)

John Adams 77 (elected vice president)

George Clinton 50

Thomas Jefferson 4

Aaron Burr 1

*Note* The Inauguration took place in Philadelphia on 4 March 1793. Washington delivered the shortest-ever Inaugural Address — 135 words.

## CONGRESS

| | | | |
|---|---|---|---|
| 1789 | 1st | Senate (26) | 17 supporters of the Admin, 9 opponents |
| | | House (64) | 38 supporters of the Admin, 26 opponents |
| 1791 | 2nd | Senate (29) | 16 Fed, 13 Dem Repub |
| | | House (70) | 37 Fed, 33 Dem Repub |
| 1793 | 3rd | Senate (30) | 17 Fed, 13 Dem Repub |
| | | House (105) | 57 Dem Repub, 48 Fed (opposition majority in the House). |
| 1795 | 4th | Senate (32) | 19 Fed, 13 Dem Repub |
| | | House (106) | 54 Fed, 52 Dem Repub |

## NOTES

1 The First Census of 1790 revealed that the population of the United States was 3,929,214 including 697,697 slaves and 59,557 free negroes.

2 New states admitted: Vermont (1791) 14th; Kentucky (1792) 15th; Tennessee (1796) 16th.

3 Constitutional Amendments: 1791, Amendments I-X, the 'Bill of Rights'.

John Adams (1735–1826), subsequently second president. Term of office: 21 April 1789 to 4 March 1797. The United States had a vice president before it had a president: George Washington was not sworn in until 30 April 1789.

---

'First in war, first in peace, and first in the hearts of his country-men', as Henry Lee put it, George Washington was a legend in his own lifetime, a giant amongst men both metaphorically and literally, for he stood six feet two and weighed over two hundred pounds — and he could crack nuts between his fingers.

Born into a planter family, he was raised as a Virginia gentle-man, but he spent much of his life surveying and soldiering in the wilderness. In 1751–2 he paid a visit to Barbados with his half-brother Lawrence. In 1754 as a lieutenant-colonel of Virginia militia he fought in one of the first skirmishes in what grew into the French and Indian War (1754–63). In 1755 as an aide to the British general Edward Braddock, whilst advancing on Fort Duquesne (Pittsburgh), four bullets passed through his coat and two horses were shot from under him.

In 1759 Washington resigned from the army and married a wealthy widow, Martha Dandridge Custis, and until 1775 he lived a placid life at the estate at Mount Vernon which he had inherited from his half-brother Lawrence, and served in the Virginia House of Burgesses. Like fellow planters, he became increasingly incensed by British policy towards the American colonies and moderately, but firmly, voiced his objections. He was elected to the First and Second Continental Congresses at Philadelphia, though, by the time the second one met in May 1775, shots had already been exchanged at Lexington and Concord. Congress now appointed George Washington as Commander-in-Chief of the ill-trained Continental Army assembled at Cambridge, Massachusetts, an appointment which he took up on 3 July 1775.

During the war he emerged as an able commander, if not a brilliant tactician, with great organising ability and fortitude especially during the bleak winter of 1777–8 at Valley Forge. In 1781, with French assistance, he forced the surrender of General

19

Cornwallis at Yorktown; after which the fighting in North America ended, though peace was not concluded until 1783.

The 'Old Fox', the 'American Fabius', now retired to Mount Vernon, but the American nation under its Confederation Government (1781) was on the verge of collapse and Washington was a prime mover in the summoning of the Constitutional Convention at Philadelphia in May 1787. Once the new Constitution had been ratified the Electoral College unanimously elected George Washington to the brand new position of President of the United States, an office which had been framed with him very much in mind, in the hope and the expectation that he would agree to fill it. He was truly indispensable at this time with his already towering prestige having been enhanced by his laying down of quasi-dictatorial authority in 1783. He was the only American capable of commanding the necessary confidence to get the new ship of state off on an even keel: no other contemporary — Benjamin Franklin who was in his eighties, Alexander Hamilton, James Madison, John Adams, or even Thomas Jefferson — could have commanded equal support.

Washington was well aware that his every action 'will serve to establish a precedent . . . (and) it is devoutly wished on my part, that these precedents may be fixed on true principles'. He took a scrupulously constitutional view of his executive position and he was reluctant to wield executive authority alone, but he did prove to be a high-class administrator — who excelled in gathering essential facts, listening to able counsel and then making decisions. He left Congress free to enact legislation without infringing upon its authority except for exploring questions of constitutionality. He chose departmental heads — Alexander Hamilton as Secretary of the Treasury, Thomas Jefferson as Secretary of State and Henry Knox, his former chief of artillery, as Secretary of War — gave them considerable latitude and depended on their advice. In 'Cabinet' meetings (the word was first used in 1793), unless opinion was evenly divided, he followed the recommendations of the majority; but Washington was always the President and all policies required his approval.

He developed the provision of the Constitution that treaties should be made with the 'advice and consent' of the Senate, to mean in practice that presidential negotiations would be followed by the Senate's ratification or rejection. Similarly, it was established that presidential appointees, who had to be approved by the Senate, could be dismissed by the president alone.

He made no major mistakes though he has been accused of being too aristocratic, too monarchical and too disposed towards legislation favouring the wealthy, indeed of becoming a 'Federalist'. His desire to be 'the President of all Americans', was dashed by the growth of political parties led by Alexander Hamilton (the 'Federalists') and Thomas Jefferson, (the 'Democratic Republicans') who resigned from the administration in 1793. By 1795 Washington was appointing to offices only conservative-minded Federalists favourable to the new Constitution. It would have been wrong to have done less and to have handed over political power to the opposition. Perhaps he suppressed the Whisky Rebellion of 1794 with undue force, but he was determined to establish the right of the Federal government to interfere in the internal affairs of the states to maintain law and order. He also suppressed Indian resistance in the North West Territory.

When war broke out in Europe in the 1790s Washington steered a middle course between the ardently pro-French Jefferson and the equally ardently pro-British Hamilton because he believed that the young America needed a twenty-year breathing space. He made treaties with Britain (Jay's Treaty) and Spain. His policy of non-involvement found its clearest expression in his 'Farewell Address' of 1796, his greatest legacy to his country. In it he advocated a policy of isolation, of opposition to what Jefferson later termed 'entangling alliances', so that America could demonstrate to Europe that 'we act for ourselves and not others'. He urged Americans to forswear party spirit and sectional passions. He refused to seek a third term as president and thus created a precedent which endured until the 1940s.

The federal capital was named after the 'Father of the Nation'. New York and Philadelphia had both served in that role but following a compromise between the 'Hamiltonians' and the 'Jeffersonians', it was agreed that by 1800 the federal capital should be a 10 mile square on the banks of the River Potomac, 40 miles southwest of Baltimore, donated by Maryland and Virginia, and selected by Washington.

Washington was the only president not to live in the White House. He selected its site and on 13 October 1792 laid the corner-stone but died before its completion. It is said that a few days before he died he walked through the still unfinished building with his wife. (The architect was an Irishman, James Hoban, who based his $500 prize-winning design on the seat of the Dukes of Leinster near Dublin.) Construction of the Capitol was begun in the following year. Washington laid its cornerstone in September 1793 with Masonic rites.

In 1797 Washington and his 'dear Patsy' — as he called his wife Martha who, as the first 'First Lady', had done so much to establish the formal style of the new republic — went home to their beloved Mount Vernon. Here, in the winter of 1799, George Washington died in his favourite four poster overlooking the Potomac: '. . . Doctor, I die hard but I am not afraid to go.'

The new United States mourned the loss of a parent. Though he was 'possessed of power, and possessed of an extensive influence,' wrote Abigail Adams, the wife of Washington's vice president and successor, John Adams, 'he never used it but for the benefit of his country.' George Washington certainly did the new republic a mighty service by proving that power can ennoble as well as corrupt.

# JOHN ADAMS

**Full name**   John Adams, 1735–1826
**Born**   Braintree (now Quincy) Massachusetts, 30 October 1735 (19 October 1734/5 Old Style). The eldest of 3 sons
**Parents**   John Adams (1691–1761), farmer, shoemaker, and Susanna Boylston Adams (1699–1797). 3 sons
**Family lineage**   English
**College**   Harvard College, Cambridge, Mass, BA 1755, MA 1758
**Married**   1764, Abigail Smith Adams (1744–1818), daughter of William Smith, Congregational Minister. 3 sons and 2 daughters
**Occupation**   Schoolmaster, lawyer, diplomat, political philosopher, vice president, 1789–97
**Religious denomination**   Unitarian
**Notable relationships**   John Adams was 17th in descent from Edward I, King of England, in three lines. His eldest son, John Quincy Adams, was the 6th president. John Adams was the first of six presidents who could claim descent from a *Mayflower* passenger (the others were J. Q. Adams, Zachary Taylor, Ulysses S. Grant, W. H. Taft and F. D. Roosevelt — who alone could claim such descent on both sides of his family)
**Died**   From debility, Quincy, Mass, 4 July 1826, aged 90 (the president who lived to the most advanced age)
**Buried**   In the United First Parish Church, Quincy, Mass. (Only two other presidents are buried in a church: John Quincy Adams and Woodrow Wilson.)

**Party** Federalist **State Represented** Massachusetts **Term of office** 4 March 1797 to 4 March 1801 **Age on taking office** 61 **Presidential administration** 3rd **Congresses** 5th, 6th

PRESIDENTIAL ELECTION 1796
276 Presidential Electors from 16 states cast their ballots as follows:

John Adams (Fed) 71
Thomas Jefferson (Dem Repub) 68 (vice president)
Thomas Pinckney (Fed) 59
Aaron Burr (Anti-Fed) 30
(48 votes were divided among nine other candidates.)

*Note* John Adams obtained 1 vote more than a majority. For the first and only time the president and the vice president represented different political parties.

### CONGRESS

| 1797 | 5th | Senate | (32) | 20 Fed | 12 Dem Repub |
|------|-----|--------|------|--------|--------------|
|      |     | House  | (106)| 58 Fed | 48 Dem Repub |
| 1799 | 6th | Senate | (32) | 19 Fed | 13 Dem Repub |
|      |     | House  | (106)| 64 Fed | 42 Dem Repub |

(The Administration retained control of Congress throughout.)

### NOTES

1 1800 2nd Census: total population, 5,310,458 including 894,452 slaves and 104,335 free negroes.
2 Constitutional Amendment: XIth (1798), limited the extent of the Federal Judiciary.

### VICE PRESIDENT

2nd Thomas Jefferson (1743–1826), subsequently 3rd president. Term of office: 4 March 1797 to 4 March 1801.

---

The new president was the son of a fourth generation Old Bay Colony farmer. He was bald, round of face and frame, and it was said that 'Old Rotundity' looked like an English country squire. Destined for the church, he entered Harvard; but after some schoolmastering he turned to the law. He made an advantageous marriage to a woman of extraordinary ability, Abigail Smith, and then events occurred that set him on the road to greatness.

He was an early opponent of Great Britain and four notable articles he wrote against the Stamp Act of 1765 helped to make him the leader of the Massachusetts 'Whigs'. 'On that night' (5 March 1770), he wrote later of events in Boston that would be known as the 'Boston Massacre', 'the foundation of American independence was laid. Not the battle of Lexington or Bunker Hill, not the surrender of Burgoyne or Cornwallis were more important events in American history . . .' What his readers had probably forgotten was that the defence of the eight British soldiers involved had been undertaken by two outstanding young Boston lawyers, one of whom was John Adams.

24

In 1771 he gave up his legal practice because of failing health (this was ironical in view of his longevity), and in 1774 he embarked upon a second career. He left his colony to represent Massachusetts in the First and Second Continental Congresses. He proposed the nomination of Colonel George Washington to command the Continental army in 1775; and, on 24 June 1776, Richard Henry Lee's motion for independence. The 'Atlas of Independence' then served on the five-man committee which drafted the Declaration of Independence. Though he played merely a reviser's part (this masterpiece was the work of Thomas Jefferson), the task of pushing it through Congress was entrusted to John Adams of whom Jefferson said: 'He was its ablest advocate and defender against the multifarious assaults it encountered.' Adams and Jefferson were the only presidents to sign the Declaration of Independence. In Congress Adams also found the time to be a member of some eighty committees — and chairman of twenty-five of them — and a member of the Board of War, as well as the author of a new constitution for his home state.

Between 1778 and 1788 he undertook several diplomatic roles in France, Holland and England. He helped to negotiate the French alliance of 1778 in Paris; and diplomatic recognition and a loan in The Hague. With Benjamin Franklin and John Jay he settled the provisional articles of a peace treaty in Paris at the end of the American War of Independence in 1783. From 1783–8 John Adams was the first American Ambassador to the Court of St James's, where he had a famous interview with George III. When he was recalled in 1788 to be Washington's partner in the first-ever presidential election, John Adams was therefore a man with a rich experience of domestic and a rare knowledge of foreign affairs.

George Washington was unanimously elected as the first president of the United States with 69 electoral votes. John Adams, second in the poll and consequently America's first vice president, received only 34, with 35 votes going to other candidates. This was because Colonel Alexander Hamilton (not for the last time) manipulated the electoral voters and persuaded many to scatter their second votes in order to avoid, so he said, any rivalry with George Washington. As vice president Adams found that he had nothing to do except to preside over the Senate where he was instrumental in developing senatorial precedents and he cast a deciding vote in a number of early crucial issues. Adams was re-elected in 1792 against formal opposition.

In 1788 and 1792 there had been no serious contest for the presidency, but 1796 was to see the first party political presidential election. It was understood that if Washington did not run again John Adams would be the Federalist candidate, but Hamilton, who wanted a more pliable candidate, again manipulated the vote.

The problem was that the electoral system had been designed for a partyless government. Each elector was entitled to cast two ballots without specifying which man he preferred for president. The winner became president, the second vice president, as in 1788 and 1792. But when parties appeared it meant that if all the electors who favoured the strongest party voted for both its candidates a tie vote would result (as in 1800). In order to elect their preferred candidate as president some electors now needed to divert their second vote from the party's second candidate to another candidate, though this would mean that the party's vice presidential candidate would receive fewer votes than a candidate from the opposing party who would become vice president instead. This happened in 1796. John Adams came within an ace of losing, and 'Mr. President by three votes' was saddled with the opposition leader, Thomas Jefferson, as his vice president.

'There is nothing I dread so much as the division of the Republic into two great parties, each under its own leader . . . This, in my humble opinion, is to be feared as the greatest political evil under our Constitution'. Adams, dreaming of a system in which the president would be above Congress and above party, was never able to build a 'party', or even a personal following, and he was to find himself, like his son, later, a statesman without a party.

He caught the full blast of Republican opposition, and opposition from inside a highly organised Congress and, worse still, he had to contend with the 'Ultras' or High Federalists, inside what was still ostensibly one Federalist party, who looked to Hamilton for their orders. There being no precedent to do otherwise he (mistakenly) maintained his predecessor's Cabinet in office, paying dearly for the fact that Washington had only been able to recruit second-rate men on salaries of a mere $3,000 a year. (The president's salary was fixed in 1789 at $25,000 and the vice president's at $5,000. These remained unchanged until 1873. No pension was provided for the president until 1958. George Washington refused to accept any salary, only expenses.) In these circumstances Adams could only have preserved the strength of the Executive branch if he had taken his own decisions; but the 'Duke

26

of Braintree' spent a lot of time at home in Quincy. The Cabinet was left alone to deliberate and Adams' government drifted into ill-advised policies.

The Inaugural Address of the 61-year-old President indicated two main areas of potential trouble: 'party' and France. He vowed to minimise any differences concerning the former and he made conciliatory noises towards the latter.

Relations with France were deteriorating rapidly against the background of the French Revolutionary Wars. The French complained that the Americans were not ensuring their 'most favoured nation' commercial status agreed in 1778; and of the recent Anglo-American Jay's Treaty of 1794. The French had already begun to seize the merchant ships of their 'perfidious friend' and had expelled the American minister in France. Mounting war fever in America contributed to, and was fanned by, Federalist gains in the 1798 mid-term elections. The pro-French Republicans were equated with 'Jacobins' and labelled 'Democrats' as a term of abuse.

Adams sent a three-man mission to France to negotiate, whilst seeking an increase in American armed strength. This olive branch was rejected by the French foreign minister, Tallyrand who, through three intermediaries, 'X, Y and Z', sought a quarter of a million dollars for himself and several millions in addition as the price of any treaty. 'Not a sixpence,' thundered C. C. Pinckney, though this is usually rendered as 'Millions for defence but not one cent for tribute'. When the 'XYZ' affair became public Adams could have had a war on his own terms. America and France were fighting an undeclared war at sea and in 1798 Adams became the father of the American Navy when he persuaded Congress to establish a Department of the Navy (ever since there has always been a USS *John Adams* in the United States Navy), but his greatest achievement as President was that he kept America at peace.

The martial spirit of the times had a domestic aspect. The High Federalists saw war as a means of aggrandisement at the expense of the Republicans: a large standing army could have internal uses. The more the High Federalists pressed for war — and Adams was forced to appoint Washington as Commander-in-Chief with Hamilton as second in command — the more apparent it became that their aims were domestic rather than foreign. John Adams appreciated however that to declare war now would be to lose all the advantages of American neutrality and sacrifice the national interest to party politics: that way would lie disaster for the Union. He decided to be president. In February 1799 without any consultation he reopened negotiations with France which led, some eighteen months later, to a treaty that ended the spoliation of American commerce, saved America from a needless war and gained greater freedom on the seas. The High Federalists were apoplectic; the Republicans were ecstatic; and party tensions eased.

Before that settlement materialised in 1800, America was shaken by political hysteria when, in June and July 1798, in an American 'Reign of Terror', the Alien and Sedition Acts were pushed through Congress curbing freedom of speech and the press in an effort to suppress 'Jacobinism' at home. Adams, like Washington before him, regarded himself and his supporters as imperial patriots and the Republican opposition as a criminal conspiracy, and consequently he acquiesced in some of the most repressive measures ever directed against political activity in the United States.

The Republicans, alarmed that such measures might preclude the return of a Republican administration, went onto the attack. In his Virginia Resolutions (1798) James Madison opined that the states could judge the constitutionality — or otherwise — of Federal legislation; and the Kentucky Resolutions, secretly drafted by Thomas Jefferson in the same year, proclaimed that any state could 'nullify', or set aside completely, any Federal legislation of which it did not approve. These resolutions posed questions that would bedevil America for years to come. The Philadelphia Convention had not decided which was sovereign, the state or the Federal government. These resolutions were a reminder that the issue was still wide open.

Now, as in 1792 and 1796, one section of the Federalists began their customary intrigues to deny office to the man who almost single-handedly had kept the nation out of war. Hamilton produced his *Letters Concerning the Public Conduct and Character of John Adams*, which revealed Cabinet secrets, denounced the French negotiations as 'capricious and undignified', and Adams as unfit for the presidency.

Peace was concluded with France on 30 September 1800. Adams' reward was to be defeated in the Electoral College in December, gaining 65 votes to the 73 tied votes of Thomas Jefferson and Aaron Burr. Republican gains in Congress brought to an end in 1801 Federalist control of the national government, except in one branch, the Judiciary. This was already manned by many

28

Federalists who held lifetime appointments and Adams with his so-called 'midnight appointments' filled up 16 new circuit courts created in February 1801 with loyal Federalists. This followed perhaps his greatest (unwitting) legacy to the young United States: the appointment in January 1801 as Chief Justice, of John Marshall who was to preside over the Supreme Court from 1801–35.

Jefferson liked to think of his victory in 1800 as the 'Revolution of 1800'. In truth the real revolution was Adams' repudiation of High Federalism, and the reduction of an ever-widening gap between Federal and Republican views of what constituted the national interest which had caused Americans to drift dangerously apart.

In the closing months of his presidency John Adams became the first president to live in the new Executive Mansion. Though the house was habitable it was barely so and 'the great unfinished audience room (the East Room) I make a drying room of . . .' wrote Mrs Adams.

The Adamses did not wait to attend the Inauguration of Thomas Jefferson ('No man who ever held the office of President would congratulate a friend on obtaining it'), but left for their home 'Peacefields' near Quincy in Massachusetts where they lived quietly together until Mrs Adams died in 1818 after fifty-four years of marriage. John Adams continued to maintain an interest in public affairs and kept up a very active correspondence with his former opponent Thomas Jefferson. He lived long enough to see his son John Quincy Adams become Chief Executive.

He once suggested that his epitaph ought to be 'Here lies John Adams who took upon himself the responsibility of peace with France in 1800.' In the event, following his death at the age of nearly 91 on 4 July 1826 (a few hours after the death of Thomas Jefferson) his final epitaph was:

John Adams, Signer of the Declaration of Independence,
Framer of the Constitution of Massachusetts.
Second President of the United States, 1735–1826.

# THOMAS JEFFERSON

**Full name**  Thomas Jefferson, 1743–1826
**Born**  Shadwell Estate, Goochland (now Albermarle) County, Virginia, 13 April 1743 (2 April 1742/3 Old Style), the third child and eldest son of 10 children
**Parents**  Col Peter Jefferson (1708–57), planter, surveyor, sheriff, magistrate, member of the Virginia House of Burgesses, and Jane Randolph Jefferson (b London, England, 1720, d 1776). 6 daughters, 4 sons
**Family lineage**  Welsh — Scottish — Irish
**College**  College of William and Mary, Williamsburg, Virginia
**Married**  1772, Martha Wayles Skelton Jefferson (1748–82), widow of Bathurst Skelton (d 1768), daughter of John Wayles, planter, attorney. 5 daughters, 1 son. (Only 2 daughters reached maturity)
**Occupation**  Lawyer; member of the Virginia House of Burgesses, 1769–75, 1776–9; member of the second Continental Congress, 1775–6; Governor of Virginia, 1779–81; member of the Confederation Congress, 1783–4; Minister to France, 1785–9; Secretary of State, 1790–3; vice president, 1797–1801
**Religious denomination**  None (though he had leanings towards the Unitarian faith)
**Notable relationships**  Through his mother he was descended from David I, King of Scots (c 1080–1153). Chief Justice John Marshall was his second cousin. Jefferson is the president with the most living descendants
**Died**  From acute diarrhoea, Monticello, near Charlottesville, Virginia, 4 July 1826, aged 83
**Buried**  Monticello

**Party** Democratic Republican **State represented** Virginia **Terms of office** 4 March 1801 to 4 March 1809 **Age on taking office** 57

### PRESIDENTIAL ELECTION 1800

276 Presidential Electors from 16 states cast their ballots as follows:

| | |
|---|---|
| Thomas Jefferson (Dem Repub) | 73 |
| Aaron Burr (Dem Repub) | 73 |
| John Adams (Fed) | 65 |
| Charles Pinckney (Fed) | 64 |
| John Jay (Fed) | 1 |

The tie vote necessitated an election in the House of Representatives (under Article II, Section 1(2) of the Constitution), where each state had one vote. Jefferson was elected president on the 36th ballot with 10 votes. Aaron Burr, 4 votes, was elected vice president.

### PRESIDENTIAL ELECTION 1804

176 Presidential Electors from 17 states cast their ballots as follows:

| | |
|---|---|
| Thomas Jefferson (Dem Repub) | |
| George Clinton (Dem Repub) | 162 from 15 states |
| Charles Pinckney (Fed) | |
| Rufus King (Fed) | 14 from 2 states |

This was the first election to take place under the provisions of the XII Amendment (1804).

### CONGRESS

| | | | | | |
|---|---|---|---|---|---|
| 1801 | 7th | Senate | (32) | 18 Dem Repub | 14 Fed |
| | | House | (105) | 69 Dem Repub | 36 Fed |
| 1803 | 8th | Senate | (34) | 25 Dem Repub | 9 Fed |
| | | House | (141) | 102 Dem Repub | 39 Fed |
| 1805 | 9th | Senate | (34) | 27 Dem Repub | 7 Fed |
| | | House | (141) | 116 Dem Repub | 25 Fed |
| 1807 | 10th | Senate | (34) | 28 Dem Repub | 6 Fed |
| | | House | (142) | 118 Dem Repub | 24 Fed |

(The Administration controlled Congress throughout.)

### NOTES

1 New state admitted: Ohio (1803) 17th.
2 Constitutional amendment: XII (1804), provided that electors shall cast separate ballots for president and vice president.
3 The slave trade was prohibited as from 1 January 1808, thus implementing Article V of the United States Constitution (1787).

### VICE PRESIDENTS

3rd Aaron Burr (New York), 1756–1836. Lawyer; Lt Colonel in Continental Army, 1775–9; Attorney General, New York State, 1789–91; US Senator, 1791–7; vice president, 4 March 1801 to 4

March 1805. Killed Alexander Hamilton in a duel, 1804. Tried for 'Treason and Misdemeanour', 1806–7, acquitted.

4th George Clinton (New York), 1739–1812. Lawyer, Brig General in Continental Army; New York delegate to 2nd Continental Congress, 1775; 1st Governor of New York, 1775–95 and 1801–4; vice presidential candidate, 1788, 1792, 1796; vice president, 4 March 1805 to 4 March 1809 (and subsequently under Madison, [qv].

---

The first American president of the nineteenth century was born in 1743. His father was a self-made man but through his English-born mother, a Randolph, he had an assured social position. When his father died in 1757 young Thomas inherited 2,500 acres and many slaves. At 19 the 6ft 2½in tall, lanky, raw country lad (he had never seen a town), with a freckled face and reddish hair, entered the College of William and Mary at Williamsburg, then the capital of Virginia. He graduated in 1762, entered the legal profession, and was admitted to the Virginia bar in 1767.

In 1769 he was elected to a seat in the Virginia House of Burgesses which he was to hold for the next six crucial years in colonial history. During this period he designed and began to build the first version of his lovely modified-Palladian villa at Monticello, perched on a densely wooded summit in Albermarle country. To the unfinished house in January 1772 he brought his bride, Martha Wayles Skelton, an attractive and well-to-do young widow, who brought him additional large land holdings and more slaves.

Jefferson's career was furthered in 1774 when he wrote *A Summary View of the Rights of British America*, in which he reached the radical conclusion that the Americans possessed the natural right to govern themselves. He became a delegate to the sixty-strong Second Continental Congress in 1775, and in June of 1776 he was appointed to head a five-man committee, which included Franklin and John Adams, to draft a Declaration of Independence. Jefferson's 'peculiar felicity of expression' was exhibited to a marked degree in a simple and eloquent appeal to fundamental values which claimed as 'self-evident' truths, human equality, the natural rights of man, the sovereignty of the people — and the right of revolution. (Jefferson's authorship of the most famous document in American history did not become widely known for several years).

Returning to a seat in the Virginia legislature (1776–9) Jefferson pressed for liberal reforms including the separation of church and state in Virginia and religious freedom. These changes were enacted later in the great Virginia Statute for Religious Freedom, 1786. He was successful in changing the laws on inheritance by securing the abolition of entail and primogeniture; but his plans for the gradual abolition of slavery failed because 'the public mind would not yet bear the proposition . . . yet the day is not far distant when it must bear and adopt it, or worse will follow . . .'

In 1779 he succeeded Patrick Henry as war-time governor of Virginia, in which unhappy position he continued until 1781 when he retired from politics exhausted. The death of his wife in 1782 drove him into the Confederation Congress in 1783–4, where he proposed the adoption of the decimal coinage system based on the dollar (subsequently introduced in 1792); and he was the author of the Land Ordinance of 1784 — the first attempt to regulate the development of the nation's trans-Appalachian domains.

He succeeded Benjamin Franklin as Minister to France in 1785 where his experiences (to October 1789) were crucial in shaping his political thinking. His republicanism was confirmed (European royalty were 'fools' and 'idiots'); as was his belief in an agrarian-based democracy — 'The yeomanry of the United States are not the *canaille* of Paris' — there would be no mobs in a 'Nation of Farmers'. He travelled extensively in France, Italy, the Rhineland and England. (He met George III at Windsor in 1786. The king was not very polite.) He came to the conclusion that his compatriots did not know when they were well off, 'How little do my countrymen know what precious blessings they are in possession of . . .' Anti-American feeling in London, 'affected his entire subsequent life'.

Because of his absence abroad Jefferson was not one of the 'Founding Fathers' who drew up the new Constitution in 1787. When the text reached him in France he thought it 'a good canvas on which some strokes only want re-touching'. He could see only two faults: the absence of a Bill of Rights (soon to be rectified), and the potential re-eligibility of the president — that way lay the degeneration of the office into a monarchy with the attendant evils of the European prototype.

He became Secretary of State (1790), in the new government, a task for which he had impressive qualifications, and high hopes that were soon to be dashed. A rift soon developed between Jefferson and Alexander Hamilton, the brilliant Secretary of the

Treasury, because of their diametrically opposed views concerning the future development of the United States. 'If I could not go to heaven but with a party, I would not go at all', Jefferson had said in 1789, but he was not prepared to go to hell with Hamilton whose policies, for a National Debt and a National Bank, for example, were he believed, designed to advance the interests of the mercantile and investing classes at the expense of the backbone of the nation, its planters, farmers and yeomen, and to destroy republicanism. Out of their implacable hostility emerged America's first two political parties, Hamilton's 'Federalists' and Jefferson's 'Democratic Republicans'. By 1792 the mutual antipathy was so great that it was only with the greatest reluctance that Jefferson agreed to stay in office until the end of 1793.

'The little spice of ambition' seemed to have vanished and he retired to Monticello where, wrote a French visitor, 'He is employed in the management of his farms and buildings; and he orders, directs, and pursues in the minutest detail every branch of the business relative to them' — including the invention of a mold-board plough for which he was awarded a gold medal by the Agricultural Society of Paris. But in 1796 at the end of his 'second retirement', he accepted nomination for the presidency as an anti-Hamiltonian Republican so as 'to put our vessel on her republican tack before she should be thrown too much to leeward of her true principles'. Though Jefferson was not a real 'party' man, he had been converted to the idea as a necessary evil. 'In every free society there must be opposite parties . . . Perhaps this party division is necessary to induce each to watch and relate to the proceedings of the other.'

The vagaries of the electoral system made Jefferson vice president in 1797 to a Federalist President. 'The second office of the government is honourable and easy,' he wrote. 'The first is but a splendid misery.' He played no part in the administration, which was dominated by Hamilton. 'He (Adams) never said one word or ever consulted me as to any measure of government.' The vice president was not idle during this period, however, which became one long campaign for the election of 1800. In 1798 he gave America the Kentucky Resolutions (see p 28) which helped to throw Adams' administration onto the defensive and to arouse that popular discontent that was to lead to its overthrow and Jefferson's eventual victory in 1801.

Jefferson and Aaron Burr both gained 73 votes in 1800 and so the election was thrown to the House of Representatives where a 'lame duck' Federalist majority would have chosen Burr had not Alexander Hamilton, to his everlasting credit, sent word from New York to elect Jefferson as the lesser of two evils, preferring his intellectual adversary to a political foe. (Three years later Burr killed Hamilton in a duel.) Jefferson was elected on the 36th ballot.

He was to pass eight unhappy years as Chief Executive. He was the first president to be inaugurated at the Capitol into an office into which he tried to inject some 'democracy'. He dropped Washington-style levées and courtly forms and ceremonies; handshaking replaced bowing and scraping. He received the fully-accoutred British ambassador in down-at-heels slippers and 'with his personal appearance so disordered that it could only be called slovenly'.

Jeffersonian simplicity was also applied in domestic politics. 'We are all Republicans, we are all Federalists,' he proclaimed in his Inaugural Address as he appealed for harmony. High Federalist legislation was overturned, the army and navy were cut back, all internal taxes and their collectors were abolished and the national debt was put in process of elimination. Jefferson, however, did not sweep away all vestiges of Hamiltonianism (for example he retained a National Bank): 'What is practicable must often control pure theory.' The nation liked his middle-course pragmatism and re-elected him in 1804 overwhelmingly, mainly because of his reduction of government expenditure, but also because of the Louisiana Purchase.

'Louisiana' was an enormous wedge-shaped territory more than twice the size of the existing United States with the port of New Orleans at its apex. Less than 1% of it was settled. It had passed from France to Spain in 1763 and recently (October 1800) back to France, thus threatening American peace, the trade of the west through New Orleans, and America's westward aspirations. Jefferson sent James Monroe, the future president, to help the American minister to negotiate with Napoleon Bonaparte for, at best, the purchase of New Orleans, or, at worst, a perpetual guarantee of an American right of deposit there; negotiations which were backed by the threat (from the Francophile Jefferson), of a treaty with Britain. Napoleon, on the eve of war with Britain, agreed to sell the whole of 'Louisiana' to the United States for some fifteen million dollars. The greatest real-estate bargain in American history added 865,000 square miles to the Union at a cost of about 8 cents an acre, from which Missouri, Nebraska, Iowa, Arkansas, North and South Dakota, most of Louisiana, Kansas, Minnesota, Montana and Wyoming, and parts of Colorado and Oklahoma were later to be carved. Jefferson eventually suppressed any qualms that he may have felt about the constitutionality of the Purchase; and dispatched his secretary, Meriwether Lewis, along with William Clark, on the first transcontinental expedition (1804–6) across the newly-acquired territory.

In his second term Jefferson struggled to keep the peace. Britain and France, at war in Europe, were abusing American neutrality. Thousands of American seamen were 'impressed' into the British navy. British and French privateers plundered what was left of American trade after its exclusion from Europe following Napoleon's 'Continental System' and the British Orders in Council. In 1807 when the USS *Chesapeake* was attacked by HMS *Leopard*, Jefferson, like Adams before him, could have gone to war with the nation behind him. Instead he inflicted economic sanctions upon the belligerents. The Embargo Act (December 1807) withdrew American commerce and navigation from the oceans. Though this did damage Britain, arguably it damaged America more, and caused a furore in mercantile New England, without forcing the European nations to lift their decrees against neutrals. In the dying moments of his presidency the Embargo was repealed.

Jefferson went into retirement like a prisoner released from his chains. He was now able to devote his time to his extensive interests. He imported plants for study and experiment and he was the first American to grow a tomato. An accomplished cook, he wrote down his favourite recipes and composed an essay on 'Soups'. He is also credited with the introduction of ice cream, waffles and macaroni into America. He designed the forerunner of today's automatic closing doors, a cannonball-weighted clock that told the days, a portable writing desk, a revolving music stand — as well as a mechanical device in his wardrobe which revolved to bring his clothes to him. He kept himself healthy by soaking his feet in cold water every morning and he was among the first Americans to be inoculated against smallpox.

He devoted himself to Monticello which was often packed with visitors, to reading and his library. This he sold to Congress in 1815 to form the nucleus of a new Library of Congress because the British had destroyed the original in 1814 — and then he started a new one. In this period also he completed the Jefferson Bible which contained the real teachings of Jesus stripped of later corruptions, proof positive that he was a true Christian. He was instrumental in securing the chartering of the University of Virginia in 1819 and it was Jefferson who designed every building, laid out the gardens, chose the staff, the students and the curriculum before it opened its doors in 1825. In his closing years he was deeply disturbed by increasing debt (friends raised money to save him from bankruptcy) and by the Missouri Compromise (1820) concerning slavery ('This momentous question like a fire bell in the night awakened and filled me with terror.') He died, symbolically, on the 50th anniversary of his Declaration of Independence, on 4 July 1826.

The sculptor Gutzon Borglum chose Jefferson to be one of the four presidents (the others are Washington, Lincoln and Theodore Roosevelt) who are carved in granite sixty feet high in the Black Hills of South Dakota in the Mount Rushmore National Park. Completed in the early 1940s (at about the same time as the Jefferson Monument in Washington DC), this has helped to crystallise the impression that Jefferson was one of the four greatest presidents. In truth it would probably be more accurate to rank him amongst the greatest individuals who ever lived. For Thomas Jefferson who helped to found a nation was a prodigy of talents — half a dozen persons rolled into one. To a group of Nobel prize winners attending a White House dinner John F. Kennedy said, 'I believe this is the most extraordinary collection of human talent, of human knowledge, that has ever been gathered together at the White House, with the possible exception of when Thomas Jefferson dined alone.' For Jefferson was statesman, scientist, architect, agriculturalist, musician, geographer, linguist, philosopher — to name only some of his talents. He chose for his epitaph on the monument he characteristically designed for himself:

Here was buried
THOMAS JEFFERSON
Author of the Declaration of American Independence,
Of the Statute of Virginia for Religious Freedom,
And Father of the University of Virginia.

# JAMES MADISON

**Full name** James Madison, 1751–1836
**Born** Port Conway, King George County, Virginia, 16 March 1751 (5 March 1750/1 Old Style), the eldest of 10 children
**Parents** James Madison (1723–1801), planter, farmer, lieutenant of Orange County, and Eleanor Rose Conway Madison (1731–1829). 5 sons, 5 daughters
**Family lineage** English
**College** College of New Jersey (now Princeton University, Princeton, New Jersey), BA 1771
**Married** 1794, Dorothea ('Dolley') Payne Todd Madison (1768–1849), widow (with one surviving child) of John Todd (d 1793), daughter of John Payne, planter and farmer. No children
**Occupation** Member of Virginia House of Delegates, 1776–7, 1784–6; 2nd Continental Congress, 1780–3, 1786–8; Annapolis Convention, 1786; Philadelphia Convention, 1787 (signatory of the Constitution); member of US House of Representatives, 1789–97; Secretary of State, 1801–9
**Religious denomination** Episcopalian
**Notable relationships** Madison was a first cousin twice removed of George Washington. Madison and Zachary Taylor, 12th president, were second cousins
**Died** From debility, Montpelier Estate, Orange County, Virginia, 28 June 1836, aged 85
**Buried** Montpelier

**Party** Democratic Republican. **State represented** Virginia **Terms of Office** 4 March 1809 to 4 March 1817 **Age on taking Office** 57 **Presidential administrations** 6th, 7th **Congresses** 11th, 12th, 13th, 14th

176* Presidential Electors from 17 states cast their ballots as follows:

| | |
|---|---|
| James Madison (Dem Repub) | 122 from 12 states |
| C. C. Pinckney (Fed) | 47 from 5 states |
| George Clinton (Dem Repub) | 6 (though not a candidate) |

*One absentee; Clinton (113 votes) declared vice president.

## PRESIDENTIAL ELECTION 1812

217* Presidential Electors from 18 states cast their ballots as follows:

| | |
|---|---|
| James Madison (Dem Repub) | 128 from 11 states |
| De Witt Clinton (Dem Repub) | 89 from 7 states |

*One vacancy; Gerry (131 votes) declared vice president.

## CONGRESS

| 1809 | 11th | Senate | (34) | 28 Dem Repub | 6 Fed |
|---|---|---|---|---|---|
| | | House | (142) | 94 Dem Repub | 48 Fed |
| 1811 | 12th | Senate | (36) | 30 Dem Repub | 6 Fed |
| | | House | (144) | 108 Dem Repub | 36 Fed |
| 1813 | 13th | Senate | (36) | 27 Dem Repub | 9 Fed |
| | | House | (180) | 112 Dem Repub | 68 Fed |
| 1815 | 14th | Senate | (36) | 25 Dem Repub | 11 Fed |
| | | House | (182) | 117 Dem Repub | 65 Fed |

(The Administration controlled Congress throughout.)

## NOTES

1 3rd Census of 1810: Total population, 7,230,903, including 1,191,364 slaves, and 186,746 free negroes.

2 New states admitted: Louisiana (1812) 18th
Indiana (1816) 19th.

## VICE PRESIDENTS

4th George Clinton (New York) continued in office until his death, in office, on 20 April 1812. Only J. C. Calhoun (7th vice president) also served under two presidents.

5th Elbridge Gerry (Mass), 1744–1814, son of Thomas Gerry of Newton Abbot, Devon, England (who emigrated in 1730). Shipowner, delegate to 2nd Continental Congress. Signatory of both the Declaration of Independence (1776) and the Articles of Confederation (1781), the only president or vice president so to do. Member of US House of Representatives, 1789–93; Commissioner to France, 1797, 'XYZ Mission'; Governor of Massachusetts, 1810–12 (where the redistribution of Electoral Districts to give unfair advantage to his own party became known as 'Gerrymandering' from 'Gerry + (sala)mander', the shape of one district); vice president 4 March 1813 to 23 November 1814. Died in office.

The smallest man ever to be president (he stood about 5ft 4in and only weighed one hundred pounds), James Madison was a giant intellectually. At his Inauguration he appeared wizened, old and worn. Washington Irving had described him as 'but a withered little apple-john'. But this diminutive, prematurely-aged Virginian already had some very notable achievements to his credit, apart from being the first president to wear long trousers.

Born a few miles from Jefferson's home into a family of 'independent and comfortable circumstances', he graduated from college where he studied history and government and did a year's postgraduate study of Hebrew. He served on the committee which drafted a new constitution for Virginia (1776), and was instrumental in securing a clause for religious freedom. Madison then became a member of the state legislature, a member of the Governor's Council of State and, at 29, the youngest member of the Second Continental Congress from 1780–3. In 1786 he was a Virginia delegate to the Annapolis Convention which recommended the summoning of a Convention to Philadelphia in 1787 to 'revise the Articles of Confederation', and he was the first of the 'demi-gods' (Jefferson) to arrive at that historic meeting.

America's first written constitution of 1781 had brought the young nation to the verge of collapse following the end of the war in 1783 when the 13 states had increasingly gone their separate ways. The confederate, congressional form of government for which it had provided, with a single chamber legislature in which each state had one vote, was totally unable to enforce its will upon states or individuals. 'That revolted State certainly for years cannot establish a stable government,' George III had confidently predicted; and indeed the Confederation had become 'a sorry excuse for government'. It was despised abroad, and Shay's rebellion in Western Massachusetts in 1786 revealed the dangers at home.

Madison had prepared for the Philadelphia meeting by studying ancient and modern forms of republican and federal government and he brought with him the outlines of a comprehensive constitution. Not all his ideas were adopted but he did more to shape the American Constitution than any other individual and well deserved the title of 'Father of the Constitution', though with characteristic diffidence he said that it was not 'the offspring of a single brain' but 'the work of many heads and hands'. Madison was one of only two presidents to sign the Constitution, the other was Washington.

The Constitution could not be put into effect until it had been ratified by the people and Madison made a major contribution to this process by writing, with Alexander Hamilton and John Jay, a series of brilliant and cogent essays, the *Federalist Papers*. The persuasiveness of these essays did much to attract support for the idea of a strong federal government, and the necessary ratification, by the people of nine states, took place by 1789.

During the next few years, however, Madison became an opponent of the new 'Federalists' led by Alexander Hamilton. He regarded Hamilton's policies as designed not only to benefit the narrow interests of the financiers and investors of the North, but also as unconstitutional, since Hamilton was prepared to interpret the wording of the document loosely, whilst Madison was a 'strict constructionist'. His opposition helped to create what became known as 'Jeffersonian Republicanism', though these principles might equally well have been known as 'Madisonianism'. He refused to serve the Federalists on a mission to France, and in 1793 he declined to replace Jefferson as Secretary of State.

Defeated in his aspirations for a Senate seat, Madison served in the House of Representatives from 1789–97. Here he was a staunch advocate (and the author of nine) of the first ten amendments to the Constitution (the 'Bill of Rights') which were ratified in 1791. He lost his seat in the 1796 elections and devoted himself to the fortunes of the Republican party under Jefferson; and it was in this period that the high point of his opposition to Hamilton came with his authorship of the Virginia Resolutions of 1798 (see page 28).

Without any diplomatic experience, Madison became Jefferson's Secretary of State from 1801–9. He found his country faced with the seemingly intractable problems posed by the attacks of both Britain and France on America's cherished neutrality. He protested against violations of international law in the only way that he could in a series of masterly State Papers; for example that of 1806, a 204 page diatribe entitled *An Examination of the British Doctrine which Subjects to Capture a Neutral Trade not Open in Time of Peace*, which had as much effect, as John Randolph put it, as 'a shilling pamphlet hurled against eight hundred ships'. As one of the ablest of the 'Founding Fathers' Madison had demonstrated that he could write a constitution, but in the developing international crisis he was completely out of his depth.

At a time when a dynamic leader of men was required it was Madison's misfortune to be elected president in 1808 as Jefferson's eldest political son, the one job for which he was the least fitted. Relations with Britain and France continued to deteriorate and Madison was duped by Napoleon into intensifying economic sanctions against Britain. This brought near-rebellion in mercantile New England. At home the vacuum of power created by Madison's indecisiveness was filled by the new members of the 12th Congress (less than half the members of the 11th Congress were returned to 'the immortal 12th') led by the new young Speaker of the House, Henry Clay of Kentucky, and abetted by the so-called 'War Hawks', prominent among whom was John C. Calhoun of South Carolina. They pressed Madison for a more militant line against the British, who were guilty not only of 'impressment' but also of aiding the Indian tribes on the Canadian frontier. Here, in November of 1811, William Henry Harrison won the battle of Tippecanoe which made him a hero of the West and helped to put him into the White House in 1840.

At length Madison became a moderate War Hawk himself and succumbed to the demands for a war for 'Free Trade and Sailors' Rights' which thinly disguised expansionist aims towards Canada ('On to Canada!'). On 1 June 1812 he sent a 'War Message' into Congress (this was presidential election year), and the so-called 'Second War of Independence' began on 18 June 1812. (Two days before the British government had announced in Parliament that its policy of seizures would be suspended immediately. This decision had in fact been taken over a month earlier, but the government had been thrown into chaos by the assassination of the Prime Minister, Spencer Perceval, on 11 May 1812.) Long afterwards Madison told the historian George Bancroft that 'he knew the unprepared state of the country, but he esteemed it necessary to throw forward the flag, sure that the people would press forward and defend it'.

Except for what Madison called 'our little naval triumphs' on the Great Lakes and elsewhere, the Anglo-American Naval War of 1812–14 went badly for America and was soon being called 'Mr Madison's War' by those who had opposed it, particularly when British successes in the Peninsular War released veterans for overseas. In August of 1814 the British burned Washington, forcing the President to flee. (Mrs Madison paused only long enough to snatch Gilbert Stuart's portrait of George Washington from its frame and the original draft of the Declaration of Independence.) All government buildings and records in Washington were destroyed; and in

1817 the Executive Mansion — so called until the presidency of Theodore Roosevelt — had to be given more of those coats of white paint (to hide scorch marks) from which it was to get its name. America did however obtain an anthem (it was made 'official' in 1931), in the form of F. S. Key's patriotic verses about 'The Star-Spangled Banner', inspired by the twenty-five hour bombardment of Fort McHenry, Baltimore (1814). America also secured, when all seemed lost — two weeks after the 'Peace of Christmas Eve' had been signed at Ghent in Belgium (it said nothing about any of the causes of the war) — a great victory and a national hero (and a future president), when General Andrew Jackson defeated Lord Pakenham's forces at New Orleans on 8 January 1815.

Peace, and Jackson's glorious victory (the British lost 2,000 men and their commander, Jackson only 62), obscured the fact that the war had been lost. As it was, Madison's last two years in office were bathed in the golden afterglow of New Orleans — Congress concurred in his proposals for a Second Bank of the United States (1816) and a protective tariff — and he was able to leave office in 1817 one of the most fortunate of presidents as far as his reputation was concerned and with a reasonable amount of credit.

Madison retired to Montpelier, Virginia, solaced by the charms of Dolley Madison, one of the most popular of all First Ladies, whose ebullience had done much to sustain his occupation of the White House. He devoted himself to reform movements, such as the young temperance movement, and the interests of the University of Virginia, of which he became rector in 1826. He became increasingly concerned about the disruptive and divisive influences that were threatening to shatter the Union in the 1820s and 1830s and his final 'Advice to My Country', opened after his death in 1836, was 'that the Union of the States be cherished and perpetuated'. His epitaph was spoken by one of his slaves, Paul Jennings, 'Mr Madison was one of the best men I ever knew.'

# JAMES MONROE

**Full name**   James Monroe, 1758–1831
**Born**   Westmoreland County, Virginia, 28 April 1758, the second of 5 children
**Parents**   Spence Monroe (d 1774), farmer, circuit judge, and Elizabeth Jones Monroe. 4 sons, 1 daughter
**Family lineage**   Scottish-Welsh
**College**   College of William and Mary, Williamsburg, Virginia
**Married**   1786, Elizabeth Kortright Monroe (1768–1830), daughter of Capt Lawrence Kortright, British Army Officer, merchant. 2 daughters, 1 son
**Occupation**   Soldier; state politician, member of Virginia House of Delegates, 1782, 1786–90, 1810; member of the Continental Congress 1783–6; US Senator, 1790–4; Minister to France, 1794–6; Governor of Virginia, 1799–1802, 1811; Minister to Great Britain, 1803–7; Secretary of State, 1811–17, and War, 1814–15
**Religious denomination**   Episcopalian
**Notable relationships**   Monroe was descended from Edward III, King of England, and Robert II, King of Scots
**Died**   From debility, New York City, NY, 4 July 1831, aged 73
**Buried**   In the Monroe Tomb, Hollywood Cemetery, Richmond, Virginia. (The cemetery also contains the graves of President John Tyler, Jefferson Davis and thousands of Confederate soldiers)

**Party** Democratic Republican **State represented** Virginia **Terms of Office** 4 March 1817 to 4 March 1825 **Age on taking Office** 58 **Presidential administrations** 8th, 9th **Congresses** 15th, 16th, 17th, 18th

## PRESIDENTIAL ELECTION 1816

217 Presidential Electors from 19 states cast their ballots as follows:

| | |
|---|---|
| James Monroe (Dem Repub) | |
| D. D. Tompkins (Dem Repub) | 183 from 16 states |
| Rufus King (Federalist) | 34 from 3 states |

232 Presidential Electors from 24 states cast their ballots as follows:
James Monroe (Dem Repub)          231 from 24 states
J. Q. Adams (Dem Repub)               1 (from New Hampshire)
Tompkins (218 votes) declared vice president.

## CONGRESS

| 1817 | 15th | Senate | (44) | 34 Dem Repub | 10 Fed |
|------|------|--------|------|--------------|--------|
|      |      | House  | (183) | 141 Dem Repub | 42 Fed |
| 1819 | 16th | Senate | (42) | 35 Dem Repub | 7 Fed |
|      |      | House  | (183) | 156 Dem Repub | 27 Fed |
| 1821 | 17th | Senate | (48) | 44 Dem Repub | 4 Fed |
|      |      | House  | (183) | 158 Dem Repub | 25 Fed |
| 1823 | 18th | Senate | (48) | 44 Dem Repub | 4 Fed |
|      |      | House  | (213) | 187 Dem Repub | 26 Fed |

(The Administration controlled Congress throughout.)

## NOTES

1 1820, 4th Census: Total population, 9,638,191 including 1,538,125 slaves and 233,504 free negroes.

2 New States:  Mississippi  (1817)    20th
               Illinois     (1818)    21st
               Alabama      (1819)    22nd
               Maine        (1820)    23rd
               Missouri     (1821)    24th

3 The 'Flag Act', 4 April 1818, provided for a flag with 13 horizontal red and white stripes and a white star for each state on a blue field.

## VICE PRESIDENT

6th Daniel D. Tompkins (New York) 1774–1825; lawyer; member of US House of Representatives, 1804; Justice of New York Supreme Court, 1804–07; Governor of New York, 1807–17; vice president, 4 March 1817 to 4 March 1825.

---

Monroe was the fourth and the last (and the unkind would say the least-gifted) of that group of early presidents known as the 'Virginia Dynasty'. He represented the last of the old in another sense — he alone continued to wear eighteenth-century knee-breeches, buckled shoes and a three-cornered hat when everyone else had taken to newer fashions. He was tall, broad-shouldered and raw-boned, with a strongly-marked, rugged face, containing blue kindly eyes. He was awkward and diffident in manner, yet the overall impression was one of dignity mixed with courtesy. He is the first president of whom a photograph exists.

James Monroe quit his studies at William and Mary College in 1776 to be a soldier, as did his classmate John Marshall. He rose to the rank of Lt Colonel and was always known as 'Colonel' Monroe until he became president. He studied law under Jefferson (who also designed a house for him, Oak Hill, which was constructed by James Hoban who built the White House), and then he went into the state legislature, before becoming a member of the Continental Congress, 1783–6. He opposed the new Constitution because he foresaw conflicts arising between the states and the federal government, but he became a Senator from 1790–4.

There then followed some twenty years of diplomatic and national political experience which was to be crowned by his victory in 1816. Washington sent him to France at the tail end of the French Revolution in 1794–6. Jefferson sent him to help to negotiate the Louisiana Purchase and then to England from 1803–7 at a critical time in Anglo-American affairs. In all these embassies, it must be said, he proved himself an able, but an unsuccessful, diplomat. From 1799–1802, and again briefly in 1811, he was Governor of Virginia until, in 1811, he was called into Madison's cabinet. He was Secretary of State from 1811–17 and also Secretary of War, 1814–15.

His record, and a form of primogeniture, made Monroe the Republican choice for the presidency and he was elected with little opposition in 1816. In 1820 only one electoral vote was cast against him out of 232. (A myth has grown up around William Plumer of New Hampshire: that he voted for Adams so that Washington should continue to be the only 'unanimous' president; he voted for Adams because he preferred him.) The Federalists did not even put up a candidate in 1816 (a few electors voted for Rufus King), and there was no real reason why they should. Ever since Jefferson's presidency 'Republicanism' had become increasingly 'Federalised', and the 'half Federalist and half Republican' Monroe believed in the three planks of what Henry Clay dubbed the 'American System', namely a tariff, a national bank and internal improvements at the expense of the federal government. Monroe capitalised upon the intense nationalism and the apparent end of party strife which followed the end of the war. He went on a three months' Grand Tour of the country through the states, North and West, as

46

far as Portland and Detroit. The heading of a leading article in the Federalist *Boston Sentinel* during his visit in July 1817 spoke of the opening of an 'Era of Good Feelings' and this term was to become synonymous with Monroe's presidency.

In his cabinet appointments Monroe tried to represent as many shades of opinion as possible and he did produce a body of more than ordinary merit. For example, John Quincy Adams of Massachusetts, whose very name was a great asset, was Secretary of State. John C. Calhoun of South Carolina (not yet the great apostate), was a devotee of Monroe and the Union, and Secretary of War. The only sour note was struck by Henry Clay of Kentucky whose refusal to serve left the 'West' unrepresented.

As events were to prove, however, behind the façade of nationalism and non-partisan politics lurked ugly sectional differences. These were fanned by a delayed post-war economic depression in the 'Panic of 1819' and were clear for all to see between 1819 and 1821. In 1819 the Missouri Territory applied for admission to the Union as a slave state — though it had few slaves and its economy scarcely required their use — and sparked off two years of bitter debate.

Slavery, believed to be a moribund institution, had been revived by the invention of Eli Witney's Cotton Gin in the 1790s. Very rapidly cotton had become King with slavery as his hand-maiden. Of the original 13 states, 7 had been 'free' and 6 'slave'; now there were 11 of each, though these figures disguised the preponderance of the North with its 5,152,000 people and 105 Congressmen, compared with the South's 4,485,000 and 81 Congressmen, 20 of whom it owed to the rule that allowed every slave to be reckoned as 'three fifths' for the purposes of taxation and representation. Missouri therefore, for the first time, raised the whole issue of the future of slavery in the Union. The proposed state straddled the accepted 'Mason-Dixon line' between slave and free; it raised the question of what was to be the future of slavery in the rest of the vast Louisiana Purchase area; but really at stake lay the political control, present and future, of the Union.

In the event, Henry Clay produced the first of three 'compromise' solutions that were to earn him the title of the 'Great Compromiser' and help to stave off Civil War for forty years. The next state to be admitted was to be Maine, a 'free' state carved out of Massachusetts, in 1820. Missouri was to be admitted as a slave state in 1821; but as the exception to the rule that in future there

47

were to be no slave states in the Louisiana Purchase area north and west of the southern boundary of Missouri along 36°30'. John Quincy Adams called the settlement 'a title-page to a great tragic volume'.

During Monroe's second term a famous State Paper was issued which, some twenty years later, came to be known as the 'Monroe Doctrine'. This was a second definitive statement of American foreign policy (Washington had uttered the first). It was issued as part of Monroe's Annual Message on 2 December 1823. Taking advantage of Spain's involvement in the Napoleonic wars her South American possessions had, one by one, been setting themselves up as independent republics. The so-called 'Holy Alliance' of Russia, Prussia and Austria, who were anxious to root out liberalism anywhere and everywhere, and who had already interfered in Spain itself to put down a liberal revolt, now seemed to be poised to restore Spanish predominance in Latin America. Russia, in addition, was trying to extend down the west coast of America and already was influential as far as San Francisco Bay.

Monroe's Message, which owed a great deal to John Quincy Adams, followed a suggestion from the British Foreign Secretary, George Canning, that Britain and the United States should act in concert to check European expansion in the New World (British trade had risen fourteen-fold with South America since 1792 — though on one occasion faulty 'intelligence' had resulted in a large consignment of ice-skates being sent out there), but this was firmly rejected by Monroe whose doctrine was directed as much against Britain as the 'Holy Alliance', despite Canning's empty boast that he had 'called in the New World to redress the balance of the old'. It asserted 'as a principle . . . that the American continents by the free and independent condition which they have assumed and maintain are henceforth not to be considered as subjects for further colonisation by any European powers'. Any attempts to do so would be interpreted as an 'unfriendly act' towards the United States, which promised, for her part, not to interfere in European affairs. The 'Monroe Doctrine' (the phrase was apparently first used in 1854) was eventually to become the corner-stone of American foreign policy in the New World, though nothing more was heard of the policy enunciated by Monroe until the mid-1840s, 'Hands off the Americas' has not always protected the latter from America herself; but the policy has been enforced with modifications and corollaries right up to the present day, as the Cuban Missile crisis of 1962 demonstrated.

Though politically the 'Era of Good Feelings' might be better described as an 'Era of Mixed Feelings', as heady nationalism gradually broke down into sectional contention, this period did herald the beginnings of an original American national literature. James Fennimore Cooper (1789–1851) emerged as a novelist. In New England a school of young writers was about to assert itself in the persons of Ralph Waldo Emerson (1803–82), Henry Wadsworth Longfellow (1807–82), John Greenleaf Whittier (1807–92), and Nathaniel Hawthorne (1804–64).

Monroe spent his last six years in active retirement at Oak Hill in Virginia in increasingly straitened circumstances finding that his government pay had never been equal to his expenditure. He died in New York City on 4 July 1831, the third out of the last four presidents to die on that historic date. Jefferson once said of Monroe in a famous eulogy that he was 'a man whose soul might be turned the wrong side outwards without disclosing a blemish to the world'. Monroe's lasting memorial is that the capital of the Republic of Liberia which he (a slave owner) helped to set up in 1822 as a home in West Africa for freed, repatriated slaves, is still called 'Monrovia' in his honour.

# JOHN QUINCY ADAMS

SIXTH PRESIDENT OF THE UNITED STATES 1825–9

**Full name**   John Quincy Adams, 1767–1848
**Born**   Braintree (now Quincy) Massachusetts, 11 July 1767, the eldest of 5 children
**Parents**   John Adams (1735–1826), 2nd president, and Abigail Smith Adams (1744–1818). 3 sons, 2 daughters
**Family lineage**   English
**College**   Harvard College, Cambridge, Mass, BA 1787
**Married**   1797 at All Hallows, Barking-by-the-Tower, London (England), Louisa Catherine Johnson Adams (b London, England, 1775, d 1852), daughter of Joshua Johnson, merchant, diplomat — US Consul in London. 3 sons, 1 daughter
**Occupation**   Lawyer; diplomat; US Senator, 1803–08; Secretary of State, 1817–25; member of the US House of Representatives, 1830–48
**Religious denomination**   Unitarian
**Notable relationships**   John Quincy Adams is the only president whose father was also president. He was eighteenth in descent from Edward I, King of England, in three lines
**Died**   From paralysis, Washington, DC, 23 February 1848, aged 80
**Buried**   In the United First Parish Church, Quincy, Mass

**Party** Democratic Republican **State represented** Massachusetts
**Term of Office** 4 March 1825 to 4 March 1829 **Age on taking Office** 57 **Presidential administration** 10th **Congresses** 19th, 20th

1824 ELECTION

| Candidates | Party | Electoral Vote (261) | States Won (24) | Popular Vote | % |
|---|---|---|---|---|---|
| J. Q. Adams | Dem Repub | 84 | 7 | 114,023 | 31.9 |
| A. Jackson | Dem Repub | 99 | 11 | 152,901 | 42.2 |
| H. Clay | Dem Repub | 37 | 3 | 47,217 | 13.0 |
| W. H. Crawford | Dem Repub | 41 | 3 | 46,979 | 12.9 |

50

The election of 1824 was the first in which the popular vote was tabulated. All 4 candidates were 'Republicans' though they represented different 'sections'. No candidate received a majority of the 261 electoral votes and the election was decided by the House of Representatives. Under the provisions of the XII Amendment (1804), Clay was eliminated, and on 9 February 1825 the 24 states cast 1 vote each. Adams received 13, Jackson 7, and Crawford 4. J. Q. Adams was declared elected with J. C. Calhoun (182 votes) as vice president. (Adams' 31.9% remains the lowest percentage of the popular vote ever obtained by any president.)

CONGRESS

| 1825 | 19th | Senate | (46) | 26 Administration supporters |
| | | | | 20 'Jacksonians' |
| | | House | (202) | 105 Administration supporters |
| | | | | 97 'Jacksonians' |
| 1827 | 20th | Senate | (48) | 28 'Jacksonians' |
| | | | | 20 Administration supporters |
| | | House | (213) | 119 'Jacksonians' |
| | | | | 94 Administration supporters |

(This was the first time that an Administration lost control of both the Senate and the House.)

VICE PRESIDENT

7th John Caldwell Calhoun (South Carolina), 1782–1850. He was the first vice president who was not a British subject at birth. Lawyer; member of the US House of Representatives, 1811–17; Secretary of War, 1817–25; vice president, 4 March 1825 to 4 March 1829, and subsequently (under Jackson) 4 March 1829 to 28 December 1832 (when he became the first vice president to resign). US Senator, 1833–44; Secretary of State (Tyler), 1844–5; US Senator, 1845–50. Died 1850.

---

Like his father, the second president, John Quincy Adams came to the presidency with a remarkable career behind him. At 8 he had been an eye-witness of the Battle of Bunker Hill (1775) from a hilltop above the family farm. At 11 he had accompanied his father to Paris and he was educated there, in Amsterdam, and at the University of Leyden. He learned fluent French, Dutch and German. At 14 he went to Russia as secretary to the American minister, returning alone from there to Paris, via Sweden,

Denmark and Germany, where his father was helping to negotiate the Treaty of Paris (1783). When his father went on to England young John returned to America to graduate at Harvard. He studied law and was called to the bar in 1790. As a young man he is described as being short of temper and of stature (he inherited his father's build, they were both about five feet six), rotund and rather untidy — it is claimed that he wore the same hat for 10 years.

George Washington sent him at the age of 26 to The Hague (1794–6). Whilst there he visited London and met his future wife, an English-born American, the niece of a signatory of the Declaration of Independence; they were married in 1797.

President John Adams, anxious to avoid a charge of nepotism, sought Washington's advice before sending his son as Minister to Prussia, 1797–1801. (When he arrived at Berlin he was held up by a Prussian officer who had never heard of the United States). He returned to America in 1801 when his father left office and practised law briefly before entering politics. He was elected to the Massachusetts Senate, and then to the US Senate, as a Federalist.

In the Senate he soon became unpopular because of his complete disregard of party affiliations. He was an Adams through and through; and on successive issues from the Louisiana Purchase to his support for Jefferson over the *Chesapeake* affair, and then his votes in favour of the Embargo Act of 1807, he consistently opposed Federalist views. Today it is possible to admire the determination and courage of his non-partisan, non-sectional approach (he has a chapter to himself on this account in John F. Kennedy's Pulitzer prize-winning book, *Profiles of Courage*), but then every Federalist turned against him and he was forced to resign. He gained some relief from politics between 1806–9 as Boylston Professor of Oratory and Rhetoric at Harvard. His lectures were so arranged as not to interfere with his Senate duties.

President Madison sent Adams back to Russia — some said into political exile — where from 1809–14 he was an eye-witness of Russia's part in the Napoleonic drama. He was then appointed as one of the five American commissioners at Ghent to negotiate a peace with England at the end of the war of 1812–14; and from there he went on to his father's old post in London as Minister to the Court of St James's (1815–17). (One day his son, Charles Francis Adams, would also fill this post (1861–8), giving rise to the aphorism that when Anglo-American relations were at their worst it was necessary to send an Adams to London.)

In 1817 after many years spent abroad — so many that doubts were later to be raised as to his qualifications to be president — John Quincy Adams was recalled to enter Monroe's cabinet as Secretary of State and, in the phraseology of the day, 'the line of safe presidents'; for ever since 1801 the Secretary of State had been heir-apparent to the presidency. He was arguably the greatest Secretary of State that the United States has ever had. Among his achievements were the Rush-Bagot Agreement (1817) with Great Britain which brought arms limitations on the Great Lakes, and the Adams-Onis Treaty (1819) with Spain by which the US acquired East and West Florida, and Spain recognised US claims in the North-West. In addition, agreement was reached with Great Britain over the joint occupancy of 'Oregon' and the northern boundary (49°) of the Louisiana Purchase. Adams also had a share in the foundation of the 'Monroe Doctrine' (qv). His Secretaryship was also marked by his 'Report on Weights and Measures', a duty laid on him by Congress, which contained a masterly summary of the history of the subject and which he regarded as a greater achievement than the cession of the Floridas.

The election of 1824 showed that the title 'Era of Good Feelings' was a misnomer. The political nationalism dubbed the 'American System' by Henry Clay which had been designed to benefit all sections had produced instead sectional rivalry and divisions: the agrarian South opposed the tariff, the debtor West the national bank, and the industrialised North-east the interference implied by federally-financed internal improvements. (This section was benefiting enormously from the privately built Erie canal, built in 1817–26, the 363 miles from Albany, New York, to Buffalo.)

There were four candidates to succeed Monroe, enough to ensure that no one could obtain a majority of the popular vote and that the election would be thrown to the House of Representatives (as in 1800). Andrew Jackson, the 'Hero of New Orleans', headed the popular poll and gained 99 electoral votes, but he lost to John Quincy Adams in the House where Henry Clay, 'Harry of the West' and Jackson's rival, the discarded candidate, put his support behind Adams. (Later, to cries of 'corrupt bargain' he accepted the post of Secretary of State.) John C. Calhoun was brought in to 'balance the ticket' as vice president.

Adams was to spend four very unhappy years in the White House. From the start he faced the opposition of those who thought Jackson should be president. His record also showed that he stood for nationalism — and his Inaugural Address advocated extreme nationalistic policies — and that he was against 'party', when the one was in decline and was being replaced by divisive sectionalism, and the other was not only being revived in an acute form but was fast becoming the *sine qua non* of effective presidential power. Without any party following, or even the charisma to attract popular support, Adams marched out of step with those around him — for example his defence of Indians and distaste for slavery offended many — and as the two-party system recovered he found himself the 'pig in the middle'.

In his famous diary Adams has left an account of the crushing responsibilities of his office. He was:

> . . . compelled to take my exercise, if at all, in the morning before breakfast. I rise usually between five and six. I walk by the light of moon or stars or none about four miles . . . Read papers till nine. Breakfast, and from nine till five receive a succession of visitors, sometimes without intermission — very seldom with an interval of half an hour . . . From five to half past six we dine after which I pass about four hours in my chamber alone, writing, reading papers about public business . . . Between eleven and twelve I retire to bed, to rise again at five or six the next morning . . .

'The weight of the office', he wrote in 1827, 'grows heavier every day.' When he did have some leisure he liked to play billiards on the new table in the White House and to swim nude in the Potomac: puritans were shocked — on both counts. He was also a dedicated amateur botanist. He established a botanical garden in Washington DC and planted hundreds of trees around the White House. He grew mulberry trees and his wife spun silk from the silkworms who inhabited them. John Quincy Adams is also the only president who was a published poet.

In the mid-term elections of 1826 an opposition party, brilliantly organised by Martin Van Buren of New York around Andrew Jackson, was strong enough to gain control of Congress and most state governments. 'Jacksonian Democracy' had been born and Jackson's election in 1828 was assured. To make matters worse Adams proceeded to make serious mistakes in domestic policy (he raised the tariff to 45% *ad valorem* in 1828) and, uncharacteristically, he bungled foreign relations with Britain and Latin America.

John Quincy Adams and his father were the only two presidents in the first fifty years of the new republic to be denied a second term. Like his father he left Washington without attending the inauguration of his successor, but the noblest portion of his long political career lay ahead. From December 1831 (aged 64) to February 1848 'the Old Man Eloquent' sat for nearly seventeen years in the House of Representatives in nine successive Congresses (22nd-30th) under five presidents. As always he was independent of party and of section. He was an opponent of South Carolina and 'nullification' in the 1830s but a supporter of the rechartering of the Bank of the United States; and he became a staunch anti-slavery protagonist, though never an Abolitionist. For 11 famous days in 1839 he was Speaker of the House. At the last he strenuously opposed the Mexican War of 1846–8. It was in the House that he suffered his final stroke (a plate still marks the spot), and he died two days later in the Speaker's room in the Capitol. In the same year he had confided to his diary in choleric vein that 'My whole life has been a succession of disappointments. I can scarcely recollect a single instance of success in anything that I ever undertook'. In truth, his presidency was his only failure; and here he 'failed' only because of his undeviating devotion to what he considered to be the nation's interests. He was undeniably a very great American — if not a great president — whether as diplomat, courageous Senator, brilliant Secretary of State, or Congressman. When he died he was accorded universal tribute and he was escorted from the Capitol to Boston and finally to Quincy where he reposes alongside his parents and his wife. Over his tomb are the words on which he rested his case — 'Alteri saeculo'. He also has a share in another monument.

In Washington DC from the Capitol to the Washington Monument stretches the Mall with the buildings of the Smithsonian Institution on either side. These buildings house scientific, historical and art collections in what has been called 'the world's greatest museum'. James Smithson (1765–1829), a natural son of the first Duke of Northumberland, an Englishman who had never seen America, left his entire fortune of £120,000 for the founding at Washington of 'an establishment for the increase and diffusion of knowledge among men'. Eleven cases of sovereigns eventually reached America, but Congress then spent ten years debating its constitutional right to accept the bequest. It was John Quincy Adams, more than anyone else, who was instrumental in winning acceptance of the gift which helped the United States to take that share in the development of the arts and the sciences which he had, far-sightedly, urged in his Inaugural Address.

# ANDREW JACKSON

**Full name**   Andrew Jackson, 1767–1845
**Born**   Waxhaw, South Carolina, 15 March 1767, the third of 3 sons
**Parents**   Andrew Jackson (b Ireland, d early March 1767), farmer, and Elizabeth Hutchinson Jackson (b Ireland, d 1781). 3 sons
**Family lineage**   Scottish-Irish
**College**   None
**Married**   1791 (and again in 1794), Rachel Donelson Robards Jackson (1767–1828), the divorced wife of Lewis Robards, daughter of John Donelson, surveyor. No children (in 1810 the Jacksons legally adopted Mrs Jackson's nephew, b 1809, who was named Andrew Jackson, Jnr)
**Occupation**   Soldier in the Revolutionary War; lawyer; member of the House of Representatives, 1796–97; US Senator, 1797–98 (resigned); judge of the Tennessee Superior Court, 1798–1804; War of 1812, Major-general; military governor of Florida, 1821. US Senator 1823–5 (resigned)
**Religious denomination**   Presbyterian
**Notable relationships**   His niece Sarah Childress married James K. Polk, eleventh president
**Died**   From consumption and dropsy at the Hermitage, Nashville, Tenn, 8 June 1845, aged 78
**Buried**   The Hermitage, Nashville, Tenn

**Party** Democratic **State represented** Tennessee **Terms of Office** 4 March 1829 to 4 March 1837 **Age on taking Office** 61 **Presidential administrations** 11th, 12th **Congresses** 21st, 22nd, 23rd, 24th

1828 ELECTION

| Candidate | Party | Electoral Vote (288) | States Won (24) | Popular Vote | % |
|---|---|---|---|---|---|
| Andrew Jackson | Dem | 178 | 15 | 687,502 | 56.0 |
| J. Q. Adams | Nat Repub | 83 | 9 | 508,074 | 44.0 |

| Candidate | Party | Electoral Vote (288) | States Won (24) | Popular Vote | % |
|---|---|---|---|---|---|
| Andrew Jackson | Dem | 219 | 16 | 687,052 | 54.5 |
| Henry Clay | Nat Rep | 49 | 6 | 530,189 | 37.5 |
| W. Wirt | Anti-Mason | 7 | 1 | 101,051 | 8.0 |
| J. Floyd | Ind Dem | 11 | 1 | — | — |

## CONGRESS

| | | | | | |
|---|---|---|---|---|---|
| 1829 | 21st | Senate | (48) | 26 Dem | 22 Nat Repub |
| | | House | (213) | 139 Dem | 74 Nat Repub |
| 1831 | 22nd | Senate | (48) | 25 Dem | 21 Nat Repub 2 Anti-Masons[1] |
| | | House | (213) | 141 Dem | 58 Nat Repub 14 Anti-Masons |
| 1833 | 23rd | Senate | (48) | 20 Dem | 20 Nat Repub 8 Anti-Masons |
| | | House | (260) | 147 Dem | 53 Anti-Masons 60 Others[2] |
| 1835 | 24th | Senate | (52) | 27 Dem | 25 Whigs[3] |
| | | House | (243) | 145 Dem | 98 Whigs |

(The Administration controlled Congress throughout.)

1 The 'Anti-Mason' Party was the first 3rd Party in US history. One of the Anti-Masons elected to the House was ex-President John Q. Adams.
2 Mainly 'National Republicans' this was the first time that the principal minority party was outnumbered by other splinter groups.
3 The 'Whig' party came into existence in 1834 as an Anti-Jackson coalition.

## NOTES

1 1830 5th census: Total population, 12,866,020 including 2,009,943 slaves and 319,599 free negroes.
2 New states admitted: Arkansas (1836) 25th; Michigan (1837) 26th.

## VICE PRESIDENTS

7th John Caldwell Calhoun, 4 March 1829 to 28 December 1832 (resigned). Formerly vice president, 1825–29 (J. Q. Adams).
8th Martin Van Buren (1833–7), subsequently 8th president. Term of Office: 4 March 1833 to 4 March 1837.

---

On 4 March 1829 a tall, erect and dignified gentleman of 61, was sworn in as the seventh President of the United States — and America entered a new age for this man was totally unlike any of his predecessors. He was a westerner, they had all come from the east. He was a frontiersman, an Indian fighter and a successful duellist (he still carried opponent's bullets in his left and right arms and lodged next to his heart). With the exception of Washington, with whom he had most in common, they had all made their marks as statesmen and diplomats. He was a popular military hero and, some obviously feared, come to put an end to the Republic.

It was perhaps possible to magnify any differences out of all proportion. In Tennessee Andrew Jackson was an aristocrat. He was a wealthy man and a slave-owner, like four of his predecessors (Washington, Jefferson, Madison and Monroe) and four of his successors (Tyler, Polk, Taylor and Johnson), with an assured social position and conservative connections. He was a gentleman-planter, judge, ex-Congressman and Senator and ranking major general (retired) in the United States army; and, despite a fierce temper and an iron will, he was an urbane and gracious gentleman. In fact, what some contemporaries feared was not so much Jackson himself as the way in which he had become president. His predecessors had not so much been chosen by the people as endorsed. This was not so with Jackson: he was 'the people's Andrew' elected to the presidency by a groundswell of popular support which had smashed old party organisations and driven established leaders to cover. Elected on a slogan of 'Jackson and Reform' that 'democracy', it seemed, had triumphed which men had feared for a thousand years and a deep and impenetrable gloom settled over Washington as the day of inauguration loomed.

That ceremony passed off well enough with the 'principal personage' displaying 'composed dignity' in front of a 'living mass' of people. But then followed a reception at the White House. Mrs Samuel Harrison Smith, a pillar of Washington society was there: '. . . What a scene did we witness! . . . the whole house had been inundated by the rabble mob . . . Ladies and gentlemen only had been expected at this Levée, not the people en masse. But it was the People's day, and the People's President and the People would rule. God grant that one day or other, the People do not put down all rule and rulers.' It was a proud day for the people, but to Judge Joseph Story, 'The reign of "King Mob" seemed triumphant'.

The new president, reputedly 'born' in more places than any other, first lived in a log cabin in the Carolinas with his Irish immigrant parents two years off the boat. His father died before his birth and the rest of the family died during the American War of Independence. At 14 Andrew was an orphan bearing a scar on his face from the sabre of a British officer whose boots he had refused to clean. At 20 he was a lawyer in the Indian wilderness in the Territorial Western District of North Carolina, on the frontier beyond the Cumberland Mountains. At 24 he 'married' a divorcée in the belief that her divorce was absolute, but finding that this was not the case he remarried Rachel Robards in 1794. This episode provided his enemies with ammunition and Jackson with his first victim in a duel.

In 1796 the Territory was organised as Tennessee and Jackson, attorney general since 1790, helped to write its constitution, was its first representative in Congress and served it briefly in the Senate from which, feeling himself to be out of place amongst such eminent men, he resigned. A contemporary described him as 'a tall, lank uncouth-looking personage, with long locks of hair hanging over his face, and a queue down his back tied in an eel-skin, his dress singular, his manners and deportment those of a rough backwoodsman'.

Back in Tennessee he became a respected judge and a major general in the state militia (though he had never risen above the rank of private before), and he devoted himself to his plantation and trade. He speculated in land and business and lost money to banks and eastern interests, but he prospered enough to buy slaves and build a fine mansion at the Hermitage plantation near Nashville.

The turning point in his life was the War of 1812. He emerged as a master of tactics and rapid movement. He crushed the Creek Indians at the battle of Horse Shoe Bend (1814) and cleared Alabama for operations against the British. He was appointed major general in the regular army and put in command of all operations in the South. A remarkable victory against seasoned British troops at New Orleans (Chalmette) on 18 January 1815 made him the hero of a whole generation of Americans. His reputation was further enhanced during the first Seminole War (1817–18) and the conquest of Florida (1818) of which, briefly, he was the temporary military governor (1821). In 1823 he was re-elected to the United States Senate from Tennessee.

By the 1820s American party politics were in a chaotic state. National party lines were increasingly blurred and obliterated by sectional issues which, skilfully manipulated by a new class of party managers, led to new style parties and factions in the states. Political developments were aided by the increasing number of voters: by 1824 all white adult males had a vote in all states except Rhode Island, Virginia and Louisiana, whereas in Great Britain in the 1820s only 5% of adult males had a vote. (By 1828 all states except Delaware and South Carolina chose their Presidential Electors by popular vote.) Political development was also aided by improved transport which made national politics possible on a wider scale; and by the proliferation of partisan newspapers.

Long before 1824 some groups were already rallying around Jackson whose prime assets were his reputation — everyone knew the 'Hero of New Orleans' — and, more particularly, his non-identification with any of the current divisive public issues. Increasingly as parties broke down so issues of policy ceased to be important; it was the man himself who mattered. Jackson piled up more popular and electoral votes than anyone else in 1824 though the plethora of candidates saw the election transferred to the House where he lost. In the manner of his defeat lay the seeds of future victory and Jackson resigned his new Senate seat to make Adams' presidency one long campaign for 1828. The sole issue was the rejection of the people's choice by the politicians in 1825 and 'Jackson the Martyr' became the symbol of the people's right to be heard. 'Democracy' and Jackson were now linked and American politics would never again be quite the same. The result in 1828 was a foregone conclusion and Jackson was swept into the White House with the largest share of the popular vote in the nineteenth century. His victory was tempered by sadness, his wife died just after the election.

Jackson was the first president to combine effectively the roles of chief of party, chief of state and chief executive, thus enhancing the power of the presidency. He asserted his authority and his independence, making it clear that he did not expect to lean upon advisers but to be the head of the executive himself. His official cabinet, with the exception of Martin Van Buren, was weak, and increasingly he surrounded himself with an inner circle of very able advisers known as his 'Kitchen Cabinet'. 'Eaton malaria' — which grew out of the snubs of the rest of the cabinet and their wives to the scandal-tainted wife of the Secretary of War — plus a growing rift between Jackson and his vice president John C. Calhoun, which led to the latter's resignation in 1832, completed the dissolution of the official cabinet.

Elected on a slogan of 'Jackson and Reform' the president set out to 'cleanse the Augean stables' of entrenched officeholders many of whom were old (veterans of the Revolution), incompetent, or both. In the previous forty years his 6 predecessors had removed only 74 officials — Jefferson's much-vaunted first introduction of

61

the so-called 'spoils system' accounting for 39 of these. Jackson in his first year removed 700 including 500 postmasters, developing the theory of rotation in office, ie that any man is capable of performing any office, and the American 'spoils system' was really born. 'To the victors belong the spoils of the enemy', said William L. Marcy, a Jacksonian senator from New York in a famous remark that is not as cynical as it sounds: the loyalty of party officials to the people who elected them should make democracy work well. Although the 'spoils system' would be badly misused under later administrations and become a source of corruption in government, Jackson's appointees were for the most part able and honest, and scoundrels like Samuel Swartwout, who milked the port of New York of over a million dollars, were the exception rather than the rule.

Jackson vetoed more bills than any of his predecessors and used the 'pocket veto' seven times. (The Constitution allows a president to hold a bill for 10 days before signing or vetoing it; if Congress adjourns during that period with the bill unsigned it does not become law.) Henry Clay and the National Republicans (or Whigs as they were soon to become known) might rail about 'King Andrew I' and his high-handed actions; but the electors disagreed and in 1832 decisively re-elected Jackson under the Democratic label.

But it is for his attitudes towards the major divisive issues of the day that Jackson's presidency is important. He faced a major challenge over the South Carolina nullification controversy. John C. Calhoun the vice president opposed the high tariffs which protected northern manufactures and he argued that states had a right to nullify, ie set at nought, federal legislation; and that *in extremis* states could secede from the Union (arguments which had been rehearsed on previous occasions). For Andrew Jackson 'union' was the most fundamental of national values and he prepared to meet this challenge to federal authority by force if necessary. A new 'Compromise Tariff', the work of Henry Clay (his second great compromise solution to a taxing problem), provided a face-saving formula for both sides; but once again a fundamental weakness in the constitution had been revealed.

Jackson vetoed the re-chartering of the Second Bank of the United States (1816–36) on the grounds that it was unconstitutional and the creature of powerful vested interests. Critics have argued that he crushed it for personal reasons and that in so doing he launched the nation upon more than a century of unsound finance.

His third victory came with his most famous veto — the Maysville Road veto in 1830. Myriads of 'internal improvement' bills were flooding in as Congressmen sought federal funds for their own districts. The role of the federal government in transportation was as yet unclear and Jackson followed Madison and Monroe in vetoing proposals because he doubted the constitutionality of such measures. He vetoed the Maysville Road on the grounds that it lay entirely inside one state (Henry Clay's Kentucky) and was a local and not a national scheme. At stake really lay the whole question of the relationship of the federal government to economic development — should it direct it? stimulate it? or leave it to private enterprise? Jackson shelved the issue.

He defied a Supreme Court decision from Chief Justice John Marshall (who was coming to the end of his very distinguished career) not to remove certain Indian tribes to the West. 'John Marshall has made his decision, now let him enforce it', said Jackson who proceeded to relocate the Five Civilised Nations of the south-east in present day Oklahoma and forced the Seminoles to comply by launching the second Seminole War (1835–42).

Jackson was equally active in foreign affairs. He tried and failed to purchase Texas and California from Mexico but sympathised with the Texas revolution of 1835 and appointed a minister to the new republic. He settled claims against France which had been dragging on since the Napoleonic War; made a reciprocal trade agreement with Great Britain over the British West Indies; and sent missions which made treaties with Siam and Muscat.

Finally, he actively campaigned for the election of his vice president Martin Van Buren to the presidency; and from The Hermitage in retirement sent the latter continuous advice — advice which was not always followed (as for example over the annexation of Texas), which led Jackson to support James K. Polk's Democratic nomination for the presidency in 1844 rather than that of 'Little Van'.

Deaf, blind in one eye and suffering from the effects of wounds and illnesses, Andrew Jackson — 'Old Hickory' — expired in 1845. He was the first president to ride on a train and the first to be the subject of an assassination attempt (1835). The first first-generation American to become president; and the first (and last) to keep a string of racehorses in the grounds of the White House.

He left the White House, so it is said, with only ninety dollars in his pocket and an honorary Harvard degree (1833), which had reduced John Quincy Adams (Phi Beta Kappa, class of '87) to near apoplexy at the thought of the honour done to 'that barbarian', who, on one occasion, had described the presidency as 'dignified slavery'.

# MARTIN VAN BUREN

**Full name**  Martin Van Buren, 1782–1862
**Born**  Kinderhook, Columbia County, New York, 5 December 1782, the third of 5 children
**Parents**  Abraham Van Buren (1737–1817), farmer, tavern keeper, and Maria Hoes Van Allen Van Buren (1737–1818), widow of Johanes Van Allen. 3 sons, 2 daughters (Mrs Van Buren had 2 sons and a daughter by her previous marriage)
**Family lineage**  Dutch (Van Buren was the first of five presidents not of British descent, the others were the two Roosevelts, Hoover and Eisenhower, qv)
**College**  None
**Married**  1807, his first cousin once removed, Hannah Hoes Van Buren (1783–1819), daughter of John Dircksen Hoes, farmer. 4 sons
**Occupation**  Lawyer; state politician; US Senator, 1821–8; Governor of New York, 1829; Secretary of State, 1829–31; Minister to Great Britain, 1831; vice president, 1833–7
**Religious denomination**  Dutch Reformed
**Notable relationships**  Through his mother Van Buren was related twice over to Theodore Roosevelt, 26th president, born 1858
**Died**  From asthma, at Lindenwald, near Kinderhook, NY, 24 July 1862, aged 79
**Buried**  Kinderhook Cemetery, NY

**Party** Democratic **State represented** New York **Term of Office** 4 March 1837 to 4 March 1841 **Age on taking Office** 54 **Presidential administration** 13th **Congresses** 25th, 26th

1836 ELECTION

| Candidates | Party | Electoral Vote (294) | States Won (26) | Popular Vote | % |
|---|---|---|---|---|---|
| M. Van Buren | Dem | 170 | 15 | 764,198 | 50.9 |
| W. H. Harrison | Whig | 73 | 7 | 549,508 | 36.6 |

| H. L. White | Whig | 26 | 2 | 145,352 | 9.7 |
| D. Webster | Whig | 14 | 1 | 41,287 | 2.7 |
| W. P. Mangum | Whig | 11 | 1 | — | — |

The Whigs ran several candidates against Van Buren in an attempt so to divide the electoral vote as to throw the election to the House (as in 1825). This tactic failed but no vice presidential candidate received a majority of the electoral vote and for the first and only time the Senate had to choose a vice president.

### CONGRESS

| 1837 | 25th | Senate | (52) | 30 Dem | 18 Whigs | 4 Others |
| | | House | (239) | 108 Dem | 107 Whigs | 24 Others |
| 1839 | 26th | Senate | (52) | 28 Dem | 22 Whigs | 2 Others |
| | | House | (242) | 124 Dem | 118 Whigs | |

(The Administration ostensibly controlled Congress throughout but a coalition of Whigs and Conservative Democrats held the balance of power in both Houses.)

### VICE PRESIDENT

9th Richard Mentor 'Tecumseh' Johnson (Kentucky), 1780–1850. Lawyer; state politician; member of the United States House of Representatives, 1807–12, 1814–19, 1829–37; US Senator, 1819–29. (He was the first vice president to serve in both Houses.) Severely wounded in the War of 1812, at the Battle of the Thames River, 1813, where he is credited with the death of Tecumseh, Chief of the Shawnees. Vice president, 4 March 1837 to 4 March 1841. Van Buren and Johnson became the first of only three teams (the others were Hoover and Curtis in 1932, and Carter and Mondale in 1980) to be defeated when they ran for re-election. Member of Kentucky Legislature 1841–2. Died 1850 unmarried.

### NOTE

1840 6th Census: Total population, 17,069,453 including 2,487,555 slaves and 386,293 free negroes.

---

Martin Van Buren, the first president to be born a citizen of the United States, probably had more nicknames than any other president. He was known variously as the 'American Talleyrand', the 'Little Magician', 'Little Matty' (he was 5ft 6in), the 'Red Fox' (what was left of his hair was red), and 'Old Kinderhook' (his birthplace), among others. 'OK' the abbreviation of the last name was used as a Van Buren political slogan and this is one of the most likely explanations of the origins of this popular term.

He was born in a Dutch village east of the Hudson near Albany. He was the first president who had taken no part, military or political, in the Revolution. He was neither Founding Father nor war hero. His long life spanned the period from the end of the Revolution to the Civil War and he has been described as one of the few distinguished Americans who might have known Washington and Abraham Lincoln. He had a good solid home background and elementary education and at 14 was apprenticed to a local attorney. The last year of his apprenticeship was spent in New York before he returned to set up office in his native village with a practice soon covering the county. In 1807 he married Hannah Hoes who died twelve years later after a very happy marriage (though she is not even mentioned in his autobiography), leaving him with four sons.

Following his marriage Van Buren moved to New York where he made rapid strides in his profession and in politics, which he had first entered in 1800 (aged 18) at the time of the success of the Democratic Republicans. He became a state Senator and by the age of 30 he was recognised as a consumate, calculating politician and the power behind the 'Albany Regency' in New York, a powerful Democratic Republican political machine based on patronage. He emerged as an adroit politician during the War of 1812 when his timely lead in swinging the State Senate from peace to war was rewarded with a four year spell as New York's Attorney General.

He was elected to the US Senate from 1821–8 where, after 1824, he became a notable Jackson protagonist believing that the latter represented the old 'Democratic' virtues and, being impressed by the general, a fellow Senator. From the mid 1820s Van Buren led the opposition to President John Quincy Adams in the Senate and became the most powerful northern supporter of Jackson; and it was the 'Little Magician' who master-minded Andrew Jackson's victory in 1828.

After a few months as Governor of New York (he was the first of four presidents — the others were Cleveland and the two Roosevelts — to hold this post), Van Buren entered Jackson's administration as Secretary of State (1829–31), as a trusted adviser and — if precedent was anything to go by — heir-apparent. A brief spell as Minister to England (the Senate refused to confirm his appointment) was followed by his vice-presidential candidature in 1832 in place of John C. Calhoun who had resigned. As vice president he was to preside over some very important debates in the Senate during Jackson's critical second term. He was nominated for the presidency by the Democrats in 1835, and in 1836, following a bitter campaign, won that office against several sectionally nominated Whigs.

An enemy, before proceeding to denigrate Van Buren, described him at this time as: '. . . reaching only precisely the middle height; in blameless toilette, his smooth, snow-white shirt bosom in complete harmony with his round face, carefully shaved, with the exception of very decent side whiskers; his large double chin finding a pleasant support on his broad black cravat . . . a settled smile, bright coloured vivacious twinkling eyes . . . a round high forehead which appears still higher from the absence of hair on the crown . . . a friendly well-meaning bourgeois . . .'

The 'Mistletoe Politician' (he was seen as a parasite clinging to the Jackson tree) was only three months into his presidency when the United States was struck by the Panic of 1837, the severest financial crisis of the century which had been brewing for many years but which owed its immediate origins to speculation, inflation and Jackson's 'hard money' policies. The result was a five-year-long depression that caused Van Buren's defeat in 1840. He followed deflationary policies and cut government expenditure but all to no avail. He refused calls to re-establish a national bank, though he did propose the establishment of an independent Treasury system that was adopted in 1840.

The economy was not his only problem: slavery was fast becoming *the* divisive issue. Slavery was touched on for the first time in an inaugural address in 1837 when Van Buren made clear his 'unflexible and uncompromising' opposition to Congressional interference with the continuation of slavery in the nation's capital, or 'the slightest interference with it in the States where it exists'. Quite clearly, as far as southerners or northern abolitionists were concerned, the president's view smacked of expediency and he was soon ranked with those who were known as 'Northern men with Southern principles'.

Another issue was becoming mixed up with the question of slavery, namely Texas. Jackson had tacitly acknowledged its independence from Mexico, but when a Texan emissary proposed that the United States annex Texas immediately, Van Buren blocked the proposal because he saw that it would lead to an extension of slave territory and would also threaten war with Mexico.

Temporarily attention was diverted away from these issues to foreign problems. Van Buren was successful in negotiating a settlement of American claims against Mexico (1840), and in resolving the boundary with Texas. In the north-east the problem of the boundary between Maine and British New Brunswick became a matter of discussions that led later, under Tyler, to the Webster-Ashburton Treaty of 1842. Van Buren also followed a policy of strict American neutrality — to the disgust of many — over the rebellions in British Upper and Lower Canada (1837).

Diplomatic successes tend not to be vote catchers and the administration fell into popular contempt as the economic crisis deepened. The Whigs prepared to capitalise upon their opponent's misfortunes and in 1839 nominated William Henry Harrison of 'Tippecanoe' fame, along with John Tyler, for the 1840 election. Van Buren received only 60 electoral votes and failed to win even his own home state, whilst Harrison received an even larger majority than Jackson had in 1832. The Jacksonian economic legacy, the collapse of Democratic party discipline, and ominous cracks between the northern and southern wings of the party over slavery and territorial expansion, meant that everything reacted against Jackson's successor and the election result of 1840 was not really surprising. In the first 'hoopla, log cabin and hard cider' campaign in American history, Van Buren was washed out of the White House in a tidal wave of apple juice and electioneering froth; and he was freed from the 'toilsome and anxious probation' that was the presidency.

The White House under his rule had been an exceptionally pleasant and dignified mansion, where the president had dispensed generous and liberal hospitality. Guests ate excellent food, prepared by a London chef, and used fine china and cutlery. His daughter-in-law Angelica, the White House hostess for the widower president, 'received' in the 'Elliptical Blue Room' which was Van Buren's creation. (His enemies depicted 'King Matty' eating with gold spoons in the 'palace' surrounded by a royal family headed by his debonair son 'Prince John'.)

Van Buren loitered long enough in Washington to be able to attend the funeral of his successor (qv) and then he set off for his newly-acquired estate at Lindenwald near Kinderhook; but at nearly sixty he was not yet done with politics. He made two attempts to regain the presidency. He failed to get the Democratic nomination in 1844 because he opposed the annexation of Texas.

In 1848 he led the 'Barnburners', a secessionist wing of the Democrats, in the formation of the 'Free Soil' party which, with the slogan of 'Free Soil, Free Speech, Free Labor and Free Men' aimed to unite all the northern anti-slavery forces. Van Buren failed to receive any electoral votes, but the divided Democrats were defeated.

He supported the Compromise of 1850 (qv) and opposed the pro-slavery policies of Presidents Pierce and Buchanan. Abraham Lincoln's efforts to preserve the Union and limit slavery met his full approval. He lived to see the Blue Regiments marching down Broadway in New York and he did so as a staunch Unionist. Martin Van Buren died on 24 July 1862, whilst the Army of the Potomac and the Army of Virginia were racing for Washington.

# WILLIAM HENRY HARRISON

**Full name**   William Henry Harrison, 1773–1841
**Born**   Berkeley Plantation, Charles City County, Virginia, 9 February 1773, the youngest of 7 children
**Parents**   Benjamin Harrison, 'The Signer' (1726–91), member, and later Speaker, of the Virginia House of Burgesses, 1749–75, 1777–81. Delegate to the first and second Continental Congresses, 1774–7; signatory of the Declaration of Independence, 1776; Governor of Virginia, 1781–4; and Elizabeth Bassett Harrison (1730–92). 4 daughters, 3 sons
**Family lineage**   English
**College**   Hampden-Sydney College, Virginia. (Did not graduate)
**Married**   1795, Anna Tuthill Symmes Harrison (1775–1864), daughter of Col John Cleves Symmes, Chief Justice of the Supreme Court of New Jersey. 6 sons, 4 daughters
**Occupation**   Medical student 1791; soldier 1791–8; Secretary of the North West Territory, 1798; territorial delegate to Congress, 1799–1800; Governor of Indiana Territory, 1800–16; War of 1812, Brigadier General; Indian Commissioner 1814–15; member of the US House of Representatives, 1816–19; Ohio Senator 1819–24; member of the US Senate, 1825–8; Minister to Colombia 1828–9; farmer; clerk of County Court, 1830–40
**Religious denomination**   Episcopalian
**Notable relationships**   Harrison was 18th in descent from Henry III, King of England. He was also descended from Sir Nicholas Bacon (1509–79); Sir Francis Bacon (1561–1626); and Col Thomas Harrison (1606–60) who was executed as a regicide. His grandson, Benjamin Harrison, was the 23rd president
**Died**   From pleurisy and pneumonia, in the White House, Washington, DC 4 April 1841, aged 68
**Buried**   North Bend, Ohio

**Party** Whig **State represented** Ohio **Term of office** 4 March 1841 to

4 April 1841 (31 days) **Age on taking office 68 Presidential administration 14th Congress** 27th (see p 76)

(see p 76)

1840 ELECTION

| Candidate | Party | Electoral Vote (294) | States Won (26) | Popular Vote | % |
|---|---|---|---|---|---|
| W. H. Harrison | Whig | 234 | 19 | 1,275,016 | 52.9 |
| M. Van Buren | Dem | 60 | 7 | 1,129,102 | 46.8 |
| J. G. Birney | Liberty | — | — | 7,069 | 0.3 |

VICE PRESIDENT

10th, John Tyler, subsequently 10th president; the vice president
who served the second shortest term — 33 days.

---

The period from 1840 to 1860 has been described as one of
momentous events and mainly mediocre presidents. The eight
presidents (beginning with Van Buren) who served a single term, or
less, have been called, not altogether fairly, the 'eight dwarfs'.
Harrison was of this number and he must rank as one of the
'unknown presidents' of the United States. Yet more 'records' cling
to him than probably any other president. He was the last president
to be born a British subject. He was the first Whig. 'Granny'
Harrison was the oldest president at inauguration until 1981. He
delivered the longest-ever Inaugural Address (nearly 8,500 words)
which lasted for an hour and three quarters and helped to kill him.
He was the first to die in office. He served the shortest ever term —
31 days. He was the first (of only two presidents) to die in the White
House. He was the only president to be the grandfather of another
president. He (and Mrs Harrison) hold the record for the most
number of children born to a presidential marriage.

The political party of which he became a pawn depicted him as a
log-cabin-living frontiersman. Nothing could be further from the
truth. Harrison was of the blood royal both literally and metaphorically. His pedigree reached back to England's kings. His
father had moved the adoption of the Declaration of Independence. His own eventful career has led to his being described as the
nearest thing to Andrew Jackson with Whig overtones.

Born into a wealthy Virginia family he abandoned a medical
career on his father's death. Washington commissioned him ensign
in the army fighting the Indians in the North West and he took part
in the battle of Fallen Timbers (1794) as an aide to General 'Mad

72

Anthony' Wayne. He gained administrative experience as the Secretary of the North West Territory and represented it in Congress. He recaptured Detroit from the British and inflicted a crushing defeat on them and their Indian allies at the battle of the Thames (1813), one of the few land victories in this (for Americans) dismal war.

For twelve years he played the role of state and federal politician and briefly, before becoming a victim of Jackson's 'spoils system', he toyed with diplomacy. But with the accession of Jackson he retired, at the age of 56, to his farm and parish-pump politics with a solid military and political career behind him and with a reputation as a sound and incorruptible figure.

He was persuaded out of his retirement in 1836 by a coalition of Whigs and Anti-Masons who needed a figure-head — and who better than the military hero, 'Old Honesty' himself? He came a good second to Van Buren and was clearly 'available' for another day, if only he did not become identified with any of the key issues of the time: 'Say not one single word about his principles or his creed,' said a party manager. 'Let him say nothing, promise nothing. Let no committee, no town meeting ever extract from him a single word about what he thinks now and will do hereafter. Let the use of pen and ink be wholly forbidden.' 'General Mum' followed the advice to the letter.

The 1840 election campaign was without precedent. The nation turned itself out of doors and monster meetings (100,000 in Dayton, Ohio), and processions stretching from town to town were commonplace. The Whigs set out to play the Democrats — the self-styled party of the people — at their own game. Their man Harrison was represented as a plain unaffected Western pioneer and Van Buren as a simpering aristocrat. Coon-skin caps abounded along with log-cabin emblems and oceans of hard cider. Mammoth paper balls covered with political slogans were pushed from town to town to 'keep the ball rolling', and behind the gathering momentum 78% of the electorate (a figure not to be equalled until 1896) prepared to turn out to put 'Tippecanoe and Tyler Too' into the White House. (No one heeded, except to jeer, the most important set of votes cast in 1840; the 7,069 votes distributed throughout the North for James G. Birney, the Abolitionist).

The Democrats were dumbfounded by the extent of their defeat. 'Who is William Harrison, and what does he stand for?' There was no time to find out. Harrison scarcely had time to get astride his

73

white charger and go over the inaugural procession route twice before delivering the longest speech on record (and it had been edited by Daniel Webster), before (like his illustrious forbear, Sir Francis Bacon), he was dead from a chill, contracted after going bare-headed in a bitingly cold Washington winter's day. 1841 was to be the first of two years (the other would be 1881), when America would have three presidents in the one year. With his death Harrison laid the foundations for yet another 'record', the 'zero factor': ever since 1840 not a single president elected in a year ending in a zero has left the White House alive. His final legacy to the nation was a constitutional conundrum: did a vice president succeeding to the presidency automatically become president of the United States?

# JOHN TYLER

**Full name**  John Tyler, 1790–1862
**Born**  Near Greenway, Charles City County, Virginia, 29 March 1790, the sixth of 8 children
**Parents**  John Tyler (1747–1813) lawyer; member, later Speaker, of the Virginia House of Burgesses; Governor of Virginia, 1808–11; US Judge, 1811; and Mary Marrott Armistead Tyler (1761–97). 5 daughters, 3 sons
**Family lineage**  English
**College**  College of William and Mary, Williamsburg, Virginia
**Married**  1. 1813, Letitia Christian Tyler (1790–1842), daughter of Robert Christian, planter. 5 daughters, 3 sons. Mrs Tyler was the first 'First Lady' to die in the White House
2. 1844, Julia Gardiner Tyler (1820–89), daughter of David Gardiner, US Senator. Julia Tyler, at 24, was the youngest 'First Lady' until Frances Cleveland (qv). 5 sons, 2 daughters
**Occupation**  Lawyer; member of the Virginia House of Delegates, 1811–16, 1823–5; Speaker, 1839–40; War of 1812, captain of militia company; member of the Virginia Council of State, 1815–16; member of the US House of Representatives, 1816–21; Governor of Virginia, 1825–7; US Senator, 1827–36; vice president, 1841; member of Confederate Congress, 1861–2
**Religious denomination**  Episcopalian
**Notable relationships**  None'
**Died**  From bilious fever, Richmond, Va, 18 January 1862, aged 71
**Buried**  Hollywood Cemetery, Richmond, Virginia

**Party** Whig **State represented** Virginia **Term of Office** 6 April 1841 to 4 March 1845. (He served the unexpired portion of his predecessor, 3 years, 332 days) **Age on taking Office** 51 **Presidential administration** 14th (continued) **Congresses** 27th, 28th

| 1841 | 27th | Senate (52) | 28 Whigs | 22 Dem | 2 Others |
| | | House (241) | 133 Whigs | 102 Dem | 6 Others |
| 1843 | | Senate (54) | 28 Whigs | 25 Dem | 1 Other |
| | | House (222) | 142 Dem | 79 Whigs | 1 Other |

(The Administration lost control of the House.)

## NOTES

1 23 January 1844: the first Tuesday after the first Monday in November was established as the future presidential election day in all states.

2 New State: Florida (1845) 27th.

### VICE PRESIDENT

Tyler was the first of four presidents (the others were Fillmore, Johnson and Arthur) who did not have a vice president.

---

Traditionally John Tyler was down on his hands and knees playing marbles on his farm in Virginia when a courier arrived from Washington with a letter, signed by Harrison's cabinet:

Washington, April 4, 1841.

To John Tyler, Vice-President of the United States:-

Sir, It becomes our painful duty to inform you that William Henry Harrison, late President of the United States, has departed this life . . .

It was the first time that *the* reason for the vice presidency was realised.

The Founding Fathers had intended that the vice president should be one of the two most favoured candidates in a presidential election, but when party politics developed their system produced problems, as in 1796. By the XII Amendment (1804), electors were henceforth to vote separately for the president and the vice president and since that date only one man (Van Buren) had been elevated directly from vice presidency to the higher post. Instead of being worth a great man's ambitions the vice presidency had become either a means of 'balancing the ticket' geographically, or of rewarding the party faithful on the weaker wing of the party. This was notably the case in 1840. When Harrison took the Whig nomination from Henry Clay, the latter, the real leader of the

Whigs, felt it beneath his dignity to take the second place on the ticket and that went to 'Honest John' Tyler, an ex-Democrat with rather watery Whig connections.

The vice president has little real power — he is the chief Senate Officer responsible for the ritualistic opening and closing sessions and the occasional tie-breaking vote (the only time that he can vote in Senate matters) and he can preside over Senate Commissions — and this had led many to decry the position. Benjamin Franklin called the vice president 'His Superfluous Excellency', whilst Franklin Roosevelt's first 'Veep', John Nance Garner, said that the office was 'Not worth a bucket of warm spit'. What they and others, before and since, have forgotten is that the vice president stands only a heart beat away from the presidency itself. John Tyler, 'His Accidency', became the first vice president to succeed on the death of his predecessor. Since 1840, 9 out of 30 presidents have been 'accidental' presidents, since 1900, 5 out of 15 — or in other words the odds on such a succession taking place are about three to one. In an actuarial sense it is less of a gamble than any of the other possible ways.

But was John Tyler the new *president*? Clearly Harrison's former cabinet in addressing him as 'Vice President' did not think so; and in the absence of any precedent to the contrary they were inclined to regard him as at best the acting president, as a trustee and executor of the late president, with themselves as co-ordinate legatees. The relevant section of the constitution was delightfully vague on this issue:

> In case of the removal of the President from office, or of his death, resignation or inability to discharge the powers and duties of the said office, the same shall devolve on the vice president . . . (Article II, section 2).

John Tyler cut straight through the Gordian knot. He had himself sworn in as President of the United States and since that time no vice president has ever been challenged upon assuming the presidency. After eight weeks both Houses of Congress voted that he was indeed 'President' Tyler. (Surprisingly, it was not until the XXV Amendment of 1967 that the issue was finally put beyond any doubt.)

'He was above the middle height, somewhat slender, clean shaven, with light hair. His light-blue eyes were penetrating, and had a humorous twinkle . . .' so wrote a contemporary of John Tyler, at 51, the youngest American president to date. He came from a Virginia family of high lineage. His father had succeeded Harrison's father in the House of Burgesses when the latter left for the Constitutional Congress in Philadelphia in 1787. He had been a bright, precocious lad who had graduated from William and Mary at 17, and had progressed from the state legislature to Congress where he had served in both Houses. He had emerged as a staunch Southern Democratic Republican, of independent leanings, who had opposed internal improvements, a national bank, the Missouri Compromise and high protective tariffs.

Increasingly during Jackson's second term he opposed what he regarded as the latter's headstrong arbitrariness and he swung towards the 'Whigs' — those who opposed the 'tyranny' of Jackson. Out of a muddle of factions came a grouping of 'States Rights Whigs', with a common denominator of hostility to Andrew Jackson, which promoted Tyler as vice president in 1836, when he obtained 47 electoral votes, and again in 1840.

Harrison's untimely demise left the Whigs, who represented mainly western and northern viewpoints, with Tyler, a southerner with a Democratic background, as Chief Executive. The Whigs hoped that Tyler would adopt their views; but many Whig ideas offended his principles — as his track record indicated, and the result was a very controversial administration. Following Tyler's second veto of a bill for a new Bank of the United States his entire cabinet resigned, with the exception of the Secretary of State, Daniel Webster; and Tyler himself was 'read out' of the Whig party (ie expelled). His repeated vetoing of legislation resulted in Tyler becoming the first president against whom an attempt was made to bring a motion of impeachment. On 10 January 1843 an impeachment resolution was brought against him on the grounds of his 'gross usurpation of power and the abuse of his power of appointment', but it was rejected by the House of Representatives by 127 votes to 83. On the last day of his administration Tyler's last veto became the first in American history to be overridden by Congress.

Tyler did however accomplish a great deal both in foreign and domestic affairs, and he betrayed an impressive capacity to get things done. The Webster-Ashburton treaty of 1842 resolved years of dispute with Great Britain over part of the Canadian border; and trade in the Far East increased after the first-ever commercial treaty with China. At home the Navy was strengthened; and Tyler signed the 'Log Cabin' Bill (the Pre-emption Act of 1841), which allowed some people to purchase 160 acres of the public lands at $1.25 an acre which has been called the most important agrarian measure ever passed by Congress.

His most significant action as president opened the way for the annexation of Texas — and lit a slow fuse under American politics. This vast area, all to the south of the Missouri Compromise line, could be carved into several slave states and was opposed by the Whigs for this reason. Tyler, though pro-slavery, took the view that the alternative to annexation was that the area would fall under foreign control and that the United States would fail to acquire a vast empire that could be pushed through to the Pacific. Well aware that he could not obtain the necessary two-thirds majority in the Senate for annexation, Tyler spent the dying moments of his 'lame duck' presidency (neither Whigs nor Democrats considered re-nominating him), pushing it through Congress by means of a joint resolution of both houses which required only a simple majority. Three days before he went out of office Texas was offered the opportunity to join the Union. At this point Tyler retired from the White House and took himself off to the estate near his birthplace which, since he regarded himself as a political outlaw, he had named 'Sherwood Forest'.

His presidency had not been without incident in other directions. On 28 February 1844 President Tyler was on board the USS *Princeton* on the Potomac to witness the firing of the world's largest naval gun, the 'Peacemaker'. The gun blew up killing Senator Gardiner, the father of Tyler's future wife, as well as the Secretary of State and the Secretary of the Navy. Tyler escaped death by a hairsbreadth.

In 1844 he married as his second wife Julia Gardiner the 'Rose of Long Island' who was thirty years his junior. Together they made sweet music, he on the violin and she on the guitar (when she was not dancing the 'new' polka), and it was Julia who saddled the presidency (in 1844) with 'Hail to the Chief', a Gaelic melody with lyrics by Sir Henry Bishop, one-time director of music at Covent Garden. The survivors of the eight children of his first marriage refused to attend the first-ever wedding of an incumbent president, which was to produce another seven Tylers, making John Tyler the president with the largest number of children. His first child was born in 1815 and his last, Pearl, born in 1860 when her father was over 70, lived until 1947 — the 200th anniversary of the birth of her grandfather.

In 1861 Tyler came out of retirement to chair the ill-fated Washington Peace Convention in the hope of averting civil war. When this failed and his state seceded, he was elected a member of the Confederate Congress (but died before he could take his seat). He was the only president to hold office in the Confederacy, and it was for this reason that Union troops despoiled his home and estate; and that, for the first and the last time, the United States ignored the death of a former president when Tyler died suddenly in 1862. Not until 1915 did Congress erect a modest monument to him in Richmond, Virginia.

# JAMES K. POLK

**Full name**  James Knox Polk, 1795–1849
**Born**  Near Charlotte, Mecklenberg County, North Carolina, 2 November 1795, the eldest of 10 children
**Parents**  Samuel Polk (1772–1827), farmer, planter, surveyor, and Jane Knox Polk (1776–1852). 6 sons, 4 daughters
**Family lineage**  Scottish-Irish
**College**  University of North Carolina, BA 1818
**Married**  1824, Sarah Childress Polk (1803–91), daughter of Joel Childress, merchant, farmer. No children
**Occupation**  Lawyer; state politician; member of US House of Representatives, 1825–39; Speaker, 1835–9; Governor of Tennessee, 1839–41
**Religious denomination**  Presbyterian (but he was received into the Methodist Church shortly before his death)
**Notable relationships**  His wife was the niece of President Andrew Jackson
**Died**  From acute diarrhoea, Nashville, Tennessee, 15 June 1849, aged 53
**Buried**  In the grounds of the State Capitol, Nashville, Tennessee

**Party** Democratic **State represented** Tennessee **Term of Office** 4 March 1845 to 4 March 1849 **Age on taking Office** 49 **Presidential administration** 15th **Congresses** 29th, 30th

1844 ELECTION

| Candidates | Party | Electoral Vote (275) | States Won (26) | Popular Vote | % |
|---|---|---|---|---|---|
| James K. Polk | Dem | 170 | 15 | 1,337,243 | 49.6* |
| Henry Clay | Whig | 105 | 11 | 1,299,062 | 48.1 |
| James G. Birney | Liberty | — | — | 62,300 | 2.3 |

*Polk was the 2nd president not to receive a majority of the popular vote.

| 1845 | 29th | Senate | (56) | 31 Dem | 25 Whigs | |
| | | House | (226) | 143 Dem | 77 Whigs | 6 Others |
| 1847 | 30th | Senate | (58) | 36 Dem | 21 Whigs | 1 Other |
| | | House | (227) | 115 Whigs | 108 Dem | 4 Others |

(The Administration lost control of the House of Representatives.)

### NOTE

New states admitted:

| Texas | (1845) | 28th |
| Iowa | (1846) | 29th |
| Wisconsin | (1848) | 30th |

### VICE PRESIDENT

11th George Mifflin Dallas (Pennsylvania), 1792–1864. Lawyer; mayor of Philadelphia, 1828; US Senator, 1831–3; Minister to Russia, 1837–9; vice president, 4 March 1845 to 4 March 1849; subsequently Minister to Great Britain, 1856–61.

---

America's first 'accidental' president was followed by the first 'dark horse'. At the Democratic nominating convention in 1844 Martin Van Buren was unable to obtain the necessary two-thirds vote and the glittering prize passed to James Knox Polk of Tennessee whose name had not even appeared on the first seven ballots. The Democrats, to hide their confusion, were quick to draw attention to the similarities between 'Old Hickory' and the new 'Young Hickory' (though he was 48) — they were both Tennesseans, Presbyterians, Scottish-Irish, lawyers, etc. The Whigs were driven either to joke about the 'pig in a polk' candidate, or to echo the Democrats' rhetorical question of 1840, with their 'Who is James Polk?'

In truth the Whigs knew all about James Polk. He was born in a log farmhouse in North Carolina but the family moved to Columbia, Tennessee in 1806. Because of ill-health (it is said that young Polk had an operation for gallstones without an anaesthetic at 17), he had a broken education and a variety of jobs before a private tutor prepared him for entry to the University of North Carolina, from which he emerged at the advanced age of 20 with the highest honours in classics and mathematics. He then studied law, built up a practice in the county seat and became a well-known advocate throughout the state of Tennessee. His oratorical skills took him into local politics as a stump orator — he was known as the 'Napoleon of the Stump' — and into the Tennessee legislature, first as its Chief Clerk and then as a member from 1823–5.

His constituents then sent him to Washington where, at the age of 30, he became one of the youngest members of the House of Representatives to which he was to be re-elected seven times between 1825 and 1839. He was a staunch supporter of Andrew Jackson, a family friend, and of Van Buren, but his 14 years in Congress were rather colourless apart from the period he spent as Speaker of the 24th Congress (Jackson's last) and the 25th. Because of his unwavering partisanship no Whig could be found to move the customary vote of thanks when he left the chair and they voted against it when it was put by a Democrat. Polk then became Governor of Tennessee in 1839, but he was defeated in 1841 and again in 1843.

In 1844, as the Democratic party convention approached, Andrew Jackson, sensing that the electorate wanted territorial expansion, urged the party to choose a candidate committed to the Nation's 'manifest destiny', ie the idea that the Nation should possess the entire continent to the Western ocean. 'Expansionism' was in the air for the first time since the War of 1812. (Explorers like John C. Frémont had been reconnoitring beyond the Rockies; wagon trains had set out to cross the mountains, and some of them had arrived.) 'Expansionism', however, too neatly provided a common denominator for essentially irreconcilable forces. It appealed to northern and western latent land hunger; but it also appealed to southern planters, who wanted Texas in particular for new slave states — and this at a time when, because of a careful 'admissions' policy, the political balance of power in the Union was relatively evenly divided between 13 'free' states and 13 'slave' states.

Martin Van Buren, the first choice of many Democrats tried, like his Whig opponent Henry Clay, to mute the demand for expansion — and behind it the issue of slavery expansion — by declaring his opposition to the annexation of Texas. Not surprisingly, Van Buren, and Clay, lost all hope of any support from the South. James Knox Polk when asked his opinion said, 'I have no hesitation in declaring that I am in favour of the immediate reannexation (sic) of Texas . . .' He was also in favour of the reconquest of 'Oregon'. He was it seems the ideal candidate for the Democrats at this juncture. 'His capacity for business is great,' wrote Andrew Jackson, 'and to extraordinary powers of labor,

83

both mental and physical, he unites that tact and judgement which are requisite to the successful direction of such an office.' His partisanship did not hurt him, nor the fact that he was a slaveholder, and he was *for* Texas. He followed Jackson's advice, to base his campaign on 'expansion' and to ignore the 'slavery' issue, to the letter. The popular election of 1844 accurately reflected the deep divisions in America, and was so close that Polk did not even win his home state, though he obtained a comfortable majority in the electoral college. At 49, the nation's youngest president to date, he set out ('with the settled purpose of not being a candidate for re-election'), to implement a programme which, according to his Secretary of the Navy, George Bancroft (recollected many years later at the age of 86), entailed reducing the tariff, establishing an independent Treasury, and acquiring Oregon and California.

In 1846 the first two aims were achieved. The Walker Tariff Act began the process of reducing the tariff to a 'revenue only' tariff. 'British all over' was the bitter complaint of protectionist northerners who were aware of the free-trade work of Sir Robert Peel in Great Britain. The Independent Treasury Act restored that which had been abolished by the Whigs in 1841; and ever since the American government has taken care of its own funds without the assistance of any banks.

'Oregon' stretched from 42° to 54°40′ (the boundary between British Canada and Russia fixed in 1825), west of the Rockies, and at various times had been disputed between Great Britain, Russia and Mexico, as well as the United States. In the north a joint occupation had been agreed with Britain by John Quincy Adams in 1827, and it was this which Polk sought to end. 'The Whole of Oregon or None' had been a popular campaign slogan in 1844; though somewhere along the line some unknown humourist had turned this into the war cry, 'Phifty Phour Phorty or Phight!' an interpretation of the 'four P's', a popular abbreviation of 'The Political Principles of President Polk'. Negotiations between the two countries (1845–6) produced a sensible compromise settlement which extended the existing American-Canadian border at 49° right across the continent as the boundary between British Columbia and American 'Oregon', with the exception of the southern tip of Vancouver Island. Northern expansionists were dismayed, but southerners were pleased; they did not want any complications arising at the same time as the Mexican question.

A war with Mexico was inevitable over Texas. Tyler's legacy had its Senators and Representatives admitted to Congress in December of 1845. This 'bloodless achievement', as Polk put it, was however about to have the same sort of repercussions on Mexico as say Louisiana, announcing her decision to leave the Union to join Mexico, would have had upon the United States. The Mexican Ambassador was withdrawn and only an internal Mexican political revolution delayed war.

Polk sent diplomat John Slidell to Mexico City to urge the Mexicans to accept the Rio Grande as their boundary with Texas and to offer to purchase for $20 million all or part of the present United States south-west, including California, but he was not received. An American army under General Zachary Taylor was then deployed in the disputed boundary area; and when in April 1846 Mexican troops fired on a US patrol Polk had no trouble in obtaining a declaration of war from Congress: 'United States blood has been spilt on United States soil'. In the war which followed America gained some spectacular victories and a whole new generation of military heroes — Taylor, Scott, Lee, Grant, Jackson, Sherman, to mention but a few — many of whom were to put their Mexican experience to good use between 1861 and 1865. The war was brought to an end by the Treaty of Guadalupe Hidalgo (1848), by which the United States gained California, New Mexico, and parts of Utah, Nevada, Colorado and Arizona, in return for the payment of $15 million — some called it 'conscience money' — and the assumption of $3¼ million worth of Mexican debts in the area.

President James K. Polk deserves to be remembered as the president who added the greatest amount of new territory to the United States. In 1845 the 27 states covered 1,357,000 square miles and the Territories (not yet states) a further 600,000. During his four years Polk added an área nearly as large as that of the whole 27 states on the day that he took his oath of office — a further million square miles. Polk's actions however, would help further to divide the Democratic party into its pro- and anti-slavery wings, and the nation itself, over the issue of the extension of slavery into the new Territories.

Polk emerges as a hard and humourless individual. His wife Sarah forbade the serving of alcoholic beverages at White House receptions. At the Inauguration Ball music and dancing stopped when the presidential couple arrived and were not resumed until after they left. He worked fourteen hours a day — 'The presidency is not a bed of roses' — and he left Washington for only six weeks in his four years. He refused to delegate anything, preferring 'to supervise the whole of the government' himself. Even during the Mexican War, though a rank amateur in military affairs (like Lincoln after him), he kept the sole direction in his own hands from grand strategy to the procurement of mules — partly because he found that some generals were Whigs. 'In four years,' said his Secretary of State (and a future president) James Buchanan, 'he assumed the appearance of an old man.' He died in 1849 aged only 53, the youngest-ever president (excluding those assassinated) to die; and he lived the shortest period after the completion of his term — only 103 days. His achievements were summed up thus by a contemporary: 'What he went for he fetched.'

# ZACHARY TAYLOR

**Full name** Zachary Taylor, 1784–1850
**Born** Montebello, Orange County, Virginia, 24 November 1784, the third of 9 children
**Parents** Richard Taylor (1744–1829), farmer, soldier, and Sarah Dabney Strother Taylor (1760–1822). 6 sons, 3 daughters
**Family lineage** English
**College** None
**Married** 1810, Margaret ('Peggy') Mackall Smith Taylor (1788–1852), daughter of Walter Smith, planter. 5 daughters, 1 son
**Occupation** Professional soldier
**Religious denomination** Episcopalian
**Notable relationships** Taylor was a second cousin of James Madison, 4th president. Taylor's daughter (Sarah) Knox Taylor (1814–35), was the first wife (1835) of Jefferson Davis, subsequently President of the Confederate States of America
**Died** From coronary thrombosis following acute gastro-enteritis, Washington, DC, 9 July 1850, aged 65
**Buried** Zachary Taylor National Cemetery, Louisville, Kentucky

**Party** Whig **State represented** Louisiana **Term of Office** 5 March 1848 to 9 July 1849 (1 year 126 days) **Age on taking Office** 64
**Presidential administration** 16th **Congress** 31st

1848 ELECTION

| Candidates | Party | Electoral Vote (290) | States Won (30) | Popular Vote | % |
|---|---|---|---|---|---|
| Zachary Taylor | Whig | 163 | 15 | 1,360,099 | 47.3* |
| Lewis Cass | Dem | 127 | 15 | 1,220,544 | 42.4 |
| M. Van Buren | Free Soil | — | — | 291,263 | 10.1 |

*Taylor did not receive a majority of the popular vote.

CONGRESS

| | | | | | |
|---|---|---|---|---|---|
| 1849 | 31st | Senate (62) | 35 Dem | 25 Whigs | 2 Free Soil |
| | | House (230) | 112 Dem | 109 Whigs | 9 Free Soil |

(This was the first of only two administrations — the other was the Nixon Administration in 1969 — that did not control Congress upon taking office.)

12th Millard Fillmore (1800–74), subsequently 13th president. He was the last vice president born in the eighteenth century.

————————————

General Zachary Taylor was another 'first' for the United States — the first completely apolitical figure to enter the White House. He was the first professional soldier to become president, he had had no elective political experience, and never had a president known less about government, law or politics. At the time of his nomination he had never even voted in an election and he did not vote for himself in 1848.

For the third time in twenty years a president was made out of a military idol and in Taylor's case, as in that of Harrison and Jackson, the main reason was that he was not identified with any of the major issues of the day, especially slavery. Neither the Whigs nor the Democrats could afford to name any statesman who had pronounced views on dangerous issues, and once again men like Henry Clay and Daniel Webster were passed over. One reason for the general inferiority of so many presidents in the period 1840 to 1860 is because the men who *were* great were not available because they had taken definite stands.

Everyone knew that there was only one issue in 1848: slavery. Should there be any new slave states? Should slavery be excluded from the Territories (as was argued by David Wilmot in 1846), allowed in the Territories (John C. Calhoun), or kept below 36°30′ — as Polk had argued in his 'Farewell Address'? Neither of the main parties however dared go before the electorate on these issues because of the disintegration that was affecting both of them (so that Northern Democrats had more in common with Northern Whigs than with Southerners in their own party). Consequently, the Whigs had no real policy at all in 1848, except Taylor himself; whilst the Democrats attempted to promote the concept of 'popular sovereignty', ie that the issue of 'slavery' or 'freedom' should be left to the inhabitants of new Territories to decide when they came to draw up their constitutions prior to statehood. American politicians, as Thomas Jefferson had forecast in 1820, had 'the wolf by the ears', and they dared not let him go.

In this nightmarish situation General Zachary Taylor was a godsend to the Whigs. His Mexican War war record made him generally acceptable; and the fact that he was a Southerner and a slave owner meant that he would appeal to Southern Whigs. His army service in Wisconsin and Iowa gave him 'western' appeal. In a very closely-fought election Taylor owed his success to the intervention of the new 'Free Soil' party, which took just enough votes from the Democrats to ensure the Whigs victory; and at the age of 64 their man was inaugurated as the twelfth president on 5 March 1849. (Taylor refused to be inaugurated on 4 March, a Sunday.)

The Taylors came originally from Carlisle in England but they had been Virginians for five generations. Taylor's father had been a colonel in the Revolution and all the Taylor sons, except one, caught soldiering from their father. Young Zachary became a regular soldier, a 1st lieutenant in the 7th Infantry, 1808, and a captain by 1810. Fighting against the Indians on the frontier under Harrison he made a name for himself and was breveted major, attaining full rank following hazardous, but inconspicuous, service in the War of 1812.

Long years of garrison duty saw him rise by degrees until in 1832 at the time of the Black Hawk War (in which Abraham Lincoln also served briefly) he was Colonel of the 1st Infantry. Along the way he had married a Maryland girl who proved to be an ideal military wife. She followed her husband to successive postings, except when he was on active service, when she stayed at home on the cotton plantation near Baton Rouge in Louisiana which Taylor had purchased, along with another plantation in Mississippi. Following active service in the Seminole War in Florida, Taylor was breveted brigadier general and made commander-in-chief of the South Western Division of the Army whilst the Mexican War was brewing. It was General Taylor who was ordered into the disputed Texas boundary area by President Polk.

Careless of his military appearance — his sloppiness had increased with his rank, he usually wore a battered straw hat and farmer's clothes — 'Old Rough and Ready', at the age of 61, was about to prove that the flexibility and resourcefulness that he had learned fighting wily Indians had been the best possible training for taking on a foe brought up in the military conventions of contemporary Europe. At Palo Alto, Resaca de la Palma, the siege of Monterey and finally Buena Vista (with an army composed of raw, volunteer recruits outnumbered two to one), Taylor inflicted crushing defeats on the Mexicans usually whilst sitting side-saddle on his old war horse, Whitey, oblivious of personal danger. (Whitey spent his last days on the White House lawn where visitors pulled hairs from his tail as souvenirs). Alarmed by Taylor's growing reputation and potential as a Whig presidential candidate President Polk dispatched General Winfield Scott (another Whig) to take Mexico City.

Taylor knew that his name was being pressed by the Whigs for the presidency but he kept out of the movement and did nothing until the war was over and he was actually nominated. (He did not acknowledge his nomination initially because he did not know about it, having refused to pay the postage on his formal letter of notification.) Polk dismissed his potential successor as 'a narrow-minded bigot' and as a 'partisan without (intellectual) resources and wholly unqualified'. Taylor certainly had no presidential ambitions and he lacked political sophistication, but he was possessed of sound commonsense and, as he was soon to demonstrate, his military service had bred in him an intense nationalism.

Taylor inherited two pressing problems: California, and a boundary dispute between Texas and New Mexico. On 24 January 1848 gold had been discovered at Sutter's Mill in the Sacramento Valley in California, a discovery which gave a distinct colour to Taylor's short administration and nearly caused the dissolution of the Union. The California gold rush soon gave that territory sufficient people (over 100,000) to form a separate state. The first stage was to adopt a constitution and in November 1848 a convention adopted a constitution, based on those of New York and Iowa, in which slavery was prohibited. Southern statesmen were horrified — they had hoped to develop 'popular sovereignty' in the new territories acquired from Mexico and thus circumvent the Missouri Compromise, but they had been checkmated at an early stage. If this constitution were allowed to pass unchallenged then there loomed large the prospect of an ever-increasing 'free' state majority in Congress which could ultimately destroy slavery everywhere. Southern bitterness threw Congress into complete chaos — it took three weeks to elect a Speaker of the House — and cries of 'secession' were in the air.

Out of the rancour emerged an attempt at a compromise solution which was largely the work of Henry Clay who, along with Daniel Webster and John C. Calhoun, represented the very last of the old guard in a Congress which was increasingly becoming the preserve of new men like William Henry Seward and Stephen A. Douglas. 'Lord Harry' provided his last signal service for the Union with several proposals which collectively were to become known as the 'Compromise of 1850' and which, it was to be argued later, saved the Union by staving off (for a decade) what Seward was to describe as the 'irrepressible conflict'.

Clay's 'Omnibus Bill' provided sops for both North and South: — the immediate admission of California as a free state; the establishment of New Mexico and Utah as Territories without reference to slavery; and adjustment of the boundary between Texas and New Mexico with compensation for Texas; the maintenance of slavery in Washington DC; the abolition of slave markets in the capital; a new (more severe) Fugitive Slave Law; (designed to break up the 'underground railroad' to Canada); and the abandonment of any restrictions on inter-state slave-trading. The bill was to be all things to all men, but it was bound to lead to furious opposition and there is every indication that Taylor was all set to veto it if it passed Congress. He regarded it as a conglomeration of incongruities which avoided the main issue, instead of meeting it head on, and in its concession to the spirit of slavery concealed treason. He had been left behind by the high level of political debate but he was prepared to use force if necessary to 'preserve the Union at all hazards'. As regards the boundary dispute, he ordered US troops to be ready to resist any Texan invasion of New Mexico and when Southern Senators remonstrated, and said that Southern officers would refuse to coerce Texas, he replied that then he would 'hang them' for treason.

On 4 July 1850 Taylor attended ceremonies at the unfinished Washington Monument in sweltering heat. He went home and consumed some cherries and iced milk, and died five days later from the after-effects of acute gastro-enteritis, saying, like a soldier, 'I have endeavoured to do my duty.' (Daniel Webster said that Taylor had died 'fortunately'.) Congress, locked in the middle of a battle royal, with none of the compromise measures passed, adjourned in awe — and all eyes turned towards America's second 'accidental' president.

# MILLARD FILLMORE

THIRTEENTH PRESIDENT OF THE UNITED STATES 1850–3

**Full name**   Millard Fillmore, 1800–74
**Born**   Locke (now Summerhill), Cayuga County, NY, 7 January 1800, second of 9 children
**Parents**   Nathaniel Fillmore (1771–1863), farmer, and his first wife Phoebe Millard Fillmore (1778–1831). 6 sons, 3 daughters. (Nathaniel Fillmore married subsequently (1834) Eunice Love Fillmore)
**Family lineage**   English
**College**   None
**Married**   (1) 1826, Abigail Powers Fillmore (1798–1853), daughter of Lemuel Powers, Baptist Minister. 1 son, 1 daughter (2) 1858, Caroline Carmichael McIntosh Fillmore (1813–81), widow of E. C. McIntosh, daughter of Charles Carmichael, merchant. No children
**Occupation**   Wool carder and cloth dresser; teacher; lawyer; state politician, 1829–31 (NY); member of US House of Representatives, 1833–5, 1837–43; vice presidential candidate, 1844
**Religious denomination**   Unitarian
**Notable relationships**   None
**Died**   From debility, Buffalo, NY, 8 March 1874, aged 74
**Buried**   Forest Lawn Cemetery, Buffalo, NY

**Party** Whig **State represented** New York **Term of Office** 10 July 1850 to 4 March 1853 (he served the unexpired portion of his predecessor, 2 years, 237 days) **Age on taking Office** 50 **Presidential administration** 16th (continued) **Congresses** 31st, 32nd

CONGRESS

| 1851 | 32nd | Senate | (62) | 35 Dem | 24 Whigs | 3 Free Soil |
|------|------|--------|------|--------|----------|-------------|
|      |      | House  | (233)| 140 Dem| 88 Whigs | 5 Free Soil |

(The administration did not control either the Senate or the House.)

VICE PRESIDENT

Fillmore was the 2nd president who did not have a vice president.

92

1 7th Census 1850: Total population: 23,191,876 including 3,204,313 slaves (all except 262 in the South), and 434,449 free negroes.
2 New state: California (1850) 31st.

---

Enslavement of negroes was not the only kind of slavery practised in the United States. The 'indentured servant' was a different kind of 'slave', bound by contract to work for a master who, in effect, owned him for the term of the contract. Young Millard was 'indentured' at the age of 14 to a clothier and hated it so much that he purchased his freedom two years before his time for the sum of $30.

Born in a log cabin in upstate New York, Millard Fillmore struggled to get an elementary education, and married his school teacher, before qualifying as a lawyer in 1823 and establishing over the next quarter of a century the most thriving legal concern in Western New York. Public office in the state — he was Attorney and Counsellor of the State Supreme Court — was followed by three terms in the state legislature. He then entered the US House of Representatives as an opponent of the Jacksonians and gravitated towards the new Whigs. In their ranks he became the leading figure in New York politics, the leader of the anti-slavery wing of the Whigs and ultimately chairman of the influential Ways and Means Committee in the House (in which capacity he had much to do with the tariff of 1842). He was unsuccessful in his vice presidential candidacy in 1844 but, following a brief spell as Comptroller of New York, ran in second place on the victorious Taylor ticket in 1848. He had been a forceful and impartial chairman of the Senate during the long, heated debates over Clay's 'Omnibus' bill, but now this 'large, impressive and handsome man of attractive manner', was, it seemed, going to need all his powers of persuasion and diplomacy to surmount America's gravest crisis to date.

In fact the removal of Taylor and his opposition to the dead-locked compromise measures had created an entirely new atmosphere. Fillmore disliked slavery but he was determined to be president of the whole country and to put his executive influence behind the compromise measures in an attempt, like a good moderate Whig, to win the middle ground between Northern

Abolitionists and Southern Secessionists. Moderate Democrats proved very receptive to the re-opening of the compromise moves — since they had the most to lose if the political system broke down. To them, and to the moderate-minded Whigs, the alternatives were either accommodation or confrontation — and both chose accommodation in preference to dissolution of the Union and the bloodshed that was sure to follow. The compromise measures could cool political passions, ease sectional conflict and, hopefully, bring Americans peace in their time.

The 'big guns' of the Senate, Calhoun, Webster and Clay, had had their say; and with the 'Great Compromiser', Clay himself, aged, ill and exhausted, management of the serious legislative business passed to Senator Stephen A. Douglas and other Democratic Senators. Their tactic was to divide the 'Omnibus' bill into its component parts and pass each separately through Congress (where only 4 Senators actually voted for every measure), after which each was approved by the president. In this way the measures were passed piecemeal by September 1850 and America had its 'Compromise'. Douglas, aided by Fillmore's bipartisan approach, had achieved the near-impossible and Humpty Dumpty had been put together again.

Fillmore had staked all on the appeasement of the South and he had 'won', in the sense that he had helped to buy for the Union more of that priceless commodity — Time. He detected an increasing note of optimism in the air, if only slavery could now be ignored. 'That agitation', he said, 'which for a time threatened to disturb the fraternal relations that make us one people, is fast subsiding . . . in all parts of the Republic.'

But in essence, compromise had been reached on an issue that could not be compromised; sooner or later it would all have to be done all over again. Their very success spelt doom for the Whigs — and in the mid-term elections (1852) the Democrats increased their hold over Congress — for if the Democrats looked to the Compromise of 1850 as a 'final solution' what was to be the role of the Whigs? It only needed mutterings about the necessity of 'further legislation' to ensure their annihilation in 1852.

As for Millard Fillmore himself, he was to be excoriated by a succession of Yankee historians as a Northern President who had bowed to the Southern slavocracy. Along with his two immediate successors, Pierce and Buchanan, he was to be depicted as one of the malleable, gingerbread men, the 'doughfaced' southern tools of the 1850s.

Even so in 1852 Fillmore almost got the Whig nomination; but on the 53rd ballot the Whigs played safe and went for yet another military idol, General Winfield Scott — 'Old Fuss and Feathers' — who went down to ignominious defeat and the Whigs to oblivion.

In foreign affairs Fillmore reopened diplomatic relations with Mexico; opposed the overthrow of the Spanish régime in Cuba by means of an 1850s 'Bay of Pigs' style expedition; sent Commodore Mathew Perry to Japan (1852) on that first expedition which was to have enormous consequences, following the entry of Japan into the nineteenth century; and he ordered that arch-imperialist, Napoleon III, not to interfere in Hawaii, though he refused plaintive requests from the Hawaiians for annexation by America.

He left the White House in 1853 (his wife caught cold at his successor's Inauguration, and died), and retired to Buffalo where he remained except for three tours of Europe. On one he refused an honorary doctorate from Oxford on the grounds that he was not qualified.

In 1856 he refused to join the new 'Republicans' and accepted the presidential nomination of the 'Know-Nothing' (1849), or 'American' (1854), party whose members, when questioned as to their policies, would only answer cryptically, 'I know nothing.' In fact this was an anti-catholic, anti-foreign, 'nativist' party with Southern pro-slavery affiliations, which was overwhelmingly defeated in 1856. Fillmore, who had based his campaign in 1856 on national unity, never again sought public office.

During the Civil War Fillmore favoured conciliation rather than coercion and he was highly critical of Lincoln's conduct of the war. In 1864 he supported the Democratic candidate, General McClellan, and was branded a 'Copperhead'. When Lincoln was assassinated Fillmore inadvertently antagonised his neighbours in Buffalo. He was preoccupied with the illness of his second wife and not aware of the request to drape private houses in mourning. He awoke to find his house smeared with black ink. Following the reunification of the Republic, he supported Andrew Johnson's plans for the reconciliation of the South.

The Fillmore's left their mark on the White House. It was the first Mrs Fillmore, former school teacher Abigail Fillmore, who laid the foundations of the White House Library with a $250 appropriation from Congress. Millard Fillmore gave it its first bathtub and its first kitchen stove, the intricacies of which he mastered before handing it over to the cook.

# FRANKLIN PIERCE

FOURTEENTH PRESIDENT OF THE UNITED STATES 1853–7

**Full name** Franklin Pierce, 1804–69
**Born** Hillsborough (now Hillsboro), New Hampshire, 23 November 1804, the sixth of 8 children
**Parents** Benjamin Pierce (1757–1839), farmer; tavern keeper; soldier; state politician, Governor of New Hampshire 1827–28, 1829–30; and his second wife Anna Kendrick Pierce (1768–1839). 5 sons, 3 daughters
**Family lineage** English
**College** Bowdoin College, Brunswick, Maine. BA 1824
**Married** 1834, Jane Means Appleton Pierce (1806–63), daughter of Jesse Appleton, President of Bowdoin College. 3 sons
**Occupation** Lawyer; member, later Speaker, of the Lower House of the New Hampshire Legislature 1829–33; member of the US House of Representatives, 1833–7; US Senator, 1837–42 (resigned); Mexican War, Brigadier General, 1847–8
**Religious denomination** Episcopalian (1865–9)
**Notable relationships** None
**Died** From stomach inflammation, Concord, New Hampshire, 8 October 1869, aged 64
**Buried** Old North Cemetery, Concord, New Hampshire

**Party** Democratic **State represented** New Hampshire **Term of Office** 4 March 1853 to 4 March 1857 **Age on taking Office** 48 **Presidential administration** 17th **Congresses** 33rd, 34th

### 1852 ELECTION

| Candidates | Party | Electoral Vote (296) | States Won (31) | Popular Vote | % |
|------------|-------|----------------------|-----------------|--------------|---|
| Franklin Pierce | Dem | 254 | 27 | 1,601,274 | 50.8 |
| W. Scott | Whig | 42 | 4 | 1,386,580 | 43.8 |
| Hale | Free Soil | — | — | 156,805 | 4.9 |
| Others | — | — | — | 12,805 | |

| 1853 | 33rd | Senate (62) | 38 Dem | 22 Whigs | 2 Others |
| | | House (234) | 159 Dem | 71 Whigs | 4 Others |
| 1855 | 34th | Senate (62) | 42 Dem | 15 Repub | 5 Others |
| | | House (234) | 108 Repub | 83 Dem | 43 Others* |

(*Mainly 'Know Nothings'; the administration lost control of the House.)

### VICE PRESIDENT

13th William Rufus Devane King (Alabama), 1786–1853, planter; member of US House of Representatives, 1811–16; US Senator, 1820–44; Minister to France, 1844–6; Senator, 1848–52. Term of Office: 24 March 1853 to 18 April 1853. He did not attend the inauguration and had his oath administered in Cuba. He died after 25 days, the shortest-ever term, never having presided over the Senate.

---

On Friday 4 March 1852, Franklin Pierce, the first president born in the nineteenth century, became the first (and only) president to 'affirm' rather than 'swear' the presidential oath. He then became the first to deliver an inaugural oration, as opposed to a prepared address, from which it emerged that he was a staunch Unionist, a States Rights man, an anti-abolitionist and hopeful that 'no sectional or ambitious or fanatical excitement might again threaten the durability of our institutions, or obscure the light of our prosperity'. 'Handsome Frank' Pierce (he was arguably one of the two best-looking presidents), the youngest president to date (he was 48), and the 'darkest of dark horses', was now Chief Executive.

How had it happened? The Democrats, dogged by distinguished politicians who could not bridge political gaps and tied by the nominating convention's two-thirds majority rule, had turned after four days of deadlock to Pierce, who had gained support from both the North and the South, and on the 49th Ballot he had become the unanimous choice. Pierce had not sought the presidency, indeed he had said that it would be 'utterly repugnant to him'. He had been propelled forward by others, including his college friend Nathaniel Hawthorne whose campaign biography much extolled Pierce's virtues, especially his wisdom. 'He is deep, deep, deep.' Now, in spite of himself, and without ever having made a single campaign speech, he had risen to 'a position so suitable for others rather than desirable for myself'. In the 1852 election the Democrats carried twenty-seven states for Pierce and the Whigs four for General

Scott, and though the popular vote was less one-sided it was clear that the Whigs were dead as a *national* party and that the Democrats were the one remaining hope of the Union.

Franklin Pierce had graduated third in his class in an exceptionally brilliant year from Bowdoin College where his contemporaries had included Henry Wadsworth Longfellow as well as Hawthorne. He became a lawyer and entered politics. He was Speaker of the General Court of his state at 26, US Congressman at 29, and Senator at 33. He was not a brilliant politician but rather 'an independent partisan of Jackson', who opposed any measures that threatened the Union. For a number of personal reasons he retired from politics in 1842 and thereafter refused tempting offers to re-enter public life — including a Senate seat and the Attorney Generalship in Polk's Cabinet. But in 1846 he chose to enter the Mexican War as a private in the Concord militia.

He was soon raised by Polk to the rank of brigadier general in command of the 9th, 12th and 15th regiments. Bullets passed through his hat and he was injured in the leg and groin but he played a gallant part at the battles of Contreras and Churabasco and he was at the fall of Mexico City (September 1848). When the Whigs tried to denigrate his military service Pierce was defended by no less an advocate than Ulysses S. Grant (though there was no love lost between them), who said that Pierce was 'a gentleman and a man of courage'. New Hampshire presented a sword of honour to their 'favourite son' and put his name forward for 1852, though more in hope than in expectation.

In 1852 there were no great issues dividing the parties and no great questions agitating the people — or so it appeared. In fact, this silence was ominous — the deceptively peaceful eye of a great national hurricane — and Franklin Pierce was hardly settled in the White House (with the new central heating system he had introduced), before the first rumbles were heard of that storm which was to culminate in the Civil War.

The big issue of his term was Kansas. Senator Stephen A. Douglas, a Democratic reject in 1852, tried to ingratiate himself with the South with his Kansas-Nebraska bill. This, which was designed to facilitate the construction of a northern-routed transcontinental railroad (Jefferson Davis, Secretary of War in Pierce's cabinet, was pressing for a southern route), offered sops to the south. The bill provided for the admission of two new states to the Union, Kansas and Nebraska, whose inhabitants would be left free 'to form and regulate their domestic institutions (ie slavery) in their own way subject only to the constitution'. To facilitate their task the Missouri Compromise (1820) was explicitly declared to be void. The bill passed the House by 113 votes to 100; the Senate without a division; and President Pierce signed it — and hastened war with the stroke of his pen. For the Kansas-Nebraska Act (1854) by repealing the Missouri Compromise destroyed the hard-won truce of 1850 and re-opened the whole question of slavery in the West.

'Bleeding Kansas' (Nebraska was unsuitable for slavery), now became a battlefield for the conflicting passions of the entire nation, as pro- and anti-slavery elements poured into the hapless area to establish 'popular' or 'squatter' sovereignty. Atrocities committed by both sides (the legendary abolitionist John Brown made his first appearance at the massacre of Pottowatomie Creek, 1856), and corrupt electoral practices, resulted in the return of a pro-slavery legislature and the framing of a pro-slavery constitution which Pierce, despite bitter protests, was prepared to accept and defend if necessary with federal forces.

As a staunch Unionist he believed that he had to play the 'honest broker', not between North and South, but between the Union and the Unthinkable. He had signed the Douglas bill in the hope that, if Kansas became 'slave' and Nebraska 'free', both sides would be mollified. Now he had to support the South; and appeasement, once again, was the price that had to be paid to prevent Southern secession. His action has been derided as a catastrophic blunder; but it is difficult to see what any of the 'giants' might, or could, have done in this situation. In 1856 a measure of peace was achieved in Kansas when Pierce sent in federal troops and a new Governor, though unrest continued until 1859. After all this, Kansas entered the Union as a 'free-soil state' in 1861.

Pierce has been accused of following a bold foreign policy in order to distract attention from internal affairs. $10 million was paid to Mexico for the Gadsden Purchase (1853) which added parts of Southern Arizona and New Mexico to the Union. There was at least talk of acquiring Hawaii, San Domingo and Alaska, and the rumour that America would offer to buy Cuba from Spain, or take it by force, leaked by three American diplomats (including future president James Buchanan), in the so-called 'Ostend Manifesto' (1854), was an acute embarrassment to the administration. Anglo-American relations were strained first, when the English minister was detected trying to recruit for the Crimean War; and then over

Central America, where the British were involved in Nicaragua in violation of what was now becoming known as the 'Monroe Doctrine'. Relations were improved by a Reciprocity treaty with Canada.

At the Democratic convention in 1856 it soon became apparent that Pierce had made many enemies North and South and that he was not capable of carrying the country. (He became the only president to date, elected in his own right, to be denied re-nomination). After a long tussle between Stephen A. Douglas and James Buchanan, who had been abroad during the recent crisis, the latter was unanimously nominated by the Democrats on the seventeenth ballot.

In 1861 the Unionist former president, still blaming Abolitionists and the anti-slavery forces for causing strife, suggested a meeting of America's five living former presidents to attempt to avert civil war. If such a meeting had taken place those attending would have been Van Buren, Tyler, Pierce himself, and his successor Buchanan. Like Fillmore, Pierce was highly critical of Lincoln's conduct of the war, especially of what he regarded as invasions of personal and property rights, and the Emancipation Proclamation. He was also branded as a 'Copperhead', and at the funeral of his friend Hawthorne in 1864 he was openly snubbed. His closing years were marred by alcoholism, severe depression and increasing ill-health.

The 'Granite State' has never been conspicuously proud of her only president, 'Young Hickory of the Granite Hills', and it took half a century to erect an unpretentious monument to him in Concord. It had been his misfortune to be elevated to a position he did not seek and to be caught up in the cross-currents of expansionism, nationalism, sectionalism and abolitionism. His had been an impossible task and it is not surprising that he had failed to bring together all factions in the Democrat party, nor that he had failed to bridge the yawning chasm between interests divided by America's 'peculiar institution'. The legacy he bequeathed to his successors was an ominous one.

# JAMES BUCHANAN

FIFTEENTH PRESIDENT OF THE UNITED STATES 1857–61

**Full name**   James Buchanan, 1791–1868
**Born**   Stony Batter, Cumberland (now Franklin) County, near Mercersburg, Pennsylvania, 23 April 1791, the second of 11 children
**Parents**   James Buchanan (b County Donegal, Ireland, 1761–1821), merchant, farmer, and Elizabeth Speer Buchanan (1767–1833). 6 daughters, 5 sons
**Family lineage**   Scottish-Irish
**College**   Dickinson College, Carlisle, Pa, BA 1809
Buchanan was the only bachelor president (though President Cleveland [qv] was a bachelor at the time of his inauguration)
**Occupation**   Lawyer; War of 1812, enlisted man; state politician; member of US House of Representatives, 1821–31; Minister to Russia, 1832–3; US Senator, 1834–45; Secretary of State (Polk), 1845–9; Minister to London, 1853–6
**Religious denomination**   Presbyterian
**Notable relationships**   Buchanan was descended from Robert II, King of Scots. The Buchanan family is a branch of the Scottish Baronial House of Buchanan *of that ilk*
**Died**   From rheumatic gout, Wheatland, Lancaster, Pa, 1 June 1868, aged 77
**Buried**   Woodward Hill Cemetery, Lancaster, Pa

**Party** Democratic **State represented** Pennsylvania **Term of Office** 4 March 1857 to 4 March 1861 **Age on taking Office** 65 **Presidential administration** 18th **Congresses** 35th, 36th

1852 ELECTION

| Candidates | Party | Electoral Vote (296) | States Won (31) | Popular Vote | % |
|---|---|---|---|---|---|
| J. Buchanan | Dem | 174 | 19 | 1,838,169 | 45.6* |
| J. C. Frémont | Repub | 114 | 11 | 1,341,264 | 33.3 |
| M. Fillmore | 'Know Nothing' | 8 | 1 | 874,534 | 21.1 |

*Buchanan did not receive a majority of the popular vote.

| 1857 | 35th | Senate | (64) | 39 Dem | 20 Repub | 5 Others |
|------|------|--------|------|--------|----------|----------|
|      |      | House  | (237) | 131 Dem | 92 Repub | 14 Others |
| 1859 | 36th | Senate | (66) | 38 Dem | 26 Repub | 2 Others |
|      |      | House  | (237) | 113 Repub | 101 Dem | 23 Others |

(The Administration lost control of the House.)

## NOTES

1 New States:   Minnesota   (1858)   32nd

                 Oregon      (1859)   33rd

                 Kansas      (January 1861)   34th

2 Secessions:

| | | |
|---|---|---|
| 1. South Carolina | 20 December | 1860 |
| 2. Mississippi | 9 January | 1861 |
| 3. Florida | 10 January | 1861 |
| 4. Alabama | 11 January | 1861 |
| 5. Georgia | 19 January | 1861 |
| 6. Louisiana | 26 January | 1861 |
| 7. Texas | 1 February | 1861 |

3 8th Census 1860: Total population: 31,443,321, including 3,953,760 slaves and 448,070 free negroes.

## VICE PRESIDENT

14th John Cabell Breckinridge (Kentucky), 1821–75. Lawyer; state politician; member of the US House of Representatives, 1851–5; vice president, 4 March 1857 to 4 March 1861 (at 36, he was the youngest vice president to be inaugurated). US Senator, 1859–61 (expelled); presidential candidate, 1860 (qv); General in the Confederate Army, 1861–5; Confederate Secretary of War, 1865; returned to legal practice, 1869–75.

---

'The Old Public Functionary' — he had been in public service for over forty years — came to the White House as one of the most experienced statesmen of his generation. Born in a log cabin in Pennsylvania he had received a good education and became a lawyer thanks largely to the determination of his mother. He had gained political experience as a state politician before serving for long terms in both the House and the Senate, and his political career had been punctuated by service in Russia (where a Princess had enquired if America belonged to England). He had then entered Polk's cabinet as Secretary of State, and he had made powerful contributions to the settlement of three major issues,

102

namely Texas, Oregon and the Mexican War, but he had turned down opportunities to become Attorney General and to fill a vacancy in the Supreme Court.

Ever since 1844 he had been spoken of as presidential material, though the sectional demands of the Democratic party had seen him passed over in 1848 and 1852. But in 1856 his party needed him. Only Buchanan had a clean record on *the* major issue of the day. He had been out of the country (in England), during the development of the 'Kansas' crisis. Buchanan stood the best chance of holding some of the less-pronounced anti-slavery states and was acceptable to the South. He was on record as upholding the institution of slavery on constitutional grounds, he had supported the admission of Texas, and his part in the recent 'Ostend Manifesto' (1854), had led some to believe that he supported slavery *per se*. He was nominated on the 17th ballot over Stephen A. Douglas.

Buchanan looked like a future president. Photographs (his was the first inauguration to be photographed) show a fine figure of a man over six feet tall, with a shock of white hair above his handsome face, which was set off by a high collar with a broad white neckcloth. He would be America's only bachelor president (his fiancée had committed suicide in 1837), and the oldest in the nineteenth century. For at this critical juncture in her affairs America was about to commit its leadership to 'Old Buck', a tired old man of 65, said his critics, who had been ill, on and off, for most of the last decade. The man who would have to 'ride the whirlwind' in 1860–1 would be within days of his seventieth birthday.

Buchanan won the 1856 election — his house at Wheatland, Pa, was the scene of one of the early 'front porch' campaigns for the US Presidency — with substantial support from the South, which he carried with the exception of Maryland, and the votes of Pennsylvania (his home state), New Jersey, Indiana, Illinois and California. But his principal opponent, the famous explorer John C. Frémont, the candidate of the brand-new Republican party, with its base firmly in the North and the West, which combined all the opponents of slavery, did ominously well. Frémont came a good second and if he could have carried Pennsylvania and either Indiana or Illinois he would have won. (In 1860 it would require only a small shift of opinion to give America a Republican president without a single vote from the South.) Clearly with the demise of the Whigs, nationally based political parties were giving way to sectional parties and the Democratic party offered one of the last hopes of national unity.

Buchanan's Inaugural revealed that he was blind and deaf to the state of feeling concerning slavery when he said that 'the tempest has subsided, all is calm'. At a time when America needed a cross between a Job and a Solomon, with dashes of a Washington and a Jackson, she had got a 65-year old lawyer who was prepared to take his stand on the letter of the Constitution and ignore its spirit: The will of the majority must prevail, he continued. 'Popular sovereignty' was to be the rule where slavery was concerned and the minority must bend. He ignored growing indignation against the *institution* of slavery and failed to recognise that a firm stand was needed against the further spread of slavery if disunion was not to result. That very issue, he indicated, was at that moment pending before the Supreme Court which was about to reach a 'speedy and final settlement'.

Indeed it was, though not in the sense he intended. Chief Justice Roger B. Taney was about to hand down the decision in one of the most famous of all American cases, *Dred Scott v Sandford* (1857). Scott, a slave, claimed his freedom on the grounds that he had twice resided in free territory north of the Missouri Compromise line. The implications of this collusive suit were enormous for the supporters and the opponents of slavery — and for the Union. Taney, in dismissing Scott's contention, opined that a slave was not a 'person' but a 'chattel'; that property rights were guaranteed by the Constitution; and that slaves, like any other form of property, could be taken legally *anywhere* in the United States. Thus was the die cast; and from now onwards it was downhill all the way. The South was jubilant and the North exasperatedly bitter — though momentarily that section was diverted by the Panic of 1857, the worst economic recession to hit America since 1837, which cast a pall of gloom over the North.

Buchanan's ill-advised recognition (1858) of the *de facto* ('mob elected', roared the North) pro-slavery legislature in Kansas, and its Lecompton pro-slavery constitution, further divided the dividing nation. The 'New Haven Memorial' claimed that the president was violating his solemn oath by supporting an 'illegal' government. In his defence Buchanan, in words that could serve as his epitaph, retorted: 'I ask what else could I have done, ought I to have done?'

In the mid-term elections of 1858 the Republicans captured the House and improved their position in the Senate. (After the

Senatorial contest in Illinois, a Republican, Abraham Lincoln, became nationally known following a series of debates with Stephen A. Douglas.) There was also clear evidence now that the Democratic party was beginning to divide into Northern and Southern wings.

National emotions were to be further inflamed in 1859. With about twenty men John Brown, the fanatical abolitionist, seized the Federal arsenal at Harper's Ferry in Virginia with the apparent objective of inciting a slave revolt. Captured two days later by troops commanded by Robert E. Lee (amongst their number was John Wilkes Booth, the assassin of Abraham Lincoln), he was tried for treason and executed. Ralph Waldo Emerson called him, 'that new saint who will make the gallows glorious like the cross', and abolitionism had its martyr whose soul was to go marching on.

But it was to be the election of 1860, the most important in American history, that was to bring matters to a head. There were four distinct political parties: the Northern Democrats, fighting on a 'popular sovereignty' programme, behind Stephen A. Douglas; the Southern pro-slavery Democrats — the inevitable final division had happened — led by John C. Breckinridge; the Constitutional Union Party, behind John Bell; and the Republican Party with their compromise 'dark horse' candidate, Abraham Lincoln. Radical, pro-slavery Southerners made it clear during the election campaign that a Republican victory would lead to the secession of certain Southern states. The election was won by Abraham Lincoln.

Buchanan had summed up his dilemma in his (January) 1860 'State of the Union' Message: 'A State has no constitutional right to secede; the Federal government has no constitutional power to prevent secession.' South Carolina was the first state to secede, in December 1860; and over the following six weeks she was joined by six other states of the deep south. On 8 February 1861, the Confederate States of America came into existence.

Buchanan has been harshly criticised for his 'failure' during his 'lame-duck' presidency (November 1860 to March 1861), to do anything to prevent secession and to avert civil war. He has been derided as an 'imbecile', and as, 'the weakest of all presidents of the United States', as 'feeble, timid, indecisive, vacillating, senile, time-serving, legalistic, pro-Southern and traitrous'. In the abolitionist-tinged history books he serves as a foil for Lincoln under whom the war erupted, but for which Buchanan gets the blame. Yet he has been grossly maligned.

He was reluctant to commit his successor to embarrassing or drastic courses, and he followed a policy of conciliation and compromise (which Lincoln followed until Fort Sumter was fired on) and this did help to keep four crucial border slave states in the Union. He has been blamed for not using powers which presidents were not expected to exercise in peace-time. It is forgotten that (unlike Lincoln's later ten-week 'dictatorship' when Congress was not in session) throughout Buchanan's four-month nightmare the Republican opposition in Congress flagrantly played politics, spurned his requests for laws, money and militia and then blamed him for inactivity. His cabinet, including several scheming Southerners, gave him no support.

Buchanan had demonstrated that he could exert firmness when he had a clear mandate — in 1857 he had sent 2,500 troops into Utah to force polygamous Mormons to abide by federal laws, and he had displayed considerable vigour in foreign affairs in dealing with Japan, China and Great Britain. He had enforced the Fugitive Slave Laws in the North. But in 1860–1 he had no army (nor constitutional authority), with which to force the seceded states back into the Union; and in any case how could he have averted war by starting it? Until shots were exchanged there was always a last-ditch hope of a peaceful settlement.

When James Buchanan left office no 'brother's blood' had been shed though 'seven erring sisters' had departed in peace. In reality the real failure at this time lay not so much with 'Buchanan the Blunderer' as in the complete breakdown of the American democratic system — of the American people themselves. In his remaining years he retained his interest in politics and supported the Union during the Civil War. He also did some writing and aided charitable causes. With the words, 'O Lord God Almighty, as Thou wilt', he died on 1 June 1868.

# ABRAHAM LINCOLN

**Full name**   Abraham Lincoln, 1809–65

**Born**   Sinking Spring Farm, near Hodgenville, Hardin (now Larue) County, Kentucky (the 1st president not born in one of the original 13 states), 12 February 1809, the second of 3 children

**Parents**   Thomas Lincoln (1778–1851), farmer, carpenter, and Nancy Hanks Lincoln (1784–1818). 2 sons, 1 daughter. Thomas Lincoln married subsequently (1819) Sarah Bush Johnston Lincoln (1788–1869). 2 daughters, 1 son. (Lincoln was the only president to have step brothers/sisters)

**Family lineage**   English

**College**   None

**Married**   1842, Mary Anne Todd Lincoln (1818–82), daughter of Robert Smith Todd, banker. 4 sons, of whom only the eldest, Robert Todd Lincoln (1843–1926), lived to maturity

**Occupation**   Labourer; clerk; soldier (in Black Hawk War, 1832); store keeper; postmaster; surveyor; state politician (Illinois); lawyer; member of US House of Representatives, 1847–49

**Religious denomination**   None ('. . . but I have never denied the truth of the Scriptures')

**Notable relationships**   Through his mother's family, the Hanks, he was 21st in descent from Edward I, King of England. He was also descended from the sister of Owen Glendower, the great Welsh hero

**Died**   From assassination by pistol shot, Washington, DC 15 April, 1865, aged 56

**Buried**   In the Lincoln Tomb, Oak Ridge Cemetery, Springfield, Illinois

**Party** (1) Republican; (2) National Union (1864) **State represented** Illinois **Terms of Office** 4 March 1861 to 15 April 1865 **Age on taking Office** 52 **Presidential administrations** 19th, 20th (part) **Congresses** 37th, 38th, 39th

| Candidates | Party | Electoral Vote (303) | States Won (33) | Popular Vote | % |
|---|---|---|---|---|---|
| A. Lincoln | Repub | 180 | 18 | 1,866,452 | 39.9* |
| S. Douglas | N. Dem | 12 | 1 | 1,376,957 | 29.4 |
| J. Breckinridge | S. Dem Constn. | 72 | 11 | 849,781 | 18.1 |
| J. Bell | Union | 39 | 3 | 588,879 | 12.6 |

*Lincoln did not receive a majority of the popular vote.

1864 ELECTION

| Candidates | Party | Electoral Vote (233) | States Won (25) | Popular Vote | % |
|---|---|---|---|---|---|
| A. Lincoln | Nat Union | 212 | 22 | 2,330,552 | 55.1 |
| G. McClellan | Dem | 21 | 3* | 1,835,985 | 44.9 |

*New Jersey, Delaware, Kentucky.

CONGRESS

| 1861 | 37th | Senate | (50) | 31 Repub | 11 Dem | 7 Others 1 Vacant |
|---|---|---|---|---|---|---|
| | | House | (178) | 106 Repub | 42 Dem | 28 Others 2 Vacant |
| 1863 | 38th | Senate | (51) | 39 Repub | 12 Dem | |
| | | House | (183) | 103 Repub | 80 Dem | |

(For 39th Congress see Andrew Johnson.)

NOTE

1 Secessions:
1. Arkansas (8th) 6 May 1861
2. N Carolina (9th) 20 May 1861
3. Virginia (10th) 23 May 1861
4. Tennessee (11th) 8 June 1861

VICE PRESIDENTS

15th Hannibal Hamlin (Maine), 1809–91. Lawyer; state politician; member of US House of Representatives, 1843–7; US Senator, 1848–57; Governor of Maine, 1857; Senator, 1857–61; vice president, 4 March 1861 to 4 March 1865. Subsequently Senator, 1869–81; US Minister to Spain, 1881–2. Died 4 July 1891.

16th Andrew Johnson (Tennessee), subsequently 17th president.

---

With Abraham Lincoln as with George Washington it is very difficult to separate the man from the myth. More has been written about Lincoln than anyone could read in a lifetime. His *Collected Works* run to more than two million words. Few men are

108

commemorated in a statue as large as that in the Lincoln Memorial in Washington DC. Even fewer have had a monument erected to honour a speech they made. It is hard to realise that Lincoln was neither a demigod nor a superman, but a real person, with ordinary human passions and limitations, of whom large numbers of people entertained a very low opinion during his lifetime. He never became a really popular president and if he had been defeated in 1864 he would have been written off as one of the great failures of American history.

'I was born 12 February 1809 in Hardin County, Kentucky. My parents were both born in Virginia of undistinguished families . . . My father removed from Kentucky to Indiana in my eighth year . . . It was a wild region with many bears and other wild animals still in the woods. There I grew up . . .'

The family, now including Thomas Lincoln's second wife who made a splendid stepmother to his children who loved her dearly, spent some 14 years in Indiana with young Lincoln working as a farmhand and general handyman. He had less than a year of formal education. 'Still somehow I could read, write and cipher to the rule of three,' and he read every book he could lay hands on. In 1828–9 he made the first of two trips on a flatboat down the Ohio and Mississippi to New Orleans, just before the family moved to Illinois in 1830.

He left home in 1831, and made another trip to New Orleans, before becoming a clerk in a store at New Salem, Illinois. He became interested in the law and began to attend court sessions with the object of becoming a lawyer. In 1832 he served as a captain of volunteers in the Black Hawk Indian war in Northern Illinois and Southern Wisconsin. In the same year he ran unsuccessfully for the lower House of the State legislature as a 'Whig', before going into partnership in a store which failed. It took him fifteen years to pay off its debts. At this time his highly developed sense of humour must have been a great comfort to him. He had a tendency to lapse into droll stories. 'This reminds me of a story', he would say, bursting into high-pitched laughter, 'like the neigh of a wild horse on his native prairie'. Mimicry, caricature, ridicule, burlesque — each was within his range, though his most telling shafts were often delivered with an elaborately innocent air: 'I was not aware until now that Mr. Douglas's father was a cooper. I am certain he was a very good one, for' — and now he bowed to Douglas — 'he has made one of the best whiskey casks I have ever seen.' In the White House, later, Lincoln explained that he needed humour as an essential outlet for his emotions: 'I laugh because I must not cry . . .'

The next few years of his life were crucial and crowded. He became Postmaster at New Salem, as well as a local surveyor; and in 1834, and in the three succeeding biennial elections, he was returned to the State legislature. At the same time he studied law. He was called to the Illinois bar in 1837 and he removed to Springfield (which became the state capital in 1839) to practise. He soon prospered as a lawyer and resigned from the legislature to concentrate on his work. In 1840 he had been chosen as a Presidential Elector on the Harrison ticket and in the ensuing campaign he first crossed swords with a newcomer, Stephen A. Douglas, who was also his rival for the hand of Mary Todd.

The belle of a leading Kentucky slaveowning family, Mary Todd had come to Springfield to live with her married sister when she met Lincoln — 'a poor nobody then'. They were married after three years of stormy courtship and a broken engagement. Lincoln failed to appear for their first marriage service in January 1841 because he was seized by that 'melancholia' — the 'hypos' Lincoln called the attacks — the fits of depression that were to wrack him throughout his life. The new couple were complete opposites in background and temperament and the pretty 5ft 2in Mary has been described as a dubious helpmeet for the 6ft 4in Lincoln who was 'so ugly that he was almost handsome':

> His face was lined, in part, by God
> In part, they say, by Mary Todd.

During the Civil War she was regarded as a traitor by the South and suspected of treason by Unionists, at a time when the death of her favourite son Willie had left her distraught. Lincoln became the second president (Washington was the first) to appear before a Congressional committee, when he was summoned to defend his wife against charges that she was a Southern spy. The next would be Gerald Ford (qv).

From 1847–9 Lincoln served a single term in the US House of Representatives as the only Whig from the heavily Democratic Illinois. He did not make a brilliant Congressman. He opposed

Polk's expansionism and the constitutionality of the Mexican War. He favoured the exclusion of slavery from the territories ceded by Mexico, though he opposed Federal interference with it where it already existed. From 1849–54 he 'practised law more assiduously than ever before', and his interest in politics was waning with the decline of the Whigs when, 'the repeal of the Missouri Compromise (1854) aroused me again'. This arousal took him back into the Illinois legislature from which he resigned in order to contest, unsuccessfully, a vacant Senate seat. So it was that in the crucial period in American history from 1855–60 he was not, except briefly in 1856, and again in 1858, involved in national politics.

In the spring of 1856 Lincoln was converted to the new (1854) Republican party with its anti-slavery (though not 'Abolitionist') platform which was linked to the major planks of the Whigs and a cheap land policy — 'Vote yourself a farm!' By May of 1856 he was the acknowledged leader of the Illinois Republicans. In June when the new party held its first national election convention Lincoln came second in the ballot for the vice presidential position and enhanced his reputation in his own state.

In June of 1858 following his adoption as the Illinois Republican candidate in the Senatorial contest against the incumbent Democrat, Stephen A. Douglas, Lincoln delivered a major speech which included lines that were to become immortal: '"A house divided against itself shall not stand." I believe this government cannot endure permanently half slave and half free. I do not expect the Union to be dissolved, I do not expect the house to fall; but I do expect it will cease to be divided . . .' Lincoln requested that he and Douglas '. . . divide time and address the same audiences during the present canvas', and the result was the widely reported Lincoln-Douglas debates of 1858. For the second time Lincoln failed to obtain a Senate seat (the Senator was chosen by the legislature where the Democrats were in the majority), and Lincoln felt, he said, '. . . like the boy that stubbed his toe — it hurt too bad to laugh and he was too big to cry . . .'; but Lincoln was now a national figure. 'No man of this generation,' wrote the New York *Evening Post*, 'has grown more rapidly before the country than Lincoln in this canvas.'

In 1860 Chicago, Illinois, staged the Republican national nominating convention. The Illinois Republicans chose Lincoln as their presidential candidate. Lincoln's strength lay in the weaknesses of his rivals. W. H. Seward, the acknowledged leader of the party, had a reputation for radicalism; and others, like Salmon P. Chase and Edward Bates, suffered from similar defects. By comparison, Abraham Lincoln was not well enough known to be regarded as either a radical or a conservative having served only one term in Congress. His humble background would appeal to the masses. His residence in Illinois, a 'doubtful' state was an asset, and these factors help to explain his emergence as a viable candidate. On the third ballot four votes were switched to Lincoln from Ohio: 'The deed was done. There were thousands cheering with the energy of insanity. Fire the salute. Abe Lincoln is nominated!'

In the election in November, Lincoln was elected by the votes of the 18 states of the North and West where he polled 54.4% of the votes. He won only 9.7% in 5 border states and his name was not even on the ballot in 10 Southern states. His total share of the vote at 39.9% was the second lowest ever for a victorious candidate; but because of his support in the populous states he obtained 180 out of a total of 303 Electoral College votes.

In his Inaugural Address in March 1861 (after the establishment of the Confederacy), he spoke out for Union:

> The Union of these states is perpetual . . . no state upon its own mere motion can lawfully get out of the Union . . . In your hands my dissatisfied fellow countrymen, and not in mine, is the momentous issue of civil war . . . You have no oath registered in heaven to destroy the government, while I shall have the most solemn one to 'preserve, protect and defend it'.

The situation which Buchanan had been unable to resolve was finally settled by the Confederate attack on Fort Sumter, which (like Roosevelt and Pearl Harbor) Lincoln has been accused of inciting. On April 15 he began counter-measures with such promptness that his critics labelled him a 'dictator'. He issued a proclamation that a state of insurrection existed and called for 75,000 militia from the states to put it down. In so doing he was committing the Federal Government to a definite theory regarding the nature of the war; the South was in rebellion, this was not a clash between rival governments. This was followed by two pro-clamations of blockade. In May Lincoln increased the size of the US Army and used two million dollars of government money to pay for 'military and naval measures', thus usurping Congressional functions. His suspension of Habeas Corpus ensured a vast expansion of presidential powers. Probably no President, not even Woodrow Wilson or Franklin D. Roosevelt, has ever wielded as much power, independent of Congress, as Lincoln did. His own view of the 'war powers' was expansive, and after 1861 he continued to assume increased powers to himself, justifying his actions by liberal interpretations of the Constitution, rather than by seeking legislation to put powers into the president's hands.

When war broke out Lincoln took quite literally the constitutional provision that: 'The President shall be Commander-in-Chief of the Army and Navy of the United States.' He assumed complete command of the Union Forces. He borrowed Halleck's *Elements of Military Art and Science* from the Library of Congress and tried to apply commonsense to military problems. The Union was about to put to the test the celebrated maxim of von Clausewitz, that the best qualifications for a commander whether king, emperor or president, are not military knowledge but 'a remarkable superior mind and strength of character'.

His immediate problem was to find a good general. The commanding general was Lt-Gen Winfield Scott, 'Old Fuss and Feathers' a veteran of the War of 1812 (and the election of 1852), but battle operations were entrusted to subordinates. Following the disaster at the first battle of Bull Run, Gen George B. McClellan became General-in-Chief of the Union armies and commander of the Army of Northern Virginia. His inactivity (as Lincoln saw it), led to four months of unrelieved gloom when the war was directed by Lincoln and his new Secretary of War, Edwin Stanton, before Maj Gen W. H. Halleck was created General-in-Chief. After the disaster at second Bull Run (August 1862) McClellan was reinstated. The only encouraging sign in the next few months was the bloody Federal victory at Antietam (17 September), but finally Lincoln tired of McClellan's hesitation and removed him in November.

Lincoln next tried Maj Gen Ambrose E. Burnside (he of the famous side whiskers), who asked to be removed after a severe defeat at Fredericksburg in December. He next turned to Maj Gen 'Fighting Joe' Hooker. Robert E. Lee inflicted a severe defeat on him at Chancellorsville in the Spring of 1863 and advanced towards Pennsylvania to be confronted by Lincoln's new commander, Maj Gen George G. Meade. Between 1 July and 3 July the Blue and the Gray clashed at Gettysburg. Lee was halted and forced to withdraw but, Lincoln believed, Meade failed to follow up this advantage.

On the day that Gettysburg ended, Maj Gen Ulysses S. Grant had captured Vicksburg on the Mississippi after a prolonged siege, and followed this with further victories. In March 1864 he was created a full Lt General and assigned to command 'the Armies of the United States' (see p 125). Lincoln's military task was now finished. He had found the general he wanted. Now he could concentrate on the political problems occasioned by the war.

In his first Inaugural Address Lincoln had said: 'I have no purpose directly or indirectly to interfere with the institution of slavery in the states where it exists. I believe I have no lawful right to do so, and I have no inclination to do so.' To that declaration he adhered strictly for over a year. But gradually Lincoln came to the conclusion that freeing the slaves would aid the cause of Union. Ideally gradual, compensated emancipation would be the solution, but there were dangers in allowing Congress to pass the necessary legislation. He set out his aims in a famous letter to Horace Greeley, the editor of the New York *Tribune*:

> My paramount object in this struggle is to save the Union, and is not either to save or destroy Slavery. If I could save the Union without freeing any slave, I would do it; and if I could save it by freeing all slaves, I would do it; and if I could do it by freeing some and leaving others alone, I would also do that. What I do about slavery and the colored race I do because I believe it helps to save the Union . . .

The Preliminary Proclamation of Emancipation was introduced in a Cabinet meeting in September 1862 'as a fit and necessary war measure for suppressing rebellion'. It was to come into force on 1 January next. It did not actually free any slaves (it would require the implementation of the 13th Amendment of January 1865 to achieve that), but it served notice that the North had added emancipation to its other declared war objectives — and ensured that no European power would now accord even diplomatic recognition to the South.

Lincoln was now turning his attention to the most pressing of all problems: what was going to happen after the war? His intention was to restore the Union as fast as possible without Congressional interference. This moderate programme was set out in his Proclamation of Amnesty and Reconstruction of December 1863. It provoked immediate hostility from the so-called 'Radical

Republicans' in Congress and they introduced their plans to punish the South in the Wade-Davis bill, just after Lincoln had been renominated for the 1864 presidential election, which he won in November. Lincoln vetoed this bill and waited for the war to end.

In his second Inaugural Address he pleaded for reconciliation: 'With malice towards none, with charity for all . . . let us bind up the nation's wounds . . . and achieve and cherish a just and lasting peace . . .' He returned to this theme in his last public address (11 April 1865); and at his last Cabinet meeting on 14 April '. . . He hoped there would be no persecution, no bloody work after the war was over . . .'

That same Good Friday evening, as part of the victory celebrations (Lee had surrendered to Grant at Appomattox on the previous Palm Sunday), Abraham Lincoln went to Ford's Theatre in Washington to see *Our American Cousin*. During the third act, John Wilkes Booth, an actor, entered the president's box and shot Lincoln in the head, as part of a widespread conspiracy to murder the leading members of the Cabinet. (Booth's brother, the famous Shakespearian actor Edwin Booth, had saved the life of young Robert Lincoln, Lincoln's son, in 1861. Robert, standing on the platform of the Pennsylvania Railroad Station in Jersey City, had fallen into the space between the platform and an incoming train. Edwin Booth pulled him up just in time.)

The president was carried across the street to a private house where he died at 7.22am the following morning without regaining consciousness. Edwin Stanton pronounced his epitaph: 'Now he belongs to the ages.'

Before his death, and immediately after, many did not regard Lincoln as an effective chief executive let alone a great man. As recently as November 1864 the best part of two million people had voted against him. 'The decease of Mr Lincoln is a great national bereavement,' said an Ohio Representative, 'but I am not so sure it is so much of a national loss.' 'How the history of this nation might have been changed,' wrote a contemporary, 'had Mr Lincoln survived to bear his influential part in reconstructing and reuniting the shattered country, no man can tell.' What the verdict of history would have been if Lincoln, born on the same day as Charles Darwin, had lived as long as the latter, can only be a matter for speculation. But, following a blow struck on a Good Friday, the Lincoln legend, by virtue of its similarity to the Christian theme of vicarious atonement and redemption, has gathered strength.

# ANDREW JOHNSON

**Full name**   Andrew Johnson, 1808–75
**Born**   Raleigh, North Carolina, 29 December 1808, the second of 3 children
**Parents**   Jacob Johnson (b Northumberland, England, 1778, d 1812), hostler, janitor, constable, and Mary McDonough Johnson (1783–1856). 2 sons, 1 daughter
**Family lineage**   English, Scottish-Irish
**College**   None
**Married**   1827, Eliza McCardle Johnson (1810–76), daughter of John McCardle, shoemaker. 3 sons, 2 daughters
**Occupation**   Tailor; mayor of Greeneville, 1830–3; member of the Tennessee Legislature, 1835–7, 1839–43; member of US House of Representatives, 1843–53; Governor of Tennessee, 1853–7; US Senator, 1857–62; military governor of Tennessee, 1862–5, commissioned as Brigadier General in US Volunteers; vice president, 1864–5; US Senator 1875
**Religious denomination**   None
**Notable relationships**   None
**Died**   From a stroke, Carter's Station, Tennessee, 31 July 1875, aged 66
**Buried**   The Andrew Johnson Cemetery, Greeneville, Tennessee

**Party** Democratic (though elected vice president in 1864 on a 'National Union' ticket) **State represented** Tennessee **Term of Office** 15 April 1865 to 4 March 1869 (Johnson served the 3 year, 323 day unexpired portion of his predecessor's term) **Age on taking Office** 56 **Presidential administration** 20th (continued) **Congresses** 39th, 40th

| | | CONGRESS | | |
|---|---|---|---|---|
| 1865 | 39th | Senate (52) | 42 Union | 10 Dem |
| | | House (191) | 145 Union | 46 Dem |
| 1867 | 40th | Senate (54) | 42 Repub | 12 Dem |
| | | House (193) | 143 Union | 49 Dem | 1 Vacancy |

(The 'Radical' Republicans gained control of the Senate and the House.)

116

1 Constitutional Amendments: XIII (December 1865) abolished slavery

XIV (June 1866) provided for racial equality.

2 New State: Nebraska (1867) 37th.

3 Alaska was purchased from Russia in 1867 for $7,200,000.

4 Impeachment of President Johnson: February-May 1868.

22 February: Motion to impeach introduced in the House.

24 February: House voted in favour, 126–47.

25 February: This was reported in the Senate.

2 March: 9 articles of impeachment framed.

3 March: 2 additional articles framed.

30 March: Trial began.

16 May: He was found guilty by a vote of 35-19 of 'High Misdemeanour as charged' but was acquitted of this, the 11th charge, since a two-thirds vote was necessary to convict. The 19th, decisive vote, was cast by Senator Edmund G. Ross of Kansas.

26 May: He was 'acquitted' on the 2nd and 3rd charges by the same vote.

### VICE PRESIDENT

Johnson was the third of four presidents who did not have a vice president.

---

Andrew Johnson was the son of 'poor whites' in North Carolina. He never attended school a single day in his life but somehow the 'illiterate tailor boy' learned to read and write. At 13 he was 'indentured' to a tailor but he ran away before his time was up; his master offered a $10 reward for his return but there were no takers. Eventually he settled down before he was 19 with his own tailor's business and a wife in Greeneville, Tennessee. He soon enjoyed a modest prosperity — 'I was punctual to my customers and did good work' — became very active in local affairs, and was elected town mayor at 22. Once established he soon made a name for himself as a resounding stump orator and as a politician who was very zealous in working-class interests, and thereafter his political rise was truly remarkable. He served two terms in the state legislature before entering the state Senate, from 1841–3; and then he was advanced to the United States House of Representatives during a crucial decade in American history. He supported the admission of Texas; he favoured, initially, a militant policy over Oregon; and he accepted the Compromise of 1850. He was a Jacksonian Democrat though he was not a doctinaire loyalist, and he was never really a 'party' man. He served a term as Governor of Tennessee — he was known as the 'mechanic Governor' — before entering the US Senate where, inevitably, he was called the 'mechanic statesman'.

The coming of secession presented him with particular problems — he was a Southerner and he owned eight household slaves. He had pronounced states rights views and he believed that Congress had no power to interfere with the extension of slavery. Yet no Northerner was more of a Unionist than this man from Eastern Tennessee and he regarded secession as unconstitutional. Consequently, though he supported Breckinridge in the election of 1860, he joined with Senator Crittenden in 1861 in support of a set of resolutions aimed at maintaining the Union and the Constitution and once secession was an accomplished fact he went over to the Union side. He made a desperate personal bid, at great risk to himself, to prevent Tennessee from seceding (it seceded in June 1861), and he was nearly lynched in Virginia on his way back to Washington where he was the only Southern Senator to stay in his seat.

When the Union armies precariously occupied certain parts of Tennessee in 1862, Lincoln asked Johnson to go to Nashville as Military Governor. For the next three difficult years he filled this post with great determination and firmness. This, it has been said, was his finest hour, and it was partly because of this that he was chosen to be Lincoln's running-mate in 1864. The Republicans chose to run under the banner of a 'National Union' party and who better to occupy the second position on the ticket than Andrew Johnson, a Southerner and a pro-war Democrat? (Johnson's enemies made a great deal of capital from the fact that he was undeniably drunk on Inauguration Day in 1865, though this was the result of spirits taken for medicinal purposes following a recent attack of typhoid fever.) It did not seem to matter that he had no real connections with the party organisation which placed him there, nor that he had had no preparation for the role of party leader, until 7.22am on 15 April 1865. He spoke no more than the truth when he said at his Inauguration that he was '. . . incompetent to perform duties so important and responsible as those which have been so unexpectedly thrown upon me'.

The problem facing Johnson was the 'Reconstruction', or as he preferred to call it (like his mentor Lincoln), the 'Restoration' of the seceded states and the establishment of a new relationship between the Southern whites and the now-freed negroes. He continued Lincoln's moderate programme throughout the summer and autumn of 1865 without any interference from Congress which was not in session. He pardoned the majority of ex-confederates, got new governments working in all the former Confederate states except Texas, and secured the ratification of the 13th Amendment abolishing slavery. He believed that the final details of readjustment could be left to the loyal peoples of the states in question, but here he was mistaken. In several states 'Black Codes' were introduced which, by means of state laws of varying harshness, placed restrictions on the freemen. Ex-confederates, even the former vice president of the Confederacy, Alexander H. Stephens, became predominant in the administration of these states.

When Congress met in December 1865 a battle royal was inevitable. The end of the war was bound, in any case, to bring acute rivalry between the president and a Congress which, largely ignored for the past four years, felt that it had been unimportant long enough. The 'National Union' party had died with Lincoln and now Johnson found himself facing the 'Radical Republicans', men who were bitterly disappointed, both by his recent policies, and their initial assessment of him: 'Johnson we have faith in you. By the gods, there will be no trouble now in running the government,' one of their leaders had said in April 1865.

These 'Radical Republicans' were a loose coalition of men of varying ideas which ranged from the idealistic and the philanthropic to the mercenary. They were ruthless and brilliantly led by men like Thaddeus Stevens, Charles Sumner and Benjamin Wade and their programme of 'Radical Reconstruction' was totally at variance with Johnson's, being based, they argued, on the realisation of the aims for which the war had been fought. The programme included the disenfranchisement of all ex-confederates; full suffrage rights and equality for negroes; land confiscation and its redistribution to negroes; and the creation of economic and educational opportunities for them. The white South was to be punished, the negro was to be advanced and, as a by-product, the predominance of the Republican party would be established for a long time to come as the grateful negro voters would be solidly Republican. The 'Radical Republicans' set to work, undid

119

Johnson's plans and started all over again, aided by their over-whelming success in the mid-term election of 1866. They refused to seat any representatives from the South in Congress, vetoed Johnson's measures and introduced their own including the Civil Rights Act of 1866, the forerunner of the later 14th Amendment, guaranteeing racial equality. By the spring of 1867 there were no legal governments anywhere in the South outside Tennessee and the South had been divided into five zones each under a major general (shades of Oliver Cromwell), where government was carried out by military *fiat* and enforced by military courts and martial law. It had been provided that states could only be readmitted to the Union if they ratified the 14th Amendment and set up governments based on 'universal suffrage', though the amendment disqualified the whole of the old political class in the South. Johnson had struggled to veto this programme but it had been passed by Congress over the presidential veto: 15 out of Johnson's 29 vetoes — the largest number ever — were dealt with in this way.

Then the Radicals turned on Johnson. By a series of laws, of which the most famous was the Tenure of Office Act, the president was deprived of control of the Army and denied the right to remove officials, including members of his own cabinet, without the consent of the Senate. If these laws were to prevail Congress would become king. To make the point clear, when Johnson tried to remove his Secretary of War in defiance of Congress, the House of Representatives voted to impeach him, under Article II, section 4 and Article I, section 3 of the Constitution of the United States. Eleven charges were formulated, ten of them referring in one way or another to the Tenure of Office Act, and the eleventh accused the president of attacking Congress in his speeches.

The issue came to a vote in May 1868 and it became clear that the Radicals had at last overplayed their hand. A vote was taken on 16 May on the eleventh charge and ten days later on the second and third. Each time the Radicals had one vote too few for the necessary 'two thirds vote' for conviction. Seven Republican Senators voted with twelve Democrats in support of Johnson and nineteen votes were enough. The attempt to subvert the Constitution, to undo the presidential form of government and to establish Congress as the sole policy maker, had failed.

Achievements of this presidency tend to be overlooked, but W. H. Seward, the Secretary of State, was active in foreign affairs. He applied the 'Monroe Doctrine' with some vigour by sending

General Philip Sheridan with 50,000 troops to the Mexican border in 1866 to check the 'Mexican Venture' of Napoleon III. In 1867 Alaska — 'Seward's Folly' or 'Andrew Johnson's Polar Bear Garden' — was purchased from Russia for $7,200,000, or about 2 cents an acre.

In 1869 Johnson, who had thought of seeking renomination, retired to Tennessee without attending the inauguration of his successor (who had said that he would neither ride with Johnson nor speak to him). But he was not yet finished with politics. In 1875 he became the only former president to be returned to the US Senate where flowers awaited him at the desk from which, he reminded his audience, he had once been the lone Southerner battling for the Union. But within seven months the 'Old Commoner' (certainly the only president who ever made all his own clothing) was dead. His last words were said to have been: 'Pillow my head on the Constitution of my country.'

# ULYSSES S. GRANT

**Full name**  Ulysses S. Grant (though his given name was Hiram Ulysses Grant), 1822–85
**Born**  Point Pleasant, Ohio 27 April 1822, the eldest of 6 children
**Parents**  Jesse Root Grant (1794–1873), leather tanner, factory owner, and Hannah Simpson Grant (1798–1883). 3 sons, 3 daughters
**Family lineage**  English-Scottish
**College**  US Military Academy, West Point, NY. Graduated 1843
**Married**  1848, Julia Boggs Dent Grant (1826–1902), daughter of Frederick Dent, merchant and planter. 3 sons, 1 daughter
**Occupation**  Professional soldier (the first officer in the history of the US Army to attain the rank of full General); Secretary of War, 1867
**Religious denomination**  Methodist
**Notable relationships**  Grant was descended from David I, King of Scots. He was a sixth cousin once removed to the future President Cleveland; and a fourth cousin once removed to the future President Franklin Delano Roosevelt
**Died**  From cancer, at Mount McGregor, near Saratoga, NY, 23 July 1885, aged 63
**Buried**  In the General Grant National Memorial, 'Grant's Tomb', Riverside Park, New York City, NY

**Party** Republican **State represented** Illinois **Terms of Office** 4 March 1869 to 4 March 1877 **Age on taking Office** 46 (youngest to date) **Presidential administrations** 21st, 22nd **Congresses** 41st, 42nd, 43rd, 44th

|  |  | 1868 ELECTION | | | |
| --- | --- | --- | --- | --- | --- |
| *Candidates* | *Party* | *Electoral Vote (294)* | *States Won (34)* | *Popular Vote* | *%* |
| U. S. Grant | Repub | 214 | 26 | 3,013,313 | 52.7 |
| H. Seymour | Dem | 80 | 8 | 2,703,933 | 47.3 |

| Candidates | Party | Electoral Vote (352) | States Won (35) | Popular Vote | % |
|---|---|---|---|---|---|
| U. S. Grant | Repub | 286 | 29 | 3,597,375 | 55.6 |
| | Dem & | | | | |
| H. Greeley* | Lib Rep | (66) | 6 | 2,833,711 | 43.8 |

*Died 29 November after the popular vote but before the electoral college vote. Greeley's 66 electoral votes were divided amongst four minority candidates.

## CONGRESS

1869　41st　Senate　(74)　　61 Repub　　11 Dem　　2 Vacancies
　　　　　　　House (243)　　170 Repub　　73 Dem
　　　　(This was the largest ever Republican majority in the Senate.)

1871　42nd　Senate　(74)　　57 Repub　　17 Dem
　　　　　　　House (243)　　134 Dem　　104 Repub　　5 Others
　　　　(The Administration lost control of the House.)

1873　43rd　Senate　(74)　　54 Repub　　19 Dem　　1 Other
　　　　　　　House (300)　　194 Repub　　92 Dem　　14 Others
　　　　(The Administration regained control of the House.)

1875　44th　Senate　(76)　　46 Repub　　29 Dem　　1 Other
　　　　　　　House (292)　　169 Dem　　109 Repub　　14 Others
　　　　(The Administration again lost control of the House.)

## NOTES

1 1870 9th Census: total population, 38,558,371.
2 Constitutional Amendment: XV (1870), the last Amendment to be ratified in the 19th century, provided that the rights of citizens to vote should not be denied 'on account of race, colour, or previous condition of servitude'.
3 New State admitted: Colorado (1876) 38th.

## VICE PRESIDENTS

17th Schuyler Colfax (Indiana), 1823–85. Editor; member of US House of Representatives, 1855–69; Speaker, 1863–9; vice president 4 March 1869 to 4 March 1873.
18th Henry Wilson (born Jeremiah Jones Colbath), (Mass), 1812–75; shoe manufacturer; US Senator, 1855–73; vice president 4 March 1873 to 22 November 1875 (died in office).

---

In 1868 it was the turn of the Republicans to go for a completely apolitical figure — *the* military idol, enormously popular in the

West and in the East, the scourge of the South — General Ulysses S. Grant: 'Let us have peace,' he implored in his acceptance speech.

Born in Ohio in 1822, into one of the oldest families in America, he was christened Hiram Ulysses Grant. With those initials he was not especially upset when, at the time of his entry into Westpoint, a clerical error (which the military authorities characteristically refused to admit), transformed him into Ulysses S. Grant (contrary to popular opinion he never laid claim to the middle name 'Simpson'), the name by which he was always known thereafter.

He received a sound grounding in the 3 Rs during a childhood spent mainly acquiring skills in the handling of horses, before he obtained a nomination to enter Westpoint Military Academy. 'A military life had no charms for me,' he wrote later, though he came from a family with a military tradition that stretched back to the French and Indian war. 'Sam' Grant, then standing only 5ft (the minimum qualifying height) and weighing only 100lb, was joining the army's college to get a good education. He excelled at maths and horsemanship (he held the Academy high jumping record for twenty-five years), but then, because he only graduated in the middle of his class in 1843, his first military appointment was as a 2nd lieutenant in the US 4th Infantry.

He fought under Zachary Taylor in the Mexican War which, like his superior — whose casual mode of dress he adopted thereafter — he totally opposed: 'It was one of the most unjust (wars) ever waged by a stronger against a weaker nation.' He took part in every major battle except Buena Vista and 'behaved with distinction and gallantry', reported a superior, Major Robert E. Lee. He served mainly as a Quartermaster and learned much of great value later about army organisation. Marriage to Miss Julia Dent (he persuaded her not to have an operation to uncross her eyes — he loved her, crossed eyes and all) was followed by boring garrison duty on the Pacific coast which led to a drinking problem. In 1854 he resigned from the army.

Grant's civilian years were discouraging and unsuccessful. 'Hard Scrabble' Farm at St Louis in Missouri did not pay its way; and he was, said a friend, too honest to make a success of his next venture as a real estate agent. 1860 found him working as a clerk in his father's leather store in Galena, Illinois. At the age of 39 this quiet, diffident, stubby little man, who was enormously popular in the town, was about to discover his true vocation.

At the outbreak of war he was appointed by the state governor to be Colonel of the 21st Illinois Volunteer Regiment, but it was not long before he was a brigadier general in command at Cairo, Illinois, at the start of a meteoric rise that three years later would see him commanding the Union armies and eight years later in the White House.

Abraham Lincoln, who recognised the importance of controlling the Mississippi, sent Grant into Missouri (February 1862) where he captured Forts Henry and Donelson in a no-nonsense fashion and 'Unconditional Surrender' Grant first made a name for himself. He was promoted major general by a grateful President. The bloody battle of Shiloh (April) — a bullet broke Grant's scabbard — and rumours of Grant's hard drinking led to demands for his removal. These were dismissed by Lincoln: 'I can't spare this man — he fights!' — and only half-jokingly he offered to send a sample of Grant's favourite whisky to all his other commanders.

On 4 July 1863 Vicksburg, the 'Western Gibraltar', the great Confederate fortress on the Mississippi, fell to Grant after a 46-day siege. This victory cut the Confederacy into two and the 'Father of waters' flowed unvexed to the sea from St Louis southwards. In October Grant took over command in the West. His victories in November at Lookout Mountain and Missionary Ridge broke the Confederates' hold on Chattanooga and opened the way for a deep thrust into the South. In March 1864 Lincoln, who had spent three anxious years looking for a commander to match Rober E. Lee, gave Grant supreme command and the revived rank of Lt General. (No soldier since George Washington had been a full Lt General.)

The Confederacy now stood on the brink of defeat and Grant's strategy was aimed at bringing about a rapid conclusion. His solution was the concept which was later labelled 'Total War' — a war behind the enemies lines which would demoralise their troops and strike terror into the hearts of its civilian population. Major General William Tecumseh Sherman, with whose name even today Southern children are awed, proceeded to cut a swathe sixty miles wide across the South from Atlanta to Savannah — traces of which are still visible. He then turned north to join up with Grant, who was pinning Lee at Richmond, Virginia, in a classic pincer movement. War, he had shown, was 'Hell'. The heart began to ebb away from the Confederacy. Confederate troops, who were filthy, hungry and disease-ridden, who were horror-struck at the news of Sherman's depredations, were only prevented from wholesale desertion by their loyalty to 'Marse Robert'. But as the spring approached Men in Gray began to slip away to their homes.

On 9 April 1865, on the edge of Appomattox village, Grant rode through the lines to answer Lee's request for surrender terms, 'to shift from myself the responsibility for any further effusion of blood'. They met: Grant, in his forties, stocky, dishevelled, unshaven and wearing a private's blouse, his sword packed somewhere in his baggage; Lee, nearly 60, tall, silver-haired, immaculate and carefully accoutred, wearing a brand-new uniform and sword. After completing the terms of unconditional surrender, Grant readily agreed that the rebels should be allowed to keep their horses for the spring ploughing and their officers their side arms, and then both men turned away near to tears. (The American Civil War finally ended on 2 June 1865 when Gen Edmund S. Kirby Smith, CSA, surrendered the trans-Mississippi forces.) Grant had given strict orders that there were to be no celebrations, though he was to castigate the South later in his *Memoirs*: '. . . the fact remains that the Confederate cause was one of the worst for which a people ever fought and one for which there was the least excuse.' A grateful Congress created Grant 'General of the Army of the United States' with the proviso that when the office became vacant 'this act shall expire and remain no longer in force'.

Both the main parties would have been delighted to support Grant in 1868. He had only ever voted once, in 1856 (and then *against* the Republican Frémont on the excellent grounds that he knew him). The opposition to the war of the 'Copperhead' Democrats was enough to make him a Republican thereafter, and he had supported the Republican-based Union party in 1864. His popular majority in 1868 was only some 300,000; and though he won 214 electoral votes, 41 of these came from 8 ex-Confederate states controlled by troops, where Democrats could not vote; so that the cynical could say that, in part, the conquering hero was elected by force, intimidation, and every available Negro vote.

On a 'tidal wave of expectation' the second greatest man thrown up by the war entered the White House. He was 5ft 8in tall, weighing 140lb with cold blue eyes and a big jaw hidden by a scrubby, messy beard. He was strong, stubborn, quiet, and a man of great integrity. He had never been known to utter a profane expletive. His presidency is generally regarded as a period of failure and Grant as one of America's worst-ever presidents, but if he was then the American people must take the blame. He was twice nominated on the first ballot by the Republicans, and elected twice, the second time by a wider margin than in 1868. In 1880 a formidable attempt to break the two-term tradition, after a four-year interlude, saw him lead on the first 35 ballots; and if he had been nominated he probably would have won. If Ulysses S. Grant was a 'failure' then millions of US citizens evidently did not think so.

His period in office coincided with the so-called 'Golden Age' of business prosperity — and corruption. Grant himself was too honest to recognise corruption in the officials under him but it went on and increased during his terms. No scandals involved Grant personally (though foolishly he accepted presents from speculators), but the administration and the Republican party were deeply shaken and the association with corruption helped to kill the party in 1884. The Crédit Mobilier scandal, uncovered in 1872, resulted in the disgrace of the vice president. Grant's private secretary was deeply implicated in the 'Whisky Ring' (1875); shamefully Grant covered up for him. The Secretaries of the Treasury and the Interior and the Attorney General were involved in serious scandals. In March 1876 the Secretary of War was charged with 'malfeasance' in office, and resigned. James G. Blaine, the Republican leader in the House, was accused of taking bribes. 'Grantism' became a byword for political avarice.

Grant's initial ignorance of government and politics meant his dependence on Republican leaders. Unfortunately, with the exception of Hamilton Fish, the Secretary of State, his was an undistinguished Cabinet and it has been said that in his two terms he never rose above the level of his advisers, not that Grant was good at taking advice. Like the trained soldier he was, he was inclined to regard the smallest opposition as 'treason', though this was offset by his susceptibility to flattery.

All this does not mean that Grant had no achievements to his credit — some more highly-regarded presidents have had much less to show for their administrations. He strengthened the presidency after Johnson's prolonged war with Congress. He took a great pride in the 15th Amendment of 1870. He allowed Reconstruction to run its course, bolstering it with military force, but by the mid-70s the North was tiring of its task and power was passing into the hands of white Southerners dedicated to ensuring white supremacy; so that though 'the North won the war, the white South won the peace'.

Inflationary pressures were checked by the pursuit of a 'sound money' policy and a high protective tariff, both of which were adhered to in spite of the 'Panic of 1873' and in the teeth of pressure from Western debt-ridden farmers and Northern industrialists, and ultimately government credit was placed on a sound footing.

Relations were improved with Great Britain. The Treaty of Washington (1871) saw the introduction of the principle of arbitration into international affairs, as a result of which the British government of W. E. Gladstone agreed to pay the United States $5½ million for depradations committed by the British-built Confederate raider, the CSS *Alabama*, during 1862–4. Grant kept America out of a war with Cuba over the *Virginius* affair (1873). This was an arms-running ship (during the Cuban rebellion of 1868–78), which was illegally flying the American flag. The Cubans shot 53 of the crew, including Americans; but ultimately agreed to pay an indemnity of $80,000 to the families of the executed Americans. The Administration made a futile attempt to annex Santo Domingo by treaty, as a future haven for the coloured people of the South.

Grant had been re-elected in 1872 following a particularly bitter campaign and Republican divisions. 'Your verdict,' he said in his second Inaugural Address (it was the coldest ever Inauguration Day, the temperature was 4°F), 'I accept as my vindication.' It would probably be more accurate to say that Americans continued to support him because his victories were still fresh, because they had no wish to 'change horses in mid-stream' and because his opponents were mediocre.

He went out of office in 1877 following the electoral crisis of 1876 (see p. 131). He embarked on a two-year world tour, during which, it was estimated, he was seen by more eyes than ever looked upon any other human being up to that time. He met, he said, four 'great men'; the Viceroy of China, Li Hung Chang; Disraeli, Bismarck and Gambetta. In 1884 he became a silent partner in an investment firm that went bankrupt. Everything that Grant owned had to go to pay his debts and there was now only one way to recoup his losses, by his pen. He set out to write his *Memoirs* but he was only half way through when it was found that he was suffering from cancer at the root of his tongue. He battled on and completed his task only four days before his death. (His *Memoirs* subsequently brought in $500,000 for his family.)

President Cleveland announcing his death to the nation said that he was 'a great military leader who was, in the hour of victory magnanimous, amidst disaster serene and self-sustained'. The fact remains that he would have had greater lustre had he never been president — 'He combined great gifts with great mediocrity' was the cutting verdict of Woodrow Wilson — and it was for his military achievements that the nation, on 27 April 1897 (the 75th anniversary of his birth), placed his remains in a 150ft-high grey granite structure, on a bluff overlooking the Hudson River in New York City.

# RUTHERFORD B. HAYES

NINETEENTH PRESIDENT OF THE UNITED STATES 1877–81

**Full name**  Rutherford Birchard Hayes, 1822–93
**Born**  Delaware, Ohio, 4 October 1822, the fifth of 5 children
**Parents**  Rutherford Hayes (1787–1822), farmer, storekeeper, and Sophia Birchard Hayes (1792–1866). 3 sons, 2 daughters
**Family lineage**  Scottish-English
**College**  Kenyon College, Gambier, Ohio. BA 1842; MA 1845; Harvard Law School, Cambridge, Mass, LLB 1845
**Married**  1852, Lucy Ware Webb Hayes (1831–89), daughter of James Webb, physician. 7 sons, 1 daughter
**Occupation**  Lawyer; Civil War, Major General (1865); member of US House of Representatives, 1865–7; Governor of Ohio, 1868–72, 1876–7
**Religious denomination**  Methodist
**Notable relationships**  None
**Died**  Following a heart attack at Fremont, Ohio, 17 January 1893, aged 70
**Buried**  Spiegel Grove Estate, Fremont, Ohio

**Party** Republican **State represented** Ohio **Term of office** 4 March 1877 to 4 March 1881 **Age on taking office** 54 **Presidential administration** 23rd **Congresses** 45th, 46th

### 1876 ELECTION

| Candidates | Party | Electoral Vote (369) | States Won (38) | Popular Vote | % |
|---|---|---|---|---|---|
| R. B. Hayes | Repub | 185* | 21 | 4,036,298 | 48.0 |
| S. J. Tilden | Dem | 184 | 17 | 4,300,590 | 50.9 |

*Following the decision of an Electoral Commission (see below). Tilden became the second candidate to receive a majority of the popular vote only to be defeated in the Electoral College.

### CONGRESS

| 1877 | 45th | Senate (76) | 39 Repub | 36 Dem | 1 Other |
|---|---|---|---|---|---|
| | | House (293) | 156 Dem | 137 Repub | |

(The Administration controlled the Senate but not the House.)

1879  46th  Senate  (76)  43 Dem  33 Repub
      House  (293)  150 Dem  128 Repub  14 Others
(The Administration lost control of the Senate. This was the first Congress since 1857 with Democratic majorities in both Chambers.)

NOTE
1880 10th Census: Total population 50,155,783.

VICE PRESIDENT
19th William Almon Wheeler (New York), 1819–87. Lawyer; banker; state politician; member of US House of Representatives, 1861–3, 1869–77; vice president, 4 March 1877 to 4 March 1881.

---

On the eve of the presidential Inauguration of 1877 Mr and Mrs Hayes left for Washington not knowing whether they *were* the First Family. The controversial election of 1876 was still under investigation.

The popular vote of November had produced 'Tilden's victory' which, translated into Electoral College votes in December, had produced 184 votes for Tilden and 165 for Hayes — with 20 contested votes. These were in the three Southern states of Louisiana, South Carolina and Florida, in which there had been conspicuous irregularities, and in Oregon. If all the disputed votes went to the Republican, Governor Rutherford B. Hayes of Ohio, he would win; a single vote would elect Governor Samuel J. Tilden of New York, the Democrat.

The US Constitution was silent on the issue of disputed elections. Congress (the 44th), the natural arbiter, was split between Republicans and Democrats. At a century's distance it is perhaps possible to underestimate the extreme gravity of this unprecedented situation, but America stood perilously close to the revival of civil conflict. As drills were held and wartime units began to reform, rumblings of a new civil war rolled ominously across America.

In this situation the initiative was seized by the House which, on 14 December, approached the Senate with a view to establishing a tribunal 'whose authority none can question and whose decision all will accept as final'. After much debate an Electoral Commission was set up on 29 December, empowered to make a final decision concerning the disputed votes. It was to consist of 5 members each of the Senate (3 Republicans, 2 Democrats), the House (2 Republicans, 3 Democrats), and the Supreme Court. 2 members of the Supreme Court were to be Republicans and 2 Democrats. It was then to be the task of the other 14 members of the Commission to select another judge as the 15th member: a Republican was chosen.

Behind the scenes frantic negotiations were taking place between Republicans and Southern Democrats because a Democratic 'filibuster' could frustrate everything. There is evidence to suggest that a *quid pro quo* was worked out, on the lines of the South agreeing to Hayes' election in return for at least one Cabinet seat, a fair share of Federal patronage, subsidies for railroad development and, most important of all, the withdrawal of Federal troops.

In the event the Commission proceeded to settle each of the four disputes along 'party' lines; and each was resolved by 8 votes to 7 in favour of Hayes; the last at 4am on 2 March. On that day, just two days before Inauguration day, the electoral vote was tabulated by Congress. R. B. Hayes (185 votes) was declared elected with W. A. Wheeler as vice president ('Who is Wheeler?' Hayes is reputed to have asked).

All eyes now turned towards Tilden. If he claimed that the will of the people had been thwarted, then America could still face civil war. All he said was: 'It is what I expected . . .' R. B. Hayes first took the oath privately on Saturday, 3 March (this created a precedent — whenever 4 March falls on a Sunday the oath has been administered privately, and then again on the 5th), prior to the official ceremony on 5 March. There was no inaugural parade or ball. There was nothing to celebrate.

'Rud' Hayes had been a delicate child and not expected to live. His father had died from plague four months before his birth and three other children in the family all died in infancy. He was raised by a doting mother, a sister and an uncle. He was given a good education and was called to the Ohio bar in 1845. He practiced locally and then in Cincinnati, where he rose to be city solicitor, and where he met his wife Lucy, who was to be the first First Lady who was a college graduate. She was to bear him a daughter and seven sons — 'We're in the boy business,' he quipped. Initially a Whig politically, like Lincoln he was converted to the Republicans by the Kansas Nebraska Act (1854). He was a staunch opponent of slavery expansion and of secession.

He served right through the Civil War in which he was seriously wounded several times. He rose from major in the 23rd Regiment of Ohio Volunteer Infantry (a certain William McKinley was in the ranks), to a colonelcy and then a brevet major-generalcy 'for gallant and meritorious service'. Gen U. S. Grant said that he was one of the best generals in the army and fit to rank alongside the best products of West Point.

War service was followed immediately by a single term in Congress and then two consecutive terms as Governor of Ohio. In 1872 he failed to obtain a seat in the House of Representatives and retired from politics to his estate at Spiegel Grove. He was called out of retirement in 1875 to run again as Governor, to combat growing Democratic influence in the state. The campaign he conducted along federal rather than state political lines, concerning 'honest money' rather than paper money, made him nationally known.

At the National Republican Convention, in Cincinnati in June 1876, Hayes was nominated as the Republican Presidential candidate on the seventh ballot as a compromise candidate. Others with a greater claim, like Roscoe Conkling of New York or James G. Blaine, were ruled out because they would have been too divisive. Hayes was acceptable because of his war record, proven integrity, party loyalty and moderate liberalism. In accepting the nomination he made clear his desire for civil-service reform and, to demonstrate that he had no intention of using patronage for personal ends, he declared that 'if elected,' he would 'not be a candidate for election to a second term'. He also spoke strongly of the need to placate the South.

His position as president following the election of 1876 was not an enviable one. 'Rutherfraud' however proved to be more than equal to the task. 'I shall show a *grit* that will astonish those who predict weakness,' he wrote in his diary, and he shook the 'Stalwart' (professional) Republicans who believed that in him they had a pliable figure.

He chose a cabinet of exceptional calibre including one ex-Confederate (David M. Key, the Postmaster General). This infuriated many and raised the question of a 'bargain'. Almost immediately he withdrew the last troops from the two Southern states where they remained, on the grounds that no government could legally be maintained in power by force of arms.

He further alienated Republican bosses by his battle for Civil Service reform. He was totally opposed to the whole concept of the 'spoils system' in politics; and in his most famous attempt to free jobs from partisan control he removed a certain Chester A. Arthur from the Collectorship of Customs in New York City. Although he paved the way for genuine civil-service reform Congress withheld support for a Civil Service Commission.

He battled against inflation and opposed (futilely) the freer coinage of silver and the proliferation of paper money. He did preside over the restoration of the gold standard, suspended since 1861. He used Federal troops to restore order after strikes and riots on the railroads (1876–7), though he sympathised with the workers. He vetoed a bill prohibiting Chinese immigration, because it violated treaty obligations, then he renegotiated a treaty with China (1880) allowing the USA to restrict it. In the only other matter of international importance which arose during his term, the Panama Canal project, he reaffirmed the national attitude of 'American control'.

'His Honesty' Hayes and his wife were remarried in the White House to celebrate their silver wedding. They were married by the same preacher and Mrs Hayes wore her original gown. The fetid moral atmosphere of the White House was cleansed — too much so for some visitors who complained that 'the water flowed like wine' at receptions presided over by prohibitionist 'Lemonade Lucy'. She it was who introduced the custom of Easter egg-rolling on the lawns of the White House, where the president indulged his passion for croquet. The first telephone was installed in the White House during this administration.

A 'lame duck' president from the start who had antagonised the party bosses, who had been faced throughout with a House dominated by Democrats, and a Senate also during his last two years, Hayes was yet a long way from being the 'third rate non-entity . . . obnoxious to no one' depicted by Henry Adams. He had taken brave and honest decisions. He had helped to restore some of the presidential prerogatives usurped by Congress since Lincoln's death. Above all he had restored faith in the integrity of Washington and in Republicanism. He deserves to be remembered as one of the strongest presidents of the second half of the nineteenth century.

# JAMES A. GARFIELD

**Full name**   James Abraham Garfield, 1831–81
**Born**   Orange, Cayuga County, Ohio, 19 November 1831, the fifth of 5 children
**Parents**   Abraham Garfield (1799–1833), farmer, canal construction supervisor, and Eliza Ballou Garfield (1801–88). 3 sons, 2 daughters
**Family lineage**   English-French Huguenot
**College**   Williams College, Williamstown, Mass, BA 1856
**Married**   1858, Lucretia Rudolph Garfield (1832–1918), daughter of Zebulon Rudolph, farmer. 5 sons, 2 daughters
**Occupation**   Teacher; lawyer, state politician; Civil War, Major General (1863); member of US House of Representatives, 1863–80; Senator Elect, 1880
**Religious denomination**   Disciples of Christ
**Notable relationships**   On his father's side he was descended from Henri I, King of France; and on his mother's side from Rhys Ap Tewdr, King of Dehenbarth. He was a fifth cousin once removed of Brigham Young, the Mormon Leader.
**Died**   At Elberon, New Jersey, 19 September 1881, aged 49, as the result of bullet wounds inflicted by Charles J. Guiteau (executed 30 June 1882) on 2 July 1881 at the Baltimore and Potomac Railroad Station, Washington DC, (the site of the present National Gallery).
**Buried**   Lakeview Cemetery, Cleveland, Ohio

**Party** Republican **State represented** Ohio **Term of office** 4 March 1881 to 19 September 1881 (199 days, the second shortest term) **Age on taking office** 49 **Presidential administration** 24th **Congress** 47th (See President Arthur)

### 1880 ELECTION

| Candidates | Party | Electoral Vote (369) | States Won (38) | Popular Vote | % |
|---|---|---|---|---|---|
| J. A. Garfield | Repub | 214 | 19 | 4,454,416 | 48.3* |
| W. S. Hancock | Dem | 155 | 19 | 4,444,952 | 48.2 |

*Garfield did not receive a majority of the popular vote.

20th Chester Alan Arthur, subsequently 21st president.

---

Garfield was the last of America's seven log cabin presidents (the others were Jackson, Taylor, Fillmore, Pierce, Buchanan and Lincoln) and he was the only one who could write Latin with one hand and Greek with the other at the same time. He was the third consecutive president from Ohio and the third consecutive former Union general.

His father died before he was two and his mother struggled to raise her four surviving children. Young Jim could read at three and he remained an omnivorous reader. He worked on the farm before trying his hand on the Ohio & Pennsylvania Canal as a mule driver and barge-man. Then he worked his way through school in nearby Chester where he first met Lucretia 'Crete' Randolph, his future pupil and wife, and was converted to the 'Disciples of Christ'. He entered their college, the Western Reserve Eclectic Institute (later Hiram College), before graduating from Williams College, Massachusetts (then under the presidency of the noted educator Mark Hopkins), with the highest honours. He returned to Hiram College as professor of Classics and within a year became its president at the age of 26. He became noted locally as a spell-binding lay preacher; and he also studied law, being admitted to the Ohio bar in 1861.

In short, he was fast becoming the epitome of the American rags-to-riches dream. He was the archetype of the 'self-made man' (as President Hayes was to note in his diary in 1880), but he was to gain experience in two more areas, politics and the army. In 1859 he was returned to the Ohio Senate as a Republican, where he opposed both slavery and secession. In April 1861 he was appointed Lt Colonel of the 42nd Regiment of Ohio Volunteers. He became a very effective soldier, and compressed a whole military career into the next five and a half years, becoming at 30 one of the youngest brigadier generals in the US Army. The battles in which he took part included Shiloh, Corinth and Chickamauga. He was promoted major general for his 'gallant conduct' as Chief of Staff to Gen Rosecrans after this last action. It seemed as though he was about to become one of the best generals of the war, but at that point (1863), at the personal instigation of President Lincoln, who could find major generals more easily than good Republicans, he went to

Washington to take up the seat in the House to which he had been elected fifteen months before.

He sat continually in Congress for the next sixteen years acquiring valuable experience over a wide field. He mastered French and German as an aid in international affairs. In 1865 he became a member of the influential Ways and Means Committee; in 1867 chairman of the Committee on Military Affairs; and in 1869 chairman of the Committee on Banking and Currency. By 1877 he was the recognised leader of the Republicans in the House. In January 1880 he was elected Senator for Ohio (so that following the presidential electoral ballot on 1 December 1880, Garfield became the only person ever to have been simultaneously a member of the House, Senator-elect and president-elect).

At the Republican Convention in Chicago in June 1880 the party split between the adherents of 'Third Term' (ex-President) Grant, and the 'Half Breeds' and James G. Blaine; and after deadlock Garfield, a very dark 'dark horse', was nominated on the 36th ballot. He was almost completely unknown to the vast majority of Americans. Hence the diary jottings of President Hayes noting his selling points; 'Let it be thoroughly presented . . . how from poverty and obscurity . . . he became a great scholar, a statesman, a Major General, a Senator, a Presidential Candidate. Give the amplest details . . . a school teacher, a labourer on the (Ohio) canal . . . *the ideal candidate.*'

The main issue in the election of 1880 was the Tariff but a skeleton was dragged from Garfield's cupboard. His name had once been found in a memo book of those, it was alleged, who had received, as a bribe, shares in the Crédit Mobilier railroad company. Garfield's 'bribe' was to be $329 and '$329' was chalked on countless walls and fences during a bitter campaign.

His election displeased the 'Stalwart' wing of the Republicans and the rift was widened by his Cabinet and other appointments. He refused to appoint 'their' Secretary of the Treasury; and his Secretary of State, Blaine, was their bête noire. Robert Todd Lincoln was the only 'Stalwart' in his cabinet, though vice president Arthur also belonged to this group. He became deeply embroiled with the Senate in a squabble over the prize patronage plum, the Collectorship of the Port of New York, just before scandals began to be uncovered relating to Post Office operations under previous administrations. 'I have sworn to execute the laws,' he told his Attorney General. 'Go ahead regardless of where and whom you hit.' After his first months in the White House he was driven to exclaim: 'My God! What is there in this place that a man should ever want to get in it.' Perhaps, he felt, he was too gentle with the myriads of office seekers who daily besieged him. 'One thing thou lackest yet,' a friend told him, 'a slight ossification of the heart.'

On 2 July 1881, when Garfield was on his way to a college reunion, he was shot in the back by Charles J. Guiteau, a Chicago lawyer and a disappointed supplicant for a consular post. (He was also a 'Stalwart' — 'Arthur is now President' he is reputed to have shouted in triumph.) The injured president was removed to the White House where air conditioning was devised to cool his bedroom. Alexander Graham Bell was brought in to search (in vain) for the bullet with his 'Induction-Balance Electrical Device'. The bullet was in fact embedded in muscle and the wound need not have proved fatal; but after being moved to New Jersey, Garfield died from blood poisoning as a result of the probings of his doctors. Garfield, who had calmed a crowd on 15 April 1865 — 'God reigns and the government at Washington still lives' — was the second president to die at the hands of an assassin.

'Martyrdom is the only way in which a man can become famous without ability,' wrote the cynic George Bernard Shaw. Garfield, the 'Martyred President', did the nation a great service by the manner of his death. It shocked America into the realisation that something had to be done about the 'spoils system' — and he was the unwitting father of the epochal Civil Service Reform Act of two years later. A stunned nation subscribed $360,000 for the family of the dead president.

# CHESTER A. ARTHUR

**Full name**  Chester Alan Arthur, 1830–86
**Born**  Reputedly Fairfield, Franklin County, Vermont. (He was most probably born in Canada, but since his parents were US citizens his eligibility for the Office of President, under Article II, Section 2, of the US Constitution, was not challenged). His date of birth was 5 October 1830. He was the fifth of 9 children
**Parents**  Rev William Arthur (b Ballymena, Northern Ireland, 1796, d 1875), Baptist Minister, and Malvina Stone Arthur (1802–69). 6 daughters, 3 sons
**Family lineage**  English-Scottish-Irish
**College**  Union College, Schenectady, NY, BA 1848, MA 1851
**Married**  1859, Ellen (Nell) Lewis Herndon Arthur (1837–80), daughter of Commander William Lewis Herndon, USN. 2 sons, 1 daughter
**Occupation**  Teacher; college principal; lawyer. Civil War, Brigadier General, 1861–2; Collector of the Port of New York, 1871–8
**Religious denomination**  Episcopalian
**Notable relationships**  None
**Died**  From Bright's disease and cerebral haemorrhage, New York, NY, 18 November 1886, aged 56
**Buried**  Rural Cemetery, Albany, NY

**Party** Republican **State represented** New York **Term of office** 20 September 1881 to 4 March 1885. (He served the unexpired portion of his predecessor, 3 years, 166 days) **Age on taking office** 50 **Presidential administration** 24th (continued) **Congresses** 47th, 48th

CONGRESS

| 1881 | 47th | Senate (76) | 37 Repub | 37 Dem | 2 Others |
|------|------|-------------|----------|--------|----------|
|      |      | House (293) | 152 Repub | 130 Dem | 11 Others |

(The Administration controlled the House; the Democrats the 'Tied' Senate.)

| 1883 | 48th | Senate (76) | 40 Repub | 36 Dem | |
|------|------|-------------|----------|--------|---|
|      |      | House (325) | 200 Dem  | 119 Repub | 6 Others |

(The Administration gained control of the Senate but suffered a severe defeat in the House to which re-apportionment had added 32 seats.)

### VICE PRESIDENT

Arthur was the last of four presidents who did not have a vice president.

---

When he was 'elected by Guiteau's bullet', the general consensus was 'Good God! Chet Arthur, President of the United States!' He had been nominated as vice president to appease the 'Stalwart' wing of the Republicans, though Conkling, its leader, had urged Arthur to 'drop it as you would a red hot shoe from the forge'. Arthur had replied: 'The office of vice president is a greater honour than I ever dreamed of attaining.' And now he was about to enter the White House — but not until it had been cleared of junk (24 wagon loads were sold off for some $3000), and redecorated and refurnished by Louis Tiffany.

The third president in 1881, Arthur at least looked like a Chief Executive. He was handsome, clean-shaven with side whiskers, tall (at 6ft 2in he ties for fourth place in the tallest president stakes with Washington), and the smartest dresser since Van Buren. He was the first president with a valet, reputed to have eighty pairs of trousers and to order his jackets two dozen at a time. He always had a flower in his button hole, a silk handkerchief in his top pocket and he wore white gloves. 'Elegant Arthur' drove around Washington in a dark green landau drawn by mahogany bays. Surprisingly, perhaps, he was considered to be one of the finest fishermen in America.

He was a minister's son and most probably born in Canada. For his first decade the family moved around in the New York-Vermont area before settling in Schenectady, NY and it was from Union College that he graduated (Phi Beta Kappa class of '48). He taught school and studied law and by 1851 was a college principal in Vermont. In 1853 he moved to New York and was called to the bar. As a very junior member of the firm of Culver and Parker he took an active part in the famous case of 'The People versus Lemmon', arising out of the Fugitive Slave Law (1850), and the Jennings case, which established the right of coloured persons to ride the city's cars.

140

He was a Whig who supported Scott in 1852 and then, like his contemporaries, he moved over to the Republicans. In 1857 he joined the state militia so that when war came he was prepared for a variety of administrative posts in New York State. The Governor made him engineer in chief, with the rank of brigadier general and acting quarter-master general, and in 1862 Inspector General of the Forces. He reported on the defences of New York harbour and the general defences of the state. With a change of Governor he resigned and returned to the law, where he built up an extensive and lucrative practice, and became prominent in city politics. (He would be the first real big city man to enter the White House.)

As one of the Republican leaders in New York he was rewarded by President Grant with the Collectorship of Customs of the Port of New York. He appointed more than he needed to the thousand or so jobs involved, mostly on merit, but the recipients were expected to be free with their time and their money in the service of the Republican party — how else could the cohesion of the party be maintained at the local level? Renominated in 1875, he was removed by the reformer President Hayes in 1878 because of his partisanship, not because of any corruption.

As vice-president under Garfield he had remained loyal to the 'Stalwarts' and had clashed with the president over patronage. Consequently, after Garfield's assassination, it was widely believed that the free wheeling 'spoils system' of New York was about to be established in Washington. But never were so many so speedily disillusioned. Chester A. Arthur, the petty politician, proved to be a statesman and one of the ablest of death-bed presidents. He abandoned his former intimates, attempted to unify the party and became an ardent reformer.

The turncoat spoilsman vigorously supported the Pendleton Civil Service Reform Act (1883), which established a bipartisan Commission and competitive examinations for certain 'classified' jobs. It did not solve all problems; but it was a start. He attempted to revise the tariff downwards. Industry was still to be protected, but the accumulation of revenue surpluses was to be discouraged. (These had encouraged reckless appropriations, for state internal improvements, from the 'pork barrel'. The tariff Act of 1883, however, made little real change — vested interests in Congress saw to that — and Westerners and Southerners began to look to the Democrats as the tariff revived as a major political issue. He vetoed an immigration bill that violated Hayes' treaty of 1880 and in 1882 enacted the first general Federal immigration law. He continued to prosecute post office frauds.

In 1883 there were only 24 outdated ships in commission. Arthur ordered the construction of four steel warships, the first vessels of a modern US navy adequate to meet the burdens imposed by her merchants and her missionaries — and her developing Imperialism — in the Far East and in South America. Ships and guns needed steel; and so Arthur's term proved to be the link between post-war Reconstruction and the period of rapid industrial growth of the late nineteenth and early twentieth century.

He asserted the 'Monroe Doctrine' in helping to end war between Chile and Peru; and made commercial treaties with Mexico and Korea. An agreement with Nicaragua, giving America communication rights across Nicaraguan territory, was rejected by the Senate. To protests from 'isolationists' an American delegate was sent to the International Berlin Conference on African Affairs in 1884.

The 'Dude President' — one of whose last public duties was to dedicate the Washington Monument in February 1885 — had risen commendably to the challenge of office and he had given Americans a far better administration than they had either expected or deserved. He was neither a 'dandified mediocrity' nor a 'non-entity with side whiskers'. He deserved a chance to be elected in his own right; but his reward for rising above 'faction', indeed above 'party', was to be turned out to pasture by the party bosses. He ran second to J. G. Blaine in the 1884 Chicago Convention and then returned to the law. He failed to win a US Senate seat from New York in 1885. Within two years he was dead at the age of 56. His was the second shortest life span of all the presidents, excluding those who were assassinated.

# GROVER CLEVELAND

TWENTY-SECOND PRESIDENT OF THE UNITED STATES 1885–9

SUBSEQUENTLY TWENTY-FOURTH PRESIDENT OF THE UNITED STATES 1893–97

**Full name** (Stephen) Grover Cleveland, 1837–1908
**Born** Caldwell, Essex County, New Jersey, 18 March 1837, the fifth of 9 children
**Parents** Rev Richard Falley Cleveland (1804–53), Presbyterian Minister, and Anne Neal Cleveland (1806–82). 5 daughters, 4 sons
**Family lineage** English-Irish-French
**College** None
**Married** 1886, Frances Folsom Cleveland (1864–1947), daughter of Oscar Folsom, Attorney. 3 daughters, 2 sons. (Mrs Cleveland married subsequently, in 1913, Professor Thomas J. Preston Jr.) Frances Cleveland was the youngest ever 'First Lady' at 21
**Occupation** Clerk; teacher; lawyer; assistant district attorney; sheriff; mayor of Buffalo (1882–3); Governor of New York State (1883–5)
**Religious denomination** Presbyterian
**Notable relationships** He was a 6th cousin once removed of President Ulysses S. Grant
**Died** Following a heart attack at Westland, Princeton, NJ, 24 June 1908, aged 71
**Buried** Princeton Cemetery, NJ

**Party** Democratic **State represented** New York **(1st) Term of office** 4 March 1885 to 4 March 1889 **Age on first taking office** 47
**Presidential administration** 25th **Congresses** 49th, 50th

1884 ELECTION

| Candidates | Party | Electoral Vote (401) | States Won (38) | Popular Vote | % |
|---|---|---|---|---|---|
| G. Cleveland | Dem | 219 | 20 | 4,914,986 | 48.5* |
| J. Blaine | Repub | 182 | 18 | 4,854,981 | 48.2 |

*Cleveland did not receive a majority of the popular vote.

143

| 1885 | 49th | Senate | (76) | 41 Repub | 34 Dem | 1 Other |
| | | House | (325) | 182 Dem | 140 Repub | 2 Others |
| | | | | | | 1 Vacant |
| 1887 | 50th | Senate | (76) | 39 Repub | 37 Dem | |
| | | House | (325) | 170 Dem | 151 Repub | 4 Others |

## NOTES

1 1886, Act providing the order of presidential succession in case of the 'removal, death, resignation or inability' of both the president and the vice president: Cabinet officers were to succeed in the following order — State, Treasury, War, Attorney General, Postmaster General, Interior. (This Act remained in effect until 1947.)

2 1887, Electoral Count Act — fixed the 2nd Monday in January as the day of meeting for presidential electors; the 2nd Wednesday in February as the day of counting electoral votes in Congress. (The intention was to prevent a repetition of the disputed Election of 1876.)

## VICE PRESIDENT

21st Thomas Andrews Hendricks (Indiana), 1819–85. Lawyer; member of US House of Representatives, 1851–5; US Senator, 1863–9; Governor of Indiana, 1873–7; vice president, 4 March 1885 to 25 November 1885 (died in office).

———————————

The only American president to serve two non-consecutive terms was born in New Jersey of a 'Northern' father and a 'Southern' mother. At a very early age he dropped his given name Stephen. In 1841 the family moved to upstate New York where young Grover attended a series of schools until he was 13. His father's death sent him into a grocery store as a clerk and put paid to his hopes of going to college. He was an assistant teacher and bookkeeper at Gotham's New York Institution for the Blind for a couple of years, and then he headed West; but he got no further than an uncle's farm at Buffalo. This proved to be his first real break. He spent the summer helping his uncle to compile volume six of *Allen's American Shorthorn Herdbook*; his uncle was so impressed that he arranged for him to enter a Buffalo law office. In 1859 he was called to the bar.

For the next two decades he built a career in Buffalo. Partly because he had to support his mother and younger sisters he remained unmarried. When the war came and he was the first man in the town to be 'drafted', he purchased a 'substitute' for $150. Though he was perfectly entitled to do this, given his family situation — and two of his brothers did go away to fight for the Union — his political opponents were to try to make much of this later.

A (Northern) Democrat as early as 1858, he was elected assistant district attorney for Erie County in 1863 and county sheriff in 1870. (In this position he personally supervised two hangings). In between he built up a law partnership and rose at the bar until he became recognised as one of the leading attorneys of Western New York and one of the most substantial and trustworthy men in Buffalo. He had shown little political ambition, but at the age of 44, he emerged — and three and a half years later he was in the White House.

First, he was elected as mayor of Buffalo (1881), and proved to be honest, able and fearless. The 'veto' mayor delighted the combination of Democrats and Republicans who had elected him when he saved them over a million dollars, and when he attacked the graft of 'machine' politics. Then, in 1882, he was elected Governor of New York state by a record majority. The 'People's Mayor' became the 'People's Governor' and he gained a national reputation for his 'strict economy' and his bipartisan approach to the state's problems, much to the disgust of the Democratic organisation in downtown New York in its 'Tammany Hall' headquarters.

In 1884 the reforming Governor was just the presidential candidate that the Democrats needed though he was bitterly opposed by 'Tammany Hall', and he was chosen to run against Republican James G. Blaine. He defeated Blaine to become the first Democrat since before the Civil War to enter the White House (and in fact the only Democrat between 1861 and 1913).

At first sight this victory seems inexplicable. Cleveland was not only a Democrat but he was neither a war hero nor a national politician and, though not corrupt, he was tainted with scandal — he had been forced to acknowledge the paternity of an illegitimate child. In the event none of this mattered, or it worked to his advantage. As a Democrat he benefited from the nation's disenchantment with a long period of very controversial Republicanism. The fact that he was not endorsed by 'Tammany'

145

bosses was in his favour. If he had not fought in the war, neither had Blaine, and no one was prepared to 'wave the bloody shirt'. National politicians were almost assumed to be corrupt and the tough, energetic ex-Governor of New York would, it was hoped, bring a breath of fresh air into Washington. Even his personal failings were manly. Though he enjoyed only a mere 0.3% advantage over Blaine in terms of the popular vote — to which a minority of Republicans, the 'Mugwumps', contributed — the 36 electoral votes of the large state of New York helped to turn this into a comfortable majority in the Electoral College.

The new president was just under 6ft tall and he tipped the scales at 260lb (only President Taft, qv, was bigger). 'You're a whopper,' said an awestruck constituent on one occasion; and he was called, among others things, 'Uncle Jumbo'. He was (for the moment), America's first bachelor president since Buchanan. Though he inherited Arthur's French chef, his favourite dish was corned beef and cabbage. Fireworks were used for the first time at his inauguration, and then he settled down to hard work — often until the early hours of the morning. He read *everything* and personally signed all documents. He wrote all his letters in longhand and answered the telephone himself.

To share this burden he took a wife. In June 1886 he became the only president to be married in the White House when, at the age of 49, he married his ward, Frances Folsom who was 21. He had, he said, been waiting for her to grow up. He had known her since the day she was born, for she was the daughter of a former law partner, and he had bought 'Frank' her first baby carriage. Mrs Cleveland became the first president's wife to give birth in the White House when the second of their five children was born in 1893.

Cleveland set out to be a 'resolute reformer'. There were to be no special favours for either the strong or the weak. 'He sailed through American history,' wrote H. L. Mencken, 'like a steel ship loaded with monoliths of granite.' He reopened for settlement 81 million acres of land which railroads had falsely appropriated and returned half a million acres of reservation land to the Indians. He further antagonised the railroad owners by signing the Interstate Commerce Act of 1887 which provided for federal regulation in the future. Almost in the same breath he vetoed a bill to appropriate $10,000 for drought-ridden farmers in Texas. He angered business-men by an attempt in 1887 to lower the tariff; and civil-war veterans by vetoing hundreds of bills providing pensions (which were not deserved in many cases) for individuals: — 'The pension list ought to remain a roll of honour.' Insult was added to injury when he vetoed the Grand Army of the Republic Act designed to compensate veterans for non-service-incurred disabilities and old age. He strongly supported the Civil Service Commission's attacks on political patronage; and Adlai Stevenson, the assistant postmaster general, lopped off thousands of Republican office holders wielding 'Adlai's Axe'.

'What is the use of being elected or reelected — unless you stand *for* something,' he had once said. In 1888 he wasn't. Facing Republican Benjamin Harrison he polled 100,000 more popular votes than his opponent but lost badly in the Electoral College. He failed to carry New York (by a mere 12,000 votes), and the vice president could not deliver Indiana. The Republican majority in the Senate had depicted the 'butcher of Buffalo' who was indifferent to the plight of starving veterans.

Mrs Cleveland was surely only making polite conversation when she told White House servants in March 1889: 'We are coming back four years today.'

# BENJAMIN HARRISON

**Full name**  Benjamin Harrison, 1833–1901
**Born**  North Bend, Ohio, 20 August 1833, the second of 10 children by his father's second marriage
**Parents**  John Scott Harrison (1804–78), farmer, and his second wife, Elizabeth Ramsey Irwin Harrison (1810–50). 7 sons, 3 daughters
**Family lineage**  English-Scottish
**College**  Miami University, Oxford, Ohio. BA 1852
**Married**  (1) 1853, Caroline Lavinia Scott Harrison (1832–92), daughter of John Witherspoon Scott, Presbyterian Minister and College professor. 1 son, 1 daughter
(2) 1896, Mary Scott Lord Dimmick Harrison (1855–1948), widow of W. E. Dimmick (d 1882). 1 daughter. (His second wife was the niece of his first wife)
**Occupation**  Lawyer; Civil War, Brigadier General (1864); US Senator 1881–87; subsequently, Professor of Law, Stanford University, California (1894)
**Religious denomination**  Presbyterian
**Notable relationships**  He was the grandson of William Henry Harrison, 9th president (qv)
**Died**  From pneumonia, Indianopolis, Indiana, 13 March 1901, aged 67
**Buried**  Crown Hill Cemetery, Indianopolis

**Party** Republican **State represented** Indiana **Term of office** 4 March 1889 to 4 March 1893 **Age on taking office** 55 **Presidential administration** 26th **Congresses** 51st, 52nd

| | | 1888 ELECTION | | | |
|---|---|---|---|---|---|
| | | *Electoral* | *States* | *Popular* | |
| *Candidates* | *Party* | *Vote (401)* | *Won (38)* | *Vote* | *%* |
| B. Harrison | Repub | 233 | 20 | 5,439,853 | 47.8* |
| G. Cleveland | Dem | 168 | 18 | 5,540,329 | 48.6 |

148

*Harrison did not receive a majority of the popular vote. Cleveland was the last (of 3) to receive a plurality of the popular vote to be defeated in the Electoral College.

CONGRESS

| 1889 | 51st | Senate | (84) | 47 Repub | 37 Dem | |
| | | House | (330) | 173 Repub | 156 Dem | 1 Other |
| 1891 | 52nd | Senate | (88) | 47 Repub | 39 Dem | 2 Populists |
| | | House | (333) | 231 Dem | 88 Repub | 14 Populists |

(The Administration lost control of the House.)

NOTES

1 1890 11th Census: Total population: 62,947,714.
2 New States Admitted (6): North Dakota (1889) 39th
South Dakota (1889) 40th
Montana (1889) 41st
Washington (1889) 42nd
Idaho (1890) 43rd
Wyoming (1890) 44th

(This was the largest number of new states during any Administration.)

VICE PRESIDENT

22nd Levi Parsons Morton (New York), 1824–1920. Banker; member of US House of Representatives, 1879–81; Minister to France, 1881–5; vice president, 4 March 1889 to 4 March 1893; subsequently, Governor of New York, 1895–7.

---

He came from the nearest thing to a royal family that the country possessed. His great grandfather had signed the Declaration of Independence; his grandfather 'Old Tippecanoe', on whose farm he was born in 1833, became, briefly, the 9th president of the United States.

Young Benjamin was educated mainly by tutors in Cincinnati before he graduated in Oxford, Ohio. Having studied law and been called to the bar, he married and went out West to seek his fortune in Indianapolis. It proved to be a hard struggle. A former Whig, like his contemporaries Hayes, Garfield and Arthur, he campaigned for the new Republicans and was elected City Attorney, 1857. His career and family concerns meant that he did not respond immediately when war broke out, but in 1862 he was appointed colonel of the 70th Regiment of Indiana Volunteer

Infantry. He took part in some bitter fighting and was breveted brigadier general, on the recommendation of Gen Hooker, for his part in the fierce battles of Sherman's Atlanta campaign of 1864, as 'an officer of superior abilities and of great professional and personal worth'.

After the war his military reputation helped him to become one of the pillars of Indiana and a leading attorney. He became identified with the 'Radical Republicans' but, in a state with a strong leaven of Democracy, 'Kid Gloves' Harrison failed to win the gubernatorial election of 1876. In 1880 he headed the state Republican delegation to Chicago, and then worked so hard for Garfield that he was offered, but declined, a Cabinet post. He preferred to go into the Senate where he stayed for one term. He spoke out against immigration and monopolistic 'trusts' and in favour of a high tariff, Indiana, veterans' pensions and civil-service reform.

He failed to secure re-election in 1886 and that might well have been the end of an unpromising political career. But in 1888 the Republicans could not agree on a presidential candidate and, on the eighth ballot, they nominated a 'rather circumspect, erudite, self-willed, dainty little aristocrat, Benjamin Harrison', who had the right qualifications. He was an ex-Senator, an ex-brigadier general with an excellent war record, and a high-tariff man. He had no marked talents, no bad habits, no taint of corruption and he was a Harrison.

He campaigned in defence of a Republican platform that was designed to be all things to all men — it even supported Irish 'Home Rule'. It was to put the Republicans back in power (and keep them there for 32 of the next 44 years) and complete the transformation of the party of Abraham Lincoln into the party of big business.

'Little Ben', he was 5ft 6in or less, 'bearded, soft-voiced, small-boned . . . meticulous of dress and in manners, in speech and in thought', proved to be almost totally out of his depth. Republican party organisers came close to running the government and he allowed executive authority to dwindle. Initiative passed more and more to that millionaires' club, the Senate. 'The President,' he was grandly informed by one of their number, 'should touch elbows with Congress. He should have no policy distinct from that of his party; and this is better represented in Congress than in the Executive.' The message was clear: Ben Harrison was not to be another Chet Arthur.

Certainly four pieces of red-letter legislation were passed in 1890 to which he contributed little more than his signature. The Disability Pension Act provided pensions for veterans for any disability, however caused, and increased the total bill by $30 million. The Sherman Anti-Trust Act — ostensibly designed to deal with the monopolistic activities of the Rockefellers (oil) and the Carnegies (steel) — was so vaguely worded as to be incomprehensible and unenforceable. The McKinley Tariff Act — despite protests from agrarian interests — raised the tariff to an average of 48% *ad valorem*. The protesters were bought off with the inflationary Sherman Silver Purchase Act.

Congress made hay with the Treasury surplus and for the first time appropriation bills totalled over one billion dollars — 'This is a billion dollar country' — for rivers and harbours, a two-ocean navy and subsidies for steamships, among other projects. Hungry for 'spoils' after four lean years, 30,000 postmasterships were turned over to Republicans; though Harrison resisted pressure for even greater patronage, extended the number of 'classified' jobs and brought in a certain Theodore Roosevelt to the Civil Service Commission.

In 1890 the administration lost control of the House and the signs were that things would not improve in 1892. America was on the edge of some of the wildest years in its history. Trouble was brewing in the economy, labour disorders were mounting, farmers were raising 'less corn and more hell' in the 'Agrarian Revolt'. The Knights of Labor, the American Federation of Labor and Farmers' Alliances were preparing to flex political muscles.

In the White House, his 'Jail' he called it, the 'Iceberg' was unmoved. Only in foreign affairs was there executive direction and even here, with the exception of the Pan-American Congress of 1889, actual achievements were meagre. As Harrison prepared to take on Cleveland in 1892 there was a general air of gloom and despondency. 'Each side,' said an observer, 'would have been glad to defeat the other if it could do so without electing its own candidate.' (There have been years like that since.)

No wonder that Harrison could say sometime after his defeat: 'There has never been an hour since I left the White House that I have felt a wish to return to it.' He went back to the law. In 1898–99 he was defence counsel in Paris for Venezuela against Great Britain following the boundary dispute in 1895. His wife had died two weeks before the 1892 election. In 1896 he married her

151

niece and secretary, thus creating a fine tangle of family relation-ships.

One critic has said of Harrison that he was 'a medium sized man with medium sized abilities'. Certainly his administration proved to be mediocre and temporising and he himself no more than a care-taker. There is however a lasting memorial to Harrison. The flags which fly on all American public buildings first did so by order of a president impressed by a bunting-bedecked Wall Street in New York during the celebrations to mark the centennial of Washington's Inauguration in 1889.

# GROVER CLEVELAND

**(2nd) Term of office** 4 March 1893 to 4 March 1897. (The only president to serve non-consecutive terms) **Age on taking office** 55 **Presidential administration** 27th **Congresses** 53rd, 54th

### 1892 ELECTION

| Candidates | Party | Electoral Vote (444) | States Won (44) | Popular Vote | % |
|---|---|---|---|---|---|
| G. Cleveland | Dem | 277 | 23 | 5,556,918 | 46.0* |
| B. Harrison | Repub | 145 | 16 | 5,176,108 | 43.0 |
| J. Weaver | Pop | 22 | 4 | 1,041,028 | 8.5 |

*Cleveland became the 1st President (Wilson was the 2nd) to be elected twice without a majority of the popular vote. He was the 1st (F. D. Roosevelt the 2nd) to receive a plurality of the popular vote in 3 elections: 1884, 1888, 1892. The 'Populist' or People's Party (Weaver) represented basically Western debtor farmers.

### CONGRESS

| | | | | | | |
|---|---|---|---|---|---|---|
| 1893 | 53rd | Senate (88) | 44 Dem | 38 Repub | 3 Oth | 3 Vac |
| | | House (357) | 220 Dem | 126 Repub | 11 Others | |
| 1895 | 54th | Senate (88) | 44 Repub | 39 Dem | 5 Others | |
| | | House (357) | 246 Repub | 104 Dem | 7 Others | |

(The Administration lost control of Congress.)

### NOTES

1 New State admitted: Utah (1896) 45th.
2 During his two terms Cleveland vetoed 584 bills and 'pocket' vetoed 238 more. Only F. D. Roosevelt used the veto more often.

### VICE PRESIDENT

23rd Adlai Ewing Stevenson (Illinois) 1835–1914. Lawyer; member of US House of Representatives, 1875–7, 1879–81; Assistant Postmaster General, 1885–9; vice president 4 March 1893 to 4 March 1897. (Grandfather of Adlai E. Stevenson, Democratic Presidential Candidate, 1952 and 1956.)

153

After spending four years practising law in New York City Grover Cleveland won a comfortable victory in 1892, though the electorate had probably voted against his opponent rather than for him. He did not get away to an auspicious start, for he required massive surgery to remove a malignant growth in the roof of his mouth. The operation, which took place on a yacht in New York's East River, was kept secret for twenty-five years.

Then the 'Panic of 1893' hit the country. There were bankruptcies, 500 bank failures, and unemployment rose dramatically. Cleveland advocated deflationary gold standard policies and the repeal of Sherman's Silver Purchase Act. He obtained a government loan from Wall Street tycoons. These policies alienated many Democrats especially in the South and West.

Financial panic led to labour unrest. When in 1894 Jacob S. Coxey led his 'army' of unemployed from Ohio to Washington DC, Cleveland approved his arrest and the use of police to break up the march. In the same year he sent troops to restore order in Chicago following the Pullman railroad strike. An injunction was sought to ensure mail deliveries — 'If it takes the entire army and navy of the United States to deliver a postal card in Chicago that card will be delivered' — and Eugene V. Debs, leader of the American Railway Union, was imprisoned.

In 1892 Cleveland had promised a downwards readjustment of the tariff, but the Wilson-Gorman Tariff Act of 1894, 'logrolled' through the Senate by Eastern Democrats and Republicans, retained very high protective levels. He denounced the bill as 'party perfidy and party dishonor', but allowed it to become law without his signature because it was some improvement on the McKinley Tariff Act of 1890.

In foreign affairs he opposed the nation's nascent imperialistic tendencies. He blocked his predecessor's treaty for the annexation of Hawii, and kept America strictly neutral when rebellion broke out in Cuba against Spain in 1895. He invoked the 'Monroe Doctrine' in the same year during a boundary dispute between Venezuela and Great Britain and persuaded the parties to seek arbitration.

His policies were either unsuccessful, or unpopular, or both. In 1894 the Republicans won landslide victories in the Congressional elections. Two years later the Democratic convention repudiated his administration and nominated the silver-tongued orator from Nebraska, William Jennings Bryan.

During his unprecedented two separate terms Grover Cleveland had demonstrated that the Confederate-tainted Democratic party could be trusted to govern in the interests of the nation as a whole. But he was perhaps too conservative to be a great constructive statesman. (When he entered the White House in 1913 Woodrow Wilson was to claim that *he* was the first post-war Democrat; Cleveland he dismissed as 'a conservative Republican'.) He opposed overgenerous veterans' pensions, land for railroads, 'gravy' for 'spoilsmen' and high tariffs for big business but it is not clear what he stood *for*. He got his satisfaction, said one critic, 'not in making good things happen but in making bad things not happen'.

He died in 1908. 'I have tried so hard to do right,' he said on his death bed. Frances Cleveland, who lived until 1947, became the first President's wife to remarry when she wed a Princeton University professor, Thomas Preston. She, who had chatted with Mrs Polk, the wife of the 11th President, once found herself seated next to Gen Eisenhower, the future 34th President. The elderly lady told him how much she missed Washington. 'Really, Mrs Preston,' said Ike, 'Where did you live?'

# WILLIAM McKINLEY

**Full name** William McKinley, 1843–1901
**Born** Niles, Trumbull County, Ohio, 29 January 1843, the seventh of 9 children
**Parents** William McKinley (1807–92), iron founder, and Nancy Campbell Allison McKinley (1809–97). 5 daughters, 4 sons
**Family lineage** English-Scottish-Irish and English-Scottish-German
**Married** 1871, Ida Saxton McKinley (1847–1907), daughter of James Asbury Saxton, banker. 2 daughters who died in infancy
**Occupation** Teacher; clerk; Civil War, Brevet Major (1865); lawyer; county attorney; member of US House of Representatives, 1877–84, 1885–91; Governor of Ohio, 1892–96
**Religious denomination** Methodist
**Notable relationships** None
**Died** At Buffalo on 14 September 1901, aged 58, as the result of bullet wounds inflicted by Leon F. Czolgosz on 6 September 1901, at Buffalo, NY
**Buried** In the McKinley tomb, Westlawn Cemetery, Canton, Ohio

**Party** Republican **State represented** Ohio **Terms of office** 4 March 1897 to 14 September 1901 **Age on taking office** 54 **Presidential administrations** 28th, 29th (Part) **Congresses** 55th, 56th

### 1896 ELECTION

| Candidates | Party | Electoral Vote (447) | States Won (45) | Popular Vote | % |
|---|---|---|---|---|---|
| W. McKinley | Repub | 271 | 23 | 7,111,607 | 50.8 |
| W. Bryan | Dem | 176 | 22 | 6,731,635 | 46.7 |

### 1900 ELECTION

| Candidates | Party | Electoral Vote (447) | States Won (45) | Popular Vote | % |
|---|---|---|---|---|---|
| W. McKinley | Repub | 292 | 28 | 7,219,525 | 51.7 |
| W. Bryan | Dem | 155 | 17 | 6,358,737 | 45.5 |

| 1897 | 55th | Senate | (90) | 46 Repub | 34 Dem | 10 Others |
| | | House | (357) | 206 Repub | 134 Dem | 16 Others |
| | | | | | | 1 Vacant |
| 1899 | 56th | Senate | (90) | 53 Repub | 26 Dem | 11 Others |
| | | House | (357) | 185 Repub | 163 Dem | 9 Others |

## VICE PRESIDENTS

24th Garrett Augustus Hobart (New Jersey), 1844–99. Lawyer; state politician; vice president, 4 March 1897 to 21 November 1899. Died in Office.

25th Theodore Roosevelt, subsequently 26th president.

## NOTE

1900 12th Census: Total population: 75,994,575.

———————

The last civil-war veteran to be president came from an old established family. His great-grandfather had fought in the Revolution and his grandfather at Tippecanoe. His father — a sign of the times — was the first president's father to be engaged in heavy industry. He was born at Niles, in Ohio — which thus furnished five of the seven presidents in the last quarter of the nineteenth century — but the family moved to Poland (Ohio) where there were better educational opportunities. In the event young William's college course came to a premature end because of his illness and family fortunes. He was working as a teacher and post-office clerk when Fort Sumter was attacked. He was one of the first to enrol in E Company of the 23rd Regiment of Ohio Volunteers (Major, R. B. Hayes), and served as a private for 14 months, before he was promoted commissary sergeant. He became an officer after taking part in the fierce fighting at South Mountain and Antietam and ended the war as a 22-year-old brevet major on the Staff of Gen Hayes who described him as 'one of the bravest and finest officers of the army'.

Then it was into the law, though his mother wanted him to be a Methodist minister, and he was called to the bar in 1867. He set up a practice in Canton a busy little (Democratic) manufacturing centre, though he adopted his father's Republicanism. He was elected District Attorney, 1869–71. In 1871 he married Ida Saxton, the elder daughter of a socially prominent and well-to-do family, who was a semi-invalid by 1873, a martyr to phlebitis and epileptic seizures. McKinley was a devoted husband. (At White House dinners, contrary to protocol, she always sat next to the president who simply threw a handkerchief over her face during a seizure until she came to.) Until 1876 he concentrated on his legal work and became so prominent in the Republican cause that in December 1877 he was returned to the House of Representatives where, with one brief break, he was to remain for the next 14 years.

In Congress 'Young Napoleon' helped to establish protectionism as the dogma of the Republican party and within three years he had replaced Garfield on the Committee of Ways and Means. In 1888, against his wishes, he was almost nominated for the presidency. By 1890, he was Chairman of the Committee of Ways and Means (1889), author of the McKinley Tariff Act (1890), which had fixed his name in the public mind, and (since 1888) protégé of Marcus A. Hanna, a Cleveland-based businessman who had become his political manager (some said his puppet master).

McKinley was also an ex-Congressman following the Republican landslide of 1890 and 'gerrymandering' (p. 39) in his own district, but this proved to be a blessing in disguise. For in 1892, the same year in which he chaired the party Convention and ran second to Harrison, he began a two-term spell as Governor of Ohio. Like Hayes and Arthur, he was about to test the theory of a young academic, Woodrow Wilson, whose recent doctoral thesis on *Congressional Government* had argued that since the presidency was primarily an administrative post the best preparation for it was the essentially comparable task of governing a state.

By 1896, McKinley had gained sufficient national prominence and popularity to be nominated on the first ballot at St Louis as the Republican presidential candidate. Talk of violence, even of secession, in 'debtor' Western and Southern states was in the air during a contest which was completely dominated by the question of 'Silver'. The Democrats, 'Populists' and renegade Republicans, nominated William Jennings Bryan on a platform favouring 'easy money' and the 'free and unlimited coinage of silver and gold' in the ratio of 16:1. The Republicans were totally opposed to freer silver and fought to maintain the gold standard and the tariff, and to elect their man as the 'Advance Agent of Prosperity', on the promise that he would 'Fill the Dinner Pail'. Whilst Bryan electioneered around the states as best he could, Mark Hanna organised a brilliant campaign for McKinley. Trains were hired to bring an estimated half a million Republicans on cheap trips to his 'front porch' at Canton; and enough election pamphlets were printed to provide three copies each for every man, woman and child in America. On the day, the biggest turn out since 1840 gave McKinley the first popular majority (but only just) since 1872. The largest crowd ever assembled in Washington up to that time saw him inaugurated in March 1897.

'We who know him regard him as a man of extraordinary ability, integrity and force of character,' wrote John Hay — and he had been Abraham Lincoln's private secretary — of the man who now had to wrestle with America's problems. That the USA was spared much trouble was due in part to his ability and in part to 'accidents'. McKinley, who had held elective offices for over two decades, has been described as 'one of the most experienced and careful politicians ever to live in the White House'. He got on well with politicians and offered leadership to Congress for the first time since Andrew Jackson.

The fortunate accidents were the discovery of very large deposits of gold in Alaska, Colorado and in South Africa, which took the sting out of the silver issue; and the fact that the American economic depression had run its course. Having introduced a new high tariff, the Dingley Tariff of 1897, the highest ever, McKinley established a new gold standard with the Gold Standard Act of 1900 (it was to last until 1933); in that year Bryan's 'Silver' campaign was greeted with total apathy.

Like his friend Hanna, McKinley was convinced that there could be an essential harmony between the interests of business and those of the whole community. Business was to be left alone to create prosperity. Monopolistic 'trusts' developed apace — between 1898 and 1904 another 236 were added to the total of 318 in existence — and though the president had qualms about them, describing them as 'dangerous conspiracies against the public good', these concentrations of industrial power were allowed to flourish unchecked in the hope that wealth created would seep down from the top and fill the nation's dinner pails.

Against an improving economic background, America was about to go to war with Spain. Since 1895 Spain had faced revolt in Cuba, an island in which there was $50 million dollars worth of American investment and an annual trade óf $100 millions. The president wanted peace. The nation, excited over Venezuela (1895), whipped up by atrocity stories in the Hearst and Pulitzer 'yellow press' (printed on cheap paper which soon yellowed), and inflamed by

159

politicians who should have known better — 'From the Rio Grande to the Arctic there should be one flag and one country' — clamoured for war. After the USS *Maine* was mysteriously destroyed in Havana harbour, McKinley, like Pontius Pilate, handed the decision to Congress, and Congress chose war — 'Remember the *Maine*' — or rather 'neutral intervention', in April 1898.

The '100 Day War' was notable for the destruction of Spanish naval power in the Pacific at the battle of Manila Bay; the storming of San Juan Hill in Cuba by ex-Assistant Secretary of the Navy, Theodore Roosevelt and his 'Rough Riders'; and the ending of Spanish power in the Caribbean at the battle of Santiago Bay. The war was concluded by the Treaty of Paris of 1898.

'It has been a splendid little war,' wrote John Hay, though it had revealed incompetence in the War Department beyond belief. Cuba became independent, in theory, in 1900 (but not fully until 1934), and America gained Puerto Rico and Guam and paid $20 million for the Philippines in order to 'educate, uplift and Christianise'. She also 'bought' determined national resistance under Aguinaldo, 1898–1902. America had emerged as a new naval and imperial power with vital interests in the Western Pacific and in Asia where she was soon to be an active force in world power politics for the first time in her history.

In 1899 Secretary of State John Hay joined with Great Britain in declaring an 'Open Door' policy in the moribund Chinese empire, guaranteeing European nations trading rights in their respective 'spheres of influence', following the outbreak of the anti-Western 'Boxer' Rising in 1898. In 1900, US troops took part in the relief of beleagured legations in Peking. America's reward was the Hay-Pauncefote Treaty with Britain in 1901 which virtually gave America a free hand in the Western hemisphere and established the 'largest sphere of influence ever seen'. As a direct consequence of these two crowded years, therefore, every American president since McKinley has been a world leader.

In the 1900 election, Bryan was against Imperialism and still for 'Silver'. The Republicans, with their now 'Full Dinner Pail', and their recognition of America's desire to play a part on the world stage with their 'Don't haul down the flag', won an even greater victory than in 1896. McKinley had never been so popular and Americans were dazzled by their new world role and their prosperity. The only sour note had been the choice of a new vice president. When Theodore Roosevelt was chosen Hanna had remarked: 'Don't any of you realise that there's only one life between this madman and the White House?'

On 6 September 1901, President McKinley was in the Temple of Music at the Pan-American Exposition in Buffalo, NY. He bent to give the lucky red carnation he always wore in his lapel to a little girl — and was shot by an out-of-work factory hand and self-styled anarchist, Leon Czolgosz, alias Fred Nieman (Nobody). 'I didn't believe that one man should have so much service and another man should have none,' he told police. (He was executed on 29 October 1901.) McKinley's thoughts were for his wife: 'My wife — be careful how you tell her . . . oh, be careful.'

The mode of his death, plus the fact that McKinley was perhaps the most popular president during his lifetime that the nation had so far had, was reflected in the magnificent tomb that was prepared for him. (Only Lincoln, Grant and Harding (qv), have been interred in anything comparable.) The tomb stands on a 75ft-high, grass-covered hill overlooking the city of Canton, Ohio. It is circular and domed and rises to a height of 96ft. The cost of half a million dollars was raised by public subscription.

# THEODORE ROOSEVELT

**Full name**  Theodore Roosevelt, 1858–1919
**Born**  33 East 20th Street, New York City, NY, 27 October 1858, the second of 4 children
**Parents**  Theodore Roosevelt (1831–78), merchant, banker, Collector of the Port of New York, and Martha Bulloch Roosevelt (1834–84). 2 sons, 2 daughters
**Family lineage**  Dutch and Scottish-Irish-French Huguenot
**College**  Harvard College, Cambridge, Mass, AB 1880; Columbia Law School, NY, 1880–2 (did not graduate)
**Married**  (1) 1880, Alice Hathaway Lee Roosevelt (1861–84), daughter of George Cabot Lee, banker. 1 daughter
(2) 1886 (at St George's, Hanover Square, London, England) Edith Kermit Carow Roosevelt (1861–1948), daughter of Charles Carow, merchant. 4 sons, 1 daughter
**Occupation**  Author; state politician; rancher; Civil Service Commissioner, 1889–95; president of the New York Police Commission, 1895–7; Assistant Secretary of the Navy, 1897–8; Spanish-American War, Colonel; vice president, 1901; subsequently, explorer and journalist
**Religious denomination**  Dutch Reformed
**Notable relationships**  Through his mother he was 17th in descent from Robert III, King of Scots. He and F. D. Roosevelt, 32nd president, were 5th cousins. His niece, Eleanor Roosevelt, married F. D. Roosevelt
**Died**  From embolism in the coronary artery, Sagamore Hill, Oyster Bay, NY, 6 January 1919, aged 60
**Buried**  Young's Memorial Cemetery, Oyster Bay, Long Island, NY

**Party** Republican **State represented** New York **Terms of office** 14 September 1901 to 4 March 1909. (He served the unexpired portion of his predecessor and one full term) **Presidential administrations**

29th (continued), 30th **Age on taking office** 42 **Congresses** 57th,
58th, 59th, 60th

1904 ELECTION

| Candidates | Party | Electoral Vote (476) | States Won (45) | Popular Vote | % |
|---|---|---|---|---|---|
| T. Roosevelt | Repub | 336 | 32 | 7,628,785 | 56.4 |
| A. Parker | Dem | 140 | 13 | 5,084,338 | 37.6 |

NOTE

New state admitted: Oklahoma (1907) 46th.

VICE PRESIDENT

26th Charles Warren Fairbanks (Indiana), 1852–1918. Lawyer;
member of US Senate, 1897–1905; vice president, 4 March 1905 to
4 March 1909.

---

Characteristically Vice President Theodore Roosevelt was on a
hunting trip half way up a mountain in the Adirondacks when the
word came that President McKinley was dying. On the following
day when he took the oath of office at Buffalo NY, he became the
youngest man ever to be sworn in as president of the United States;
he was 42 years and 322 days old. 'Now look', moaned Mark
Hanna, whose exasperation knew no bounds, 'that damned
cowboy is President!' His feelings were shared by 'Boss' Tom Platt
of New York who had worked hard to have 'Old Four Eyes', the
Governor of New York, made vice president.

Theodore Roosevelt was born into a rich family in New York
City in 1858. He would be the very first rich man's son to become
president; the first who would have to work his way down. His

163

father's family had been amongst the earliest Dutch settlers in the then New Amsterdam; the correct pronounciation of the Dutch name is Rose-y-velt. Amongst his mother's forebears could be counted English, Scottish, Welsh and Irish, as well as some German and French Huguenot blood. His millionaire father's family were Northerners, whilst his aristocratic mother from Georgia had one brother who was a Confederate admiral and another who served on the CSS *Alabama*.

Young 'Teedie' was a sickly, asthmatic, puny child and very near-sighted. He was educated at home by tutors and by means of two extended overseas trips which the family had made by the time he was 15. On these trips the life-long struggle first began between the instincts of the naturalist and the hunter. (His later reputed refusal to shoot a small bear on a hunting trip inspired the 'Teddy Bear' craze.)

After an inauspicious start at Harvard, Theodore (he hated being called 'Teddy'), became one of the club set. He was a conscientious student who made Phi Beta Kapa in his senior year, he first took up boxing (a bout later in 1908 was to leave him blind in his left eye), and he became fastidious in dress. He also fell in love and in his graduation year married a 19-year-old beauty from Boston, Alice Hathaway Lee.

He first tried to make his way in the law and by writing; then, in 1882, the Honorable Theodore Roosevelt at 23 became the youngest Assemblyman in the New York State Legislature at Albany, as a conservative Republican from the 21st District. He intended, he said, 'to be of the governing class'. The Harvard man who wore his rimless pince-nez on a black silk cord, with teeth 'almost as big as colt's teeth', was initially regarded as a joke; but soon it was conceded that he was very earnest and active. In 1884 he was sent as a delegate to the Republican National Convention in Chicago.

That year was to be a turning point in his life both politically and personally. On St Valentine's Day his mother and his wife died in his house within hours of each other. His beloved wife died from Bright's disease two days after giving birth to a daughter, Alice Lee. (Subsequently, Mrs Alice Roosevelt Longworth, she lived until 1980.) His personal tragedy (and the political tragedy of Democrat Grover Cleveland's election) drove him into exile. 'The light went from my life for ever,' he wrote. The door once closed was never reopened: there is not a word about his first wife in his autobiography to indicate that she had ever existed.

For the next two years he immersed himself on two ranches he had bought in the 'Badlands' of Dakota Territory. He tried to do some writing, he was appointed deputy sheriff of Billings County, and his Harvard exhortation to dilatory cowboys during a roundup — 'Hasten forward there quickly' — became a catchphrase in local saloons. He turned his face to the East in 1886 to remarry and to try to re-enter politics.

On 2 December 1886 Theodore Roosevelt, ranchman (according to the register), married a childhood friend, Edith Carow, at St George's Church, Hanover Square, in London, England. Over the next ten years they were to have five children, and Alice made six. Edith Roosevelt proved to be a superb wife and mother — 'When Mother was a little girl she must have been a boy!' one small son remarked — and a gracious First Lady. She began the custom of placing 'likenesses' of the First Ladies in the ground-floor corridor of the White House.

Roosevelt's venture into politics failed. He ran, unsuccessfully, as Mayor of New York and a magazine printed his political obituary: 'You are not the timber of which Presidents are made.' He then turned back to writing. He was to write some forty books all told — the best were *The Naval War of 1812* (1882) and *The Winning of the West* (1889–96). But after a three-year interlude he returned to his true vocation.

He was appointed a Civil Service Commissioner by President Harrison in 1889. He brought incredible energy to the task: 'He was Gargantuan in his capacity for work . . . he was pure action,' said a friend, as he went about his difficult job in a blaze of publicity and controversy. He stayed on under Cleveland until 1895, when he became president of the Board of Police Commissioners for New York City. His bubbling, noisy, strenuous administration earned him enemies, as well as both a national and an international reputation, and there were many who were not sorry to see him leave to join McKinley as Assistant Secretary of the Navy in 1897.

In this post he began to make the navy ready for war with Spain, before he resigned in 1898 to become Lt Colonel of the 1st Volunteer Cavalry Regiment: a motley collection, they were dubbed the 'Rough Riders'. Their storming of San Juan Hill in Cuba became legendary and their leader a colonel and a national hero.

Roosevelt's disappointment at his failure to receive the Medal of

Honor was soon offset by even greater recognition. 'Boss' Tom Platt of New York needed the hero in order to draw attention away from state scandals and offered to support Roosevelt's candidacy for the post of Governor of New York. Promising to 'play fair' he accepted, adding, 'I have always been fond of the West African proverb: "Speak softly and carry a big stick and you will go far".' He went further than Platt intended. Governor Roosevelt's vigorous, honest administration was the reason why Platt strove to give him the political kiss of death in 1900, by helping to make him vice president.

Roosevelt became president when the philosophy of *laissez faire* individualism was giving way to what might be termed the idea of a 'Welfare State' among certain progressive thinkers, including some of the Republican rank and file. As their leader from 1901 to 1909 he had to balance their demands against those of the conservative 'Old Guard' who dominated the party in Congress. Consequently the sum of his legislative achievements was small, but he rendered the 'reform' movement great assistance by the publicity he gave it, constantly sermonising against the evils of big business and high finance.

His 'Square Deal' was aimed at holding the ring between capital and labour and checking the abuses of industrialisation by moderate reform. In 1902 he intervened in an anthracite strike and got both sides to agree to arbitration. In 1903 the Department of Commerce and Labor was established. Anti-trust suits were brought against industrial combines (the most famous case led to the break up of a J. P. Morgan-controlled railroad empire). Roosevelt however, like McKinley, believed in the value of industry (he also believed in the potential menace of organised labour), and consequently he distinguished between 'good' and 'bad' trusts. Overall, no drastic transformation was achieved by Roosevelt the 'trust buster'.

Some of T.R's greatest achievements (he was the first president to become known by his initials), concerned conservation. President Grant had set up the first national park, Yellowstone, in 1872. Roosevelt established the Yosemite National Park in 1906, and 150 million acres of national forest, 51 wildlife refuges and numerous national monuments. Coal deposits and the sites of future dams were 'reserved' for later public use. In 1908 a National Conservation Conference was held.

Upton Sinclair's novel *The Jungle* (1906), exposing industrial evils in the Chicago stockyards, and the pressure of the 'Muckraking' movement, led to valuable consumer protection legislation like the Meat Inspection Act and the Pure Food and Drugs Act, of 1906. Roosevelt was the first president to receive a negro officially when Booker T. Washington dined in the White House. During his administration the name 'White House' became the official designation of the president's residence in Washington.

America wanted a vigorous foreign policy consonant with her new imperial strength. Roosevelt was the man of the hour. He wielded his 'big stick' to good effect. Sixteen US battleships were sent on a fourteen-month world cruise: the 'Great White Fleet' was designed to impress potential enemies, both at home and abroad. In order to facilitate rapid transit from the Atlantic to the Pacific T.R. played godfather to the new Republic of Panama, which gratefully allowed the US Army Corps of Engineers to build a canal across the isthmus, 1904–14. When he went down to inspect progress, Roosevelt became the first president to leave US soil while in office.

The 'Roosevelt corollary' to the Monroe Doctrine (1904), at a time of threatened European intervention in the Caribbean, established the 'right' of America to interfere wherever and whenever she chose in Latin America, as the policeman of the Western hemisphere. Treaty maker and mediator, Roosevelt was awarded the Nobel Peace prize in 1906 for his part in ending the Russo-Japanese War (1904–5) by the Treaty of Portsmouth, New Hampshire.

He kept up the pace during his second term — in 1904 he became the first non-elected president to win the presidency in his own right — and then retired, the youngest ever ex-president, as he had pledged to do, in 1909. He had made only one great mistake, based on a personal error of judgement, he had chosen William Howard Taft to succeed him.

In 1909 he plunged into Africa on safari, before touring Europe and representing America at the funeral of King Edward VII. The big game he shot in Africa provided the Smithsonian in Washington with the world's most complete collection. In 1914 he gravely undermined his health with a trip into the wilds of Brazil:-'I had to go it was my last chance to be a boy.' Its River of Doubt was later renamed 'Rio Teodore'.

Bitterly disappointed with Taft — 'no more backbone than a chocolate éclair' — Roosevelt began to advocate a 'New

Nationalism' from 1910. In the 1912 election he ran for president on a 'Progressive' or 'Bull Moose' ticket ('I feel as strong as a bull moose,' he had told Hanna in 1900; thereafter that was his trade mark). However he only succeeded in splitting the Republicans and ensured the election of Woodrow Wilson. During the campaign he narrowly escaped assassination: a bullet passed into his right lung through his overcoat, spectacle case and the manuscript of a speech.

He opposed Wilson's neutrality policy in the First World War after 1914; begged, in vain, to be allowed to command a regiment in France (where his four sons fought and his youngest son was killed) after 1917; and, at the end, opposed the idea of a League of Nations. He put what energies he had left into editorials for the Kansas City *Star*. He went to bed early on 5 January 1919. 'Please put out the light,' he told his Negro valet. At four o'clock the next morning he died.

# WILLIAM H. TAFT

**Full name**   William Howard Taft, 1857–1930
**Born**   2038 Auburn Avenue, Cincinnati, Ohio, 15 September 1857, the second of 5 children
**Parents**   Alphonso Taft (1810–91), lawyer, politician, Ambassador, and his 2nd wife Louisa Maria Torrey Taft (1827–1907). 4 sons, 1 daughter. (Taft had 2 half-brothers from his (father's first marriage)
**Family lineage**   English, Scots-Irish
**College**   Yale College, New Haven, Conn, BA 1878; Cincinnati Law School, LLB 1880
**Married**   1886, Helen Herron Taft (1861–1943), daughter of John Williamson Herron, attorney. 2 sons, 1 daughter
**Occupation**   Lawyer; state official; judge of the Ohio Superior Court, 1887–1900; US Solicitor General (and Acting Attorney General) 1890–2; US circuit court judge, 1892–1900; President of the Philippines Commission, 1900–1; Governor of the Philippines, 1901–4; Secretary of War, 1904–8; subsequently: Professor of Constitutional Law, Yale University, 1913–21; 10th Chief Justice of the Supreme Court of the United States, 1921–30
**Religious denomination**   Unitarian
**Notable relationships**   Taft was twenty-fourth in descent from David I, King of Scots. Through his mother's family he was a seventh cousin twice removed of Richard M. Nixon, 37th president
**Died**   From arteriosclerosis, Washington DC, 8 March 1930, aged 72
**Buried**   Arlington National Cemetery, Arlington, Virginia

**Party** Republican **State represented** Ohio **Term of office** 4 March 1909 to 4 March 1913 **Age on taking office** 51 **Presidential administration** 31st **Congresses** 61st, 62nd

169

| Candidates | Party | Electoral Vote (483) | States Won (46) | Popular Vote | % |
|---|---|---|---|---|---|
| W. H. Taft | Repub | 321 | 29 | 7,679,114 | 51.6 |
| W. J. Bryan | Dem | 162 | 17 | 6,410,665 | 43.1 |

## CONGRESS

| 1909 | 61st | Senate | (92) | 59 Repub | 32 Dem | 1 Vacant |
|---|---|---|---|---|---|---|
| | | House | (391) | 219 Repub | 172 Dem | |
| 1911 | 62nd | Senate | (92) | 49 Repub | 42 Dem | 1 Vacant |
| | | House | (391) | 228 Dem | 162 Repub | 1 Soc |

(Although the Administration nominally controlled the Senate, control was actually in the hands of the Democrats and 'insurgent Republicans'. The Republicans lost control of the House for the first time since 1892.)

## NOTES

1 1910 13th census: Total population: 91,972,266.
2 New States Admitted:   Arizona (1912) 47th
                         New Mexico (1912) 48th.

## VICE PRESIDENT

27th James Schoolcraft Sherman (New York), 1855–1912, lawyer; state politician; member of US House of Representatives, 1887–91, 1893–1909; vice president 4 March 1909 to 30 October 1912 (died in office).

---

He was a jovial, warm-hearted mountain of a man. Easily the largest president of the United States, he was 6ft tall and he entered the presidency weighing 332lb. A special bath was installed in the White House for him, big enough for four lesser mortals. His passion was baseball and he became the first president to open the season when he threw out the first ball of 1910. He was the last president to keep a cow on the White House lawn. She was a Holstein called 'Pauline Wayne' who shared the garage with four official limousines and provided all the milk for the kitchen.

Taft is one of the very few presidents to have been born in a big city. He is the only president whose father had been a cabinet minister and he is one of only two *alumni* of Yale (the other is Gerald Ford) to have entered the White House. He followed his father into the law and then, though not a political animal, he rose in his profession by means of a string of Republican-sponsored judiciary appointments: 'I always had my plate the right side up when offices were falling.' Before he was 35 he was a Federal Court Circuit Judge, where he emerged as a conservative legal scholar. He had made a brief appearance on the national scene two years before this as US Solicitor General. By this time he was married to the daughter of one of the leading Republicans in Ohio. 'Nellie' Herron Taft was to be instrumental in planting the 3,000 Japanese cherry trees which so delight visitors to the Tidal Basin in the nation's capital every Spring.

Taft's friend since the Harrison era, Theodore Roosevelt, sent him out to the newly-acquired Philippines, first as a Commissioner and then as Governor General. He threw himself into the reorganisation of everything from the roads to the economy with such success that the Filipinos called him a saint. (Dedicated to the work in hand, Taft had had to pass up two chances of that Supreme Court seat which had long been his greatest ambition.) From 1904–8 he was Secretary of War and 'the ambassador to stubborn tasks at the far corners of the earth'; from Panama, where he had overall control of construction work on the canal, to Tokyo and Cuba, where he was the provisional governor (1907). It was, then, a man with a brilliant legal mind, a proven administrator and 'trouble shooter', with a long record of exceptional public service behind him, who was virtually chosen by Roosevelt to be his successor to carry forward the banner of the 'Square Deal'. Some people were delighted: 'T.R. has cut enough hay. Taft is the man to put it in the barn.'

Not since Henry II saddled himself with Beckett can there have been such a swift feeling of disillusionment. The trouble was that the crown prince not only had to follow Roosevelt, but Taft was not a politician and he had never really wanted the presidency in the first place. T.R. had left behind a smooth party machine that had controlled the presidency and both houses of Congress for the past twelve years and had just triumphantly been re-elected for a new term. Within two years the Republicans had lost the House, their control of the Senate was more apparent than real, and the Administration was a small civil war against itself.

Active presidents always make things difficult for their successors, especially if the incoming president disclaims the executive pretensions of his predecessor. Taft's views on executive power were published in a famous book in 1916, but the theory was based on practice. The president, he wrote, can only exercise constitutional authority. There is no 'undefined residuum of power' to be exercised because he thinks it is in the public interest. In other words, where Roosevelt would do anything not expressly prohibited by the constitution, Taft would not do anything which was not specifically provided for in the constitution. There was the rub. Taft, who in any case had a distaste for party politics, fumbled the baton of dynamic executive power passed on by his predecessor and left public opinion, Congress and the Republican party leaderless.

The result was predictable and catastrophic. Roosevelt's style of leadership and his avoidance of controversial issues had maintained party unity. Now clear rifts began to appear between the progressives and the 'Standpatters' — the conservatives who dominated Congress. Taft fell down straight away over the tariff issue which had been studiously avoided by Roosevelt. His proposals for a new, lower tariff, supported by the progressives, were slaughtered in the Senate. Taft simply signed the bill (the Payne-Aldrich tariff), but then added that it was 'the best bill Republicans ever produced'. His removal of Roosevelt's Secretary of the Interior, Ballinger, made him appear to be slowing down Roosevelt's conservation work. Increasingly he appeared to be the prisoner of the conservatives. He was, said a critic, 'an amiable island entirely surrounded by men who knew exactly what they wanted'.

In 1910 the party was in a self-destructive mood. In the elections for the 62nd Congress there was a Democratic landslide and the progressives, straddling party lines, held the balance of power. This was used wisely. They passed, and Taft signed, a long series of useful bills for, amongst other things, conservation, a postal savings bank, a parcel post and the establishment of a Childrens' Bureau. The Interstate Commerce Commission was strengthened and a commission was established to promote efficiency and economy in government. There were two constitutional amendments and two new states were admitted. Anti-trust suits, many instituted under Roosevelt, were brought to fruition and oil and tobacco trusts were dissolved. This was quite a substantial domestic record.

Foreign policy had been less successful. Taft, a strong advocate of international arbitration, saw two treaties with England and France amended to death by the Senate. The Canadians rejected a Reciprocity Agreement; and Taft's honest efforts to secure the position of American exporters and investors overseas was derided by some as 'dollar diplomacy'. Preaching an all-embracing 'New

Nationalism' which was distasteful to the 'Standpatters', Roosevelt prepared to contest the Republican nomination for 1912 and then 'bolted' the party when the establishment supported Taft. The result was the 'Progressive' or 'Bull Moose' party of 1912. A hastily concocted party of mainly middle-class enthusiasts from every section except the South, it split the Republican vote and let in the Democrats. Wilson had 435 electoral votes, Roosevelt 88 and Taft 8 (from Utah and Vermont). This was the worst-ever defeat of an incumbent president. But it did not mean as many thought, that the Republicans were about to go the way of the mid-nineteenth century Whigs. Roosevelt knew better; 'There are no loaves and fishes,' he said. 'Progressivism' was only an ideal.

'The nearer I get to the inauguration of my successor, the greater the relief I feel,' said Taft. An outspoken Kentucky journalist had once proposed that the answer to the problem of what to do with ex-presidents would be to 'Take 'em out and shoot 'em'. Taft went to Yale as a professor until 1921, when he got the position he had always wanted. President Harding appointed him as the 10th Chief Justice of the Supreme Court of the United States. Here he zestfully planned reforms to make the Federal judiciary more efficient — 'I don't remember that I ever was President.' He administered the oath of office to Presidents Coolidge and Hoover. He secured Congressional approval for a new Supreme Court Building to match the dignity of that branch of government. He died one month after retiring.

# WOODROW WILSON

**Full name**  (Thomas) Woodrow Wilson, 1856–1924
**Born**  24 North Coalter Street, Staunton, Virginia, 28 December 1856, the third of 4 children
**Parents**  Dr Joseph Ruggles Wilson (1822–1903), Presbyterian Minister, and Janet Woodrow Wilson (b Carlisle, England, 1826, d 1888)
**Family lineage**  Scottish-Irish
**College**  College of New Jersey (now Princeton University), Princeton, NJ, BA 1879. University of Virginia Law School (did not graduate); Johns Hopkins University, Baltimore, Doctor of Philosophy, 1886
**Married**  (1) 1885, Ellen Louise Axson Wilson (1860–1914), daughter of Samuel Axson, Presbyterian Minister. 3 daughters
(2) 1915, Edith Bolling Galt Wilson (1872–1961), (widow of Norman Galt), daughter of W. H. Bolling, attorney and judge
**Occupation**  Lawyer; university professor; president of Princeton University, 1902–10; Governor of New Jersey, 1911–13
**Religious denomination**  Presbyterian
**Notable relationships**  His second wife was a direct descendant of the Indian Princess Pocahontas
**Died**  From apoplexy, Washington DC, 3 February 1924, aged 67
**Buried**  In the Protestant Episcopal Cathedral of St John the Divine, Washington DC

**Party** Democratic **State represented** New Jersey **Terms of office** 4 March 1913 to 4 March 1921 **Age on taking office** 56 **Presidential administrations** 32nd, 33rd **Congresses** 63rd, 64th, 65th, 66th

|  |  | 1912 ELECTION | | | |
|---|---|---|---|---|---|
| *Candidates* | *Party* | *Electoral Vote (531)* | *States Won (48)* | *Popular Vote* | *%* |
| W. Wilson | Dem | 435 | 40 | 6,283,019 | 41.8* |
| T. Roosevelt | Prog | 88 | 6 | 4,119,507 | 27.4 |

| W. Taft | Repub | 8 | 2 | 3,484,956 | 23.2 |
| E. Debs | Soc | — | — | 962,573 | 6.0 |

(*Wilson did not receive a majority of the popular vote, but his was the largest Electoral majority to date.)

### 1916 ELECTION

| Candidates | Party | Electoral Vote (531) | States Won (48) | Popular Vote | % |
|---|---|---|---|---|---|
| W. Wilson | Dem | 277 | 30 | 9,129,606 | 49.3* |
| C. Hughes | Repub | 254 | 18 | 8,532,221 | 46.1 |

*For the 2nd time Wilson failed to receive a popular majority.

### CONGRESS

| 1913 | 63rd | Senate (96) | 51 Dem | 44 Repub | 1 Vacant |
| | | House (435) | 290 Dem | 127 Repub | 18 Others |
| 1915 | 64th | Senate (96) | 56 Dem | 39 Repub | 1 Other |
| | | House (435) | 231 Dem | 193 Repub | 8 Others |
| | | | | | 1 Vacant |
| 1917 | 65th | Senate (96) | 53 Dem | 42 Repub | 1 Other |
| | | House (435) | 216 Repub | 210 Dem | 9 Others |

(The Democrats controlled the House with minority support.)

| 1919 | 67th | Senate (96) | 48 Repub | 47 Dem | 1 Other |
| | | House (435) | 237 Repub | 191 Dem | 7 Others |

(The Administration lost control of the Senate and the House.)

### NOTES

1 1920 14th Census: Total population: 105,710,620.
2 Constitutional Amendment: XVIII (1919), prohibited the manufacture distribution and sale of alcohol.
3 Constitutional Amendment: XIV (1920), gave the vote to women.

### VICE PRESIDENT

28th Thomas Riley Marshall (Indiana), 1854–1925. Lawyer; state politician; Governor of Indiana, 1909–13; vice president 4 March 1913 to 4 March 1921. ('What this country needs is a good 5c cigar.')

---

Two myths persist about Woodrow Wilson — he early discarded his given first name, of 'Tommy', in favour of something more distinctive — that he could not read until he was 10 or 11, because he was mentally slow, and that he was a Southerner from Virginia. He was probably dyslexic, he used to try to read words backwards. As regards the South, he was in it but not of it.

175

He was born in Virginia of first and second generation Ohioan parents (his mother was born in England). His father was a Presbyterian minister and the Wilson family moved from manse to manse. In his second year they left Virginia (for ever), for Augusta, Georgia, where they remained, out of the line of battle, during the war years, in which two of his father's brothers became Union generals. In 1870 they moved to Sherman-wrecked Columbia, South Carolina, winding up in 1874 in North Carolina. This son of the Middle West, raised in the South during the period of Civil War and Reconstruction could say later: 'Because I love the South I rejoice in the failure of the Confederacy.'

He was educated in New Jersey and emerged from Princeton with a reputation for scholarship and skill in debate. Ill-health forced him to give up law school but he went into a law partnership in Atlanta, Georgia, and was called to the state bar in 1883. He found legal practice both uncongenial and unremunerative and in 1883 entered the Johns Hopkins University at Baltimore for post-graduate work in politics and history. His book on *Congressional Government* (1885) brought him offers of academic positions and the only doctorate earned by an American President.

He taught history at a brand new college for women, Bryn Mawr in Pennsylvania, from 1885–8, and then moved to the Wesleyan College at Middletown, Connecticut, for two years. In 1890, at the age of 34, he was appointed Professor of Jurisprudence and Political Economy at Princeton University. Twelve years later he was unanimously elected President of Princeton on a 'reform' ticket.

Two brief trips to England and Scotland had included visits to Oxford where he had been captivated by the 'entrancing beauty', and impressed by the ethos, of the university. He now set out to make Princeton a centre of academic excellence with a tutorial system of instruction at its heart. He fought for educational democracy and against privilege and he made many enemies; but in those progressive times the university professor attempting reforms in his institution earned both state and national attention. There were even political whispers that he could become Senator for New Jersey, or Vice President, in 1912; Wilson dismissed such ideas as 'absurd'.

But the Democratic 'bosses' in New Jersey, with the tide running against the Republicans, were seriously, desperately, searching for a gubernatorial candidate, and the academic theoretician of the art of government, increasingly exasperated at Princeton, was eventually persuaded to run in the 1910 election. He fought a vigorous, independent campaign on a progressive platform and was elected by a large majority.

The 'bosses' soon found that they were unable to control this amateur in politics. Wilson began to fulfil his campaign pledge and he rapidly moved New Jersey into the vanguard of the progressive movement. His reforms had a deep impression on the nation at large. They were studied as practical examples of possibilities and their initiator also came under close scrutiny. A presidential nominee was needed to replace William Jennings Bryan who had led the Democrats to three of their last four defeats. Colonel Edward House of Texas, the nearest thing there was to a Democratic 'Kingmaker', came north to see the rising star of New Jersey. Prepared to be sceptical, he left entranced. There was an instant mutual liking and respect between the two men. 'Never before,' said House, 'have I found both the man and the opportunity.' With this support Wilson campaigned strenuously up and down the land for the leadership of the Democratic party.

At the Democratic National Convention in Baltimore in 1912 the Governor of New Jersey was put forward by the progressive wing of the party against the party politicians, the plutocrats, 'big business' and Tammany Hall. When the 'Peerless Leader', William Jennings Bryan, the 'Old Commoner' himself, rose to cast his vote for Wilson, he helped to start a movement that gave the latter the necessary two-thirds vote and nomination on the 46th ballot.

Wilson campaigned on the 'New Freedom' programme offering restoration of the Government to the people, 'freedom for the man who is knocking and fighting at the closed doors of opportunity', and placing stress on individualism and state's rights. He was elected by a record majority of electoral votes in an election that saw the culmination of twenty years of popular revolt against the control of affairs by a privileged few. He was 56. His face was 'curiously geometrical . . . The mouth is small, sensitive, with full lips, a mouth almost too well-shaped for a man, and a woman might envy the arched eyebrows. But the almost brutal strength of the general bony structure of the face, and that aggressive jaw promise an active, iron willed, fighting man . . .'

'Our work is a work of restoration', he said in his First Inaugural. He became the first president since John Adams to address joint sessions of Congress thus emphasising the connection between the executive and the legislature and the role of the president as the leader of the government. This also contributed to a successful legislative record during his first administration. The Underwood Tariff Act provided for a lower tariff (and a graduated income tax), and virtually took the tariff out of politics. The Federal Reserve Act established 12 Regional Reserve Banks and provided America with a more elastic money supply. (This system, set up in 1914, enabled the country to take the strain of the war). A Federal Trade Commission was set up to guard against unfair business practices; anti-trust legislation was strengthened; the legality of trade unions was recognised, along with their right to strike; the Farm Loan Act of 1916 provided low-interest credit over long terms. Wilson followed Roosevelt in attempting to use Federal power for the public good; attacks were made on the problem of child labour; and a maximum 8-hour day for interstate railroad workers was brought in to prevent a threatened massive railroad strike.

Abroad, he struggled to keep America at peace. When revolution broke out in Mexico (1914–17), he followed a policy of 'watchful waiting', though he did interfere in the Caribbean to protect American interests in Haiti and Dominica. When the Great War began in 1914, ever-mindful of American traditions and the cosmopolitan nature of the population, he urged Americans to be 'neutral in fact and name and impartial in thought and deed'. German attacks on allied and American shipping made this a difficult policy to sustain. The sinking of the British liner *Lusitania* (May 1915), with the loss of 128 American lives, was followed by three strong diplomatic notes to Germany. Slowly he began to prepare the nation for the inevitable: 'The rest of the world is on fire and our house is not fireproof. We must keep ourselves in readiness to quench the fires of war.' Unfortunately a phrase that he used at this time — about a man being 'too proud to fight' — was taken out of context around the world and undermined the effect of his warning.

In 1916, against Congressional opposition, he enlarged the Army and the Navy though, as late as January 1917, he made an appeal for mediation and for a 'peace without victory'. This came shortly after he had narrowly defeated Charles Evans Hughes in the presidential election of 1916 which had been fought on the slogan — 'He kept us out of the war.'

Increasingly American neutrality was becoming very difficult and a series of events bought her to the edge of war. First, Germany made a bold gamble for victory by announcing the start of unrestricted submarine warfare. As a result, diplomatic relations between Germany and the United States were severed in February 1917. The final straw was the interception by British intelligence of a telegram from the German Foreign Secretary, Zimmerman, to the German Minister in Mexico, promising Mexico the recovery of the land she had lost in Texas, New Mexico and Arizona if she would declare war on the United States and try to bring in Japan as well. Wilson's 'War Message' to Congress of 2 April 1917 was followed by America's entry into the war.

Under the energetic direction of Secretary of War, Newton D. Baker, to whom Wilson left the detailed planning, 2 million men were drafted in the next fifteen months. Eventually, 5 million Americans were under arms commanded by General Pershing, and from early 1918 fresh American troops began to tip the balance in favour of the Allies. In January 1918 Wilson enunciated America's war aims in what came to be known as his 'Fourteen Points': the fourteenth of which advocated the establishment of a 'general association of nations', to help to keep the peace in future.

After the Armistice (November 1918), Wilson became the first American president to visit Europe when he attended the peace negotiations at Versailles, following a tremendous reception in France, England and Italy. The Versailles Treaty of 1919, although it embodied the Covenant of the League of Nations, imposed very harsh terms on Germany and departed from the idealism of his 'Fourteen Points'. Even though Wilson was awarded the Nobel Peace Prize for 1919 for his efforts, he could not carry his own people with him. The mid-term elections of 1918 had competely shifted the political balance of power in America and Wilson had made the mistake of not taking Republican leaders into his confidence. Consequently, when Wilson refused to compromise on details, the Treaty of Versailles failed by 7 votes to obtain the necessary two-thirds vote for ratification in the Senate in March 1920. (The United States concluded a separate peace with Germany, the Treaty of Berlin, in 1921 and did not join the League of Nations.)

President Wilson had set out on a nationwide 'whistle stop' tour in an attempt to whip up public support for the League of Nations. He had collapsed from exhaustion in Pueblo, Colorado, and had suffered a severe stroke in Washington (in October 1919). For the last few months in office he was totally incapacitated, shielded by his doctors, and his (second) wife, who had shared his burden of office since 1915. The unkind said that for the first time America had a woman president: 'We have petticoat government. Mrs Wilson is President.' Certainly the situation highlighted the need for some form of constitutional safeguard in the event of the president's total incapacity. (This was not provided until 1967.) The president who had worn himself out in the service of America lived barely three years after leaving office. The private man was totally different from his gaunt, austere public self. He loved playing golf, '. . . because while you are playing golf you *cannot* worry and be preoccupied with affairs'. He read detective stories, composed limericks and did a brilliant impersonation of Teddy Roosevelt. He was a good tap dancer and once said that he would have liked to have gone into vaudeville. 'He failed,' said James Truslow Adams, 'but he failed nobly.'

# WARREN G. HARDING

TWENTY-NINTH PRESIDENT OF THE UNITED STATES 1921–3

**Full name**  Warren Gamaliel Harding, 1865–1923
**Born**  Corsica (now Blooming Grove), Morrow County, Ohio, 2 November 1865, the eldest of 8 children
**Parents**  Dr George Tryon Harding (1843–1928), homeopathic physician, and his first wife, Phoebe Elizabeth Dickerson Harding (1843–1910). 5 daughters, 3 sons
**Family lineage**  English, Scottish-Irish
**College**  Ohio Central College, Iberia, Ohio, BS, 1880
**Married**  1891, Florence Kling De Wolfe Harding (1860–1924), divorced wife of Henry De Wolfe, daughter of Amos Kling, banker, merchant. No children. (There was one son by her previous marriage)
**Occupation**  Newspaper owner; state politician; Lt Governor of Ohio, 1904–6; US Senator, 1915–21
**Religious denomination**  Baptist
**Notable relationships**  None
**Died**  From apoplexy, San Francisco, California, 2 August 1923, aged 57
**Buried**  In the Harding Memorial, Marion, Ohio

**Party** Republican **State represented** Ohio **Term of office** 4 March 1921 to 2 August 1923 (died in office) **Age on taking office** 55
**Presidential administration** 34th **Congress** 67th

### 1920 ELECTION

| Candidates | Party | Electoral Vote (531) | States Won (48) | Popular Vote | % |
|---|---|---|---|---|---|
| W. Harding | Repub | 404 | 37 | 16,153,115 | 61.0* |
| J. Cox | Dem | 127 | 11 | 9,133,092 | 34.6 |

*This was the largest percentage of the popular vote to date.

### CONGRESS

| 1921 | 67th | Senate | (96) | 59 Repub | 37 Dem | |
|---|---|---|---|---|---|---|
| | | House | (435) | 300 Repub | 132 Dem | 1 Other |
| | | | | | | 2 Vacant |

29th Calvin Coolidge (Vermont), subsequently, 30th president.

---

America had seen nothing like it since the mourning for Lincoln. Millions turned out to watch Harding's funeral train during its four-day journey across the continent in August 1923. Americans suddenly became aware that they had loved their popular white-haired president with the face of a Roman senator. Three quarters of a million dollars were rapidly subscribed to build him a memorial in his home town: it was to be a vast hollow drum of white marble with forty-eight columns (one for each state).

Warren Gamaliel Harding (he was named after a Methodist minister uncle) was the first president born after the Civil War and the last of seven from the Buckeye State of Ohio where the family had lived since the days of his great-great grandfather. He grew up in Blooming Grove in a large family of which his mother, a self-taught midwife, was the mainstay. After graduation he went off to the county seat at Marion where, at the age of 19, he bought a local newspaper, the Marion *Star*, to which he was to devote the remainder of his non-political life.

He worked hard and in 1891 married a divorcée, Florence de Wolfe, the daughter of a prosperous local man. She represented the pinnacle of small-town achievement with her wealth, position and assurance, but she had to break with her father in order to marry her 'Wurr'n'. Amos Kling, in his anger at his daughter's marriage, revived the unsubstantiated rumours about Harding's supposedly negro descent which were to stalk him to his dying day. 'How do I know, Jim?' he once remarked exasperatedly to a friend. 'One of my ancestors may have jumped the fence.'

With the help of his wife — he called her 'Duchess' — the *Star* became a regular daily newspaper and Warren Harding a prosperous and influential civic leader with something of a reputation as an orator — 'bloviating' he called it. (It was undeserved; nobody could really understand *what* he said, but he *said* it very well.) From there it was only a small step into local Republican politics, though Marion County was Democratic. This progression was punctuated by more than one attack of 'nerves', which put him in the local sanitorium, and the first of the restless, aimless travels which would eventually take him through the United States, the Caribbean and Europe.

He was elected county auditor in 1895 and then, as he grew in importance, State Senator, 1899–1903. An Ohioan Republican leader, H. M. Daughterty, who was to be intimately associated with his fortunes thereafter, saw something in him and helped him to the Lt Governorship of the state, 1904–6. He was later to be defeated in the race for the governorship and he put all his energies back into the *Star*. He was still important and prominent enough, however, to be chosen to make the nominating speech for Taft at the 1912 Republican convention. In 1916 it was as the newly-elected Senator from Ohio that he presided over the Republican convention as its chairman.

He was to spend one term in the Senate, 1915–21, on which he left not the slightest legislative mark and where both his attendance and voting record were below average. But at least, during the bitter war years, the conservative Republican and defender of big business made no enemies. There he would have been quite content to stay for he found the Senate 'a very pleasant place' and he liked the social life of Washington. But he was persuaded to be a Republican presidential candidate in 1920, despite his frequent statements that he was unfitted for the office. This was not because the party lacked candidates, but because his presence on the ticket was needed to ensure control of Ohio; no Republican had ever been elected president without Ohio's electoral vote. At Chicago however, with only one day to go, the Republican nominating convention was deadlocked. In suite 404-5-6 on the thirteenth floor of the Blackstone Hotel — the famous smoke-filled room of American folk-lore — at 1am on the final day of the convention, the Republican party bosses let it be known that they wanted Senator Warren Harding to be tried out for a few ballots on the morrow. At 6.15pm that evening, when Pennsylvania cast its 61 votes for Harding on the tenth ballot, the impossible had happened. Poker-playing Harding was impassive: 'We drew to a pair of deuces and filled.' An old Senator put it another way: 'There ain't any first raters this year . . . We've got a lot of second raters and Warren Harding is the best of the second raters.'

In the 1920 election the Republicans fought against Wilson and against the League of Nations. Harding, from his front porch in Marion, waged a confused and equivocal campaign — his verbose pronouncements on the League could be taken either way — as he promised a return to 'normalcy' and peace and prosperity, following the economic crisis of 1920. 'Warren Harding is just folks like other folks', urged his campaign managers and folks rose up in their millions on his birthday in November 1920 to give him the greatest share ever of the popular vote and the most overwhelming victory since James Monroe's a century earlier. Average Americans elected an Average man as president for what he wasn't rather than for what he was; his defects were his virtues for a generation brought up on the heady philosophical diet of the Wilson era. 'Main Street has arrived in the White House,' said a witty woman alluding to a popular small-town novel of that year.

Well aware that he was not a Lincoln or a Wilson, Harding determined to have the 'Best Minds' in his cabinet; and the cabinet which included men like Hughes, Hoover, Mellon, Wallace, Hay and Weeks, was one of the strongest in a generation. (Unfortunately it also contained some men who were totally unfit for office — but that lay in the future.) His aim was to have 'Less government in business and more business in government', and this was to be achieved (in a Taft-like way) by letting each branch of government fulfil its constitutional functions: — 'Congress proposes, the President disposes.' Being president, he felt, should be 'an easy job'.

During the life of the administration there were achievements that in any other would have been regarded as substantial. The Washington Naval Disarmament Conference, which established building ratios for the world's leading navies, and the establishment of the Federal Bureau of the Budget are two prime examples. Unfortunately, the top-heavy Republican 67th ('Do Nothing') Congress split into its regional groups and Harding signed some legislation of dubious merit, such as the Fordney-McCumber Tariff, the highest-ever, and a new anti-immigration law. Even so, as the post-war depression began to give way to that prosperity which would be linked inextricably with the name of his successor, the administration seemed worthy of respect and Harding was being hailed by the press as a wise statesman. The 1922 mid-term elections did show a swing to the Democrats, but that was not unusual; for there had been unemployment, economic problems and opposition from farmers, trades unionists, army veterans and both the 'Wets' and the 'Drys' who opposed Prohibition for different reasons.

Complaints had already reached Harding about the activities of some of his subordinates; since they tended to come through sources which he regarded as less than impartial they were dismissed as 'libels'. But, unknown to the president, his administration was becoming riddled with corruption. A so-called 'Ohio Gang', operating from a little green house at 1625 K St, was making enormous profit from the sale of liquor licences, offices, concessions, legal immunity and pardons — and these were only the tip of the iceberg. Attorney General Harry Daughterty, Secretary of the Interior Albert Fall, and Veterans' Bureau director Charley Forbes were deeply involved in very questionable pursuits.

What was to become the symbol of the Harding era -- the 'Teapot Dome scandal' — involved Fall. One of his first actions had been to arrange for the transfer of control of the naval oil reserves at Teapot Dome in Wyoming and Elk Hills Fields in California to his department. These had then been turned over for exploitation to two oil magnates in a deal which involved their oil companies developing new oil installations at Pearl Harbor, Hawaii. At the same time Fall began to become personally more prosperous: the cynical made certain deductions.

Not until the autumn of 1922 did Washington gossip swell to a crescendo with rumours of a scandal involving 'waste, extravagance and irregularity' in the Veterans' Bureau. (Forbes cost the government, it was later estimated, some $200 million.) Harding broke: 'My God-damn friends they're the ones that keep me walking the floor nights,' he said, with increasing reports of resignations and even suicides in high places.

It was against this background of a growing awareness of corruption among his subordinates that Warren Harding turned his attention to foreign affairs. Announcing that he could see 'rudiments of good in both the League (of Nations) and the Hague Tribunal' — thus further dividing the Republican party — he set out to work for American membership of the International Court of Justice at the Hague. As Woodrow Wilson had set out on a pilgrimage on behalf of the League, so Harding planned a 'swing round the circle' on behalf of the Hague Tribunal. His 'Voyage of Understanding' would dwarf that of his predecessor, taking in a trans-continental trip to Alaska as well as a visit to the West coast. He was, it appears, on the verge of blossoming into a statesman, when he died at San Francisco during this journey.

Other presidents have died just in time to save their reputations. Harding died too soon. Scandals, both public and personal, broke immediately after his death. His mistress spared the public no details of their love life and a love child. Each month and each succeeding year brought fresh revelations — there was even a claim that the 'Duchess' had poisoned her husband in San Francisco to save him from impeachment — and as Pelion was piled on Ossa the public became increasingly willing to believe the worst of Harding unable, unlike his contemporaries, to give his version of events. Long-draw out legal processes conspired further to diminish what was left of his reputation; not until 1929 did Secretary Fall go on trial and not until 1931 was he sent to prison.

In 1925 the cornerstone of the Harding Memorial was laid. He and his wife were buried in it in December 1927. Not until June 1931 could a Republican successor (his own repute almost as diminished as Harding's) be found to dedicate the colonnaded marble drum of Alexandrian immensity, though there were only forty-six columns because the funds had abruptly dried up. Already Warren Gamaliel Harding had become the most neglected of presidents.

# CALVIN COOLIDGE

**Full name**   (John) Calvin Coolidge, 1872–1933
**Born**   Plymouth Notch, Windsor County, Vermont, 4 July 1872, the elder of 2 children
**Parents**   John Calvin Coolidge (1845–1926), farmer, storekeeper, Justice of the Peace, and his first wife, Victoria Josephine Moor Coolidge (1846–85). 2 son, 1 daughter. (In 1891 he married secondly, Caroline Brown Coolidge [1857–1920])
**Family lineage**   English
**College**   Amherst College, Amherst, Mass, BA 1895
**Married**   1905, Grace Anna Goodhue Coolidge (1879–1957), daughter of Andrew Goodhue, Steamboat Inspector. 2 sons
**Occupation**   Lawyer; state politician; Governor of Massachusetts, 1919–21
**Religious denomination**   Congregationalist
**Notable relationships**   An ancestor, Joseph Coolidge, married Thomas Jefferson's grand-daughter, in 1825. His step-mother was a descendant of Gen Israel Putnam (1718–90), a hero of the American Revolution
**Died**   From coronary thrombosis, Northampton, Mass, 5 January 1933, aged 60
**Buried**   Plymouth Notch Cemetery, Plymouth, Vermont

**Party** Republican **State represented** Massachusetts **Terms of office** 3 August 1923 to 4 March 1929 (he served the unexpired portion of his predecessor and one full term) **Age on taking office** 51 **Presidential administration** 34th (cont), 35th **Congresses** 68th, 69th, 70th

1924 ELECTION

| Candidates | Party | Electoral Vote (531) | States Won (48) | Popular Vote | % |
|---|---|---|---|---|---|
| C. Coolidge | Repub | 382 | 35 | 15,725,016 | 54.1 |
| J. Davis | Dem | 136 | 12 | 8,386,704 | 28.8 |
| R. La Follette | Prog | 13 | 1 | 4,832,532 | 16.6 |

| 1923 | 68th | Senate | (96) | 51 Repub | 43 Dem | 2 Others |
| | | House | (435) | 225 Repub | 207 Dem | 3 Others |
| 1925 | 69th | Senate | (96) | 54 Repub | 40 Dem | 1 Other |
| | | | | | | 1 Vacant |
| | | House | (435) | 247 Repub | 183 Dem | 5 Others |
| 1927 | 70th | Senate | (96) | 48 Repub | 47 Dem | 1 Other |
| | | House | (435) | 237 Repub | 195 Dem | 3 Others |

## VICE PRESIDENT

30th Charles Gates Dawes (Illinois), 1865–1951. Lawyer; banker; Chairman of the German Reparations Committee which produced the Dawes Plan of 1924; Nobel Peace Prize, 1925; vice president 4 March 1925 to 4 March 1929; subsequently Ambassador to Great Britain, 1929–32; president of the Reconstruction Finance Corporation, 1932–3.

---

The sixth president to reach the White House following the death of his predecessor was first sworn in during the early hours of 3 August 1923 by his father, a public notary, by the light of a kerosene lamp in the boyhood home which he happened to be visiting.

Calvin Coolidge (he had dropped his given name 'John' and the 'Jr' that went with it) was descended from five generations of strong, silent, thrifty Vermonters who had been respectable, hard-working, public-spirited men, almost all of whom had become mayors, aldermen and sheriffs. He had grown up in an intensely political atmosphere to be a serious young man — he was never a child — steeped in the traditions of New England Town Hall government.

He was educated in the local one-room school before being sent to a private high school and then on to Amherst from which he graduated *cum laude*. He was then twenty-two, with the medium height and wiry figure of an Indian — he was proud of being part Indian. He had carroty red hair, sharp features, a pale skin with big freckles, a thin mouth and blue eyes. His voice, when he used it ('He ain't gabby', said his folks), was a high, twangy, unmusical, New England drawl.

He practised law in Northampton, Mass, and was called to the state bar in 1897, but he was to make his career in Republican politics. For the next quarter of a century he was to be out of elective office for the sum total of only twenty months; and of the twenty occasions he ran for office he was successful in nineteen — a defeat in 1905 he attributed to wasting his time on honeymoon. In 1905 he married, much against his mother's wishes, Grace Anna Goodhue a University of Vermont educated lady of outstanding qualities who taught at the local deaf and dumb school. Her tact and gaiety offset her husband's shyness and she took a full share in his political rise.

Coolidge became a Northampton city councillor in 1908 and then a city official. Then, by a series of inexorable steps, he became a member of the state House of Representatives, Mayor of Northampton, and member of the state Senate of which, ultimately, he was to be the president. He served three consecutive terms as Lt Governor of the state before becoming Governor of Massachusetts, 1918–21.

On his way up he had shown few enthusiasms (though he had toyed briefly with progressivism), he had made no promises, no bargains, no deals and he had won enormous respect. He did very little in a positive sense in any of his local or state offices. In his *Autobiography* he takes pride in his non-activity, for instance, in having cut the number of bills by 30% as President of the Massachusetts Senate. As Governor of Massachusetts he made government both more efficient and economical; and this slimming-down process was to be a constant thread of all the particular offices he held — 'He was an efficiency expert to decrease production.'

Part of Coolidge's success was owed to a political patron, Frank W. Stearns, a millionaire Boston store owner, who came to admire, worship and then love his protégé. He put his vast fortune and considerable advertising resources behind Coolidge and he did more than anyone else to get him nominated as vice president to Harding by a convention protesting against 'boss' dictation in 1920. In the previous year Coolidge had first come to national prominence during the Boston Police Strike when he had, as Governor, refused to do anything, until it was too late and the damage had been done, and then the State militia had been called in to restore law and order. Along with his zeal for economy and efficiency, this nihilism was to be carried into the White House where, said one critic, it made *laissez faire* look like a programme for dynamic action.

America's new accidental president was in fact a vestigial

remnant of the Jeffersonian Democratic Republicans of the late eighteenth century; for they had also believed that 'that government governs best which governs least'. Coolidge set out to be America's least-ever president, and he succeeded. As the embodiment of everything that was best about fast-vanishing rural America, this son of a small store-keeper with his frugality, independence, morality and personal integrity did restore public confidence in the presidency and the Republican party. But he did little else; though apparently this inactivity was what was wanted by the electorate which gave him a resounding victory in 1924 with the slogan 'Keep Cool with Coolidge'.

For the five years and seven months of his presidency his philosophy was summed up by his view that 'The business of America is business'. Apparently he worshipped both God and Mammon. The men who ran industry, he believed, and made the most money, were the right people to run the economy, for from their efforts would flow prosperity for all. At a time when business was being regarded with something akin to veneration as it produced 'Coolidge Prosperity', the status quo was maintained for the benefit of big business. The Tariff (and other) Commissions were loaded with the representatives of special interests; four reductions of federal taxation aided the small man but aided even more conspicuously the rich. Government support was given to bankers and brokers whose speculative credit was being used to fuel the boom as the nation invested in business prosperity. When ordinary Americans rushed to buy stocks 'on margin' against the collateral of their homes, farms, factories and businesses, conservative businessmen and the officials of the Federal Reserve Board urged Coolidge to take some dampening action. He and his Treasury Secretary, Andrew Mellon (who realised a profit on the stock market estimated at three thousand million dollars) issued a statement that the prosperity would continue; and stocks jumped 26 points in one day on their say-so.

At no time during his political rise had Coolidge ever betrayed any qualities of leadership or vision, and now in domestic affairs Congress was given no direction whatever because, he believed, the use of federal power threatened individual freedom and initiative. Congress ignored dozens of his (often half-hearted) recommendations, or overrode his vetoes. He believed that it was more important to kill bad legislation than to promote good; so, for example, he vetoed two farm-aid bills to relieve that section of the

190

community which was not sharing in the general prosperity. He kept himself fit, he once said, 'by avoiding big problems', including Prohibition, and by working fewer hours — an average of four hours a day — than any of his predecessors.

'He did not have an international hair on his head,' said Elihu Root and there is certainly no mention of foreign policy in his *Autobiography*. He deferred to his Secretaries of State, Hughes and Kellogg, and the most conspicuous achievement of this administration was the Kellogg-Briand Pact of 1928 outlawing war, though it was to be honoured more in the breach than in the observance. American marines put down a revolt in Nicaragua and a dispute with Mexico over oil was resolved peacefully. Coolidge went down to Havana himself to preside over the 6th Inter-American conference.

The White House had not been such a dreary place since Franklin Pierce's presidency, though Coolidge was the last president to hold regular receptions for the general public where he shook hands with thousands of people. The chef quit because of his parsimony — he made daily inspections of the kitchens and store rooms — and guests were served plain ice water in paper cups.

'Silent Cal' is best remembered for his taciturnity. His conversation, it was said, bloomed like the eidelweiss, rarely and in a cold and forbidding atmosphere. Words with him were not a medium of exchange and whenever he opened his mouth to speak 'a moth flew out'. Stories about him abound. The best known tells of a charming young lady seated next to him when he was dining out who had made a bet, 'That I can get you to speak three words this evening.' 'You lose', was the laconic retort.

At a time when his re-election was being spoken of as an accomplished fact, Coolidge shook everyone (including his wife), by issuing a ten word message: 'I do not choose to run for President in 1928.' The reasons for this have been pondered long and often. Could it be that he had had enough of politics? Did he hesitate to raise the issue of a 'third term'? Or was he aware of the looming economic crisis? Certainly, when the bubble of 'Coolidge Prosperity' burst in 1929 Americans lost far more than Coolidge's charming dinner companion. His categorical refusal to govern had cost them their shirts. H. L. Mencken was only half-right when he said that Calvin Coolidge '. . . had no ideas, but he wasn't a nuisance'.

# HERBERT C. HOOVER

**Full name**  Herbert Clark Hoover, 1874–1964
**Born**  Downey Street, West Branch, Iowa, 10 August 1874, the second of 3 children
**Parents**  Jesse Clark Hoover (1846–80), blacksmith, agricultural implement maker, and Huldah Randall Minthorn Hoover (1848–83). 2 sons, 1 daughter
**Family lineage**  Swiss-German
**College**  Stanford University, Stanford, California, AB 1895
**Married**  1899, Lou Henry Hoover (1874–1944), daughter of Charles Henry, banker. 2 sons
**Occupation**  Mining engineer; voluntary relief worker, 1914–19; US Food Administrator, 1917–19; Secretary of Commerce, 1921–8. Subsequently, relief worker; Chairman of Commissions on organisation of government
**Religious denomination**  Society of Friends
**Notable relationships**  Through his mother Hoover was an eighth cousin once removed of Richard M. Nixon, 37th president
**Died**  From internal haemorrhage, New York City, NY, 20 October 1964, aged 90 (the second oldest president)
**Buried**  West Branch, Iowa

**Party** Republican **State represented** California **Term of office** 4 March 1929 to 4 March 1933 **Age on taking office** 54 **Presidential administration** 36th **Congresses** 71st, 72nd

### 1928 ELECTION

| Candidate | Party | Electoral Vote (531) | States Won (48) | Popular Vote | % |
|-----------|-------|----------------------|-----------------|--------------|------|
| H. Hoover | Repub | 444 | 40 | 21,437,277 | 58.2 |
| A. Smith | Dem | 87 | 8 | 15,007,698 | 40.8 |

### CONGRESS

| | | | | | | |
|------|------|--------|------|----------|--------|---------|
| 1929 | 71st | Senate | (96) | 56 Repub | 39 Dem | 1 Other |

|        |      | House (435)       | 267 Repub | 163 Dem   | 1 Other   |
|--------|------|-------------------|-----------|-----------|-----------|
|        |      |                   |           |           | 4 Vacant  |
| 1931   | 72nd | Senate  (96)      | 48 Repub  | 47 Dem    | 1 Ind     |
|        |      | House (435)       | 220 Dem   | 214 Repub | 1 Other   |

(The Administration lost control of the House.)

## NOTES

1 1930 15th Census: Total population: 122,775, 046.
2 Constitutional Amendment: XX (1933), abolished the 'lame duck' session of Congress from December to March, during which period, in election years, congressmen who had failed to be re-elected had continued to legislate. Moved all Congressional sessions forward to 3 January; advanced the date of the president's Inauguration to 20 January.

## VICE PRESIDENT
31st Charles Curtis (Kansas), 1860–1936. Lawyer; member of US House of Representatives, 1893–1907; US Senator, 1907–13, 1915–29; vice president 4 March 1929 to 4 March 1933. Hoover and Curtis were the first team to be defeated since 1840, when they ran for re-election in 1932.

---

The first president born west of the Mississippi was an orphan by the age of eight. 'Bertie' was brought up by uncles, first in Iowa and then in Oregon. He attended public schools and worked for his doctor/land-agent uncle as an office boy, before entering the new university at Stanford, California. He was a member of the first class to be graduated from Stanford, graduating in mining engineering and geology in 1895.

His first job was as a gold miner at $2 a day on a ten-hour night shift and a seven-day week; but before long he was an assistant mining engineer in the gold mines of Nevada and New Mexico. In 1897 he went out to the gold fields of Western Australia on behalf of a British firm, Bewick, Moreing and Company. Then in 1899 he was sent to China as Chief Engineer to the Chinese Engineering and Mining Company at Tientsin. He travelled out via London and California, where he stopped only long enough to marry his university sweetheart. Lou Henry Hoover had a talent for home-making which was to ease their adventurous life over the next two decades on several continents. She was a brilliant linguist and an expert on metals (she collaborated with her husband on a translation of Agricola's *De Re Metallica*), who was to become a poised and dignified First Lady.

Surviving the Boxer siege of Tientsin in 1900 (where the Hoovers distinguished themselves by their coolness and their powers of leadership and organisation), Herbert Hoover's technical skills and, even more, his integrity and his administrative and diplomatic abilities, had combined to make him a famous figure in the mining world by the early 1900s. He became a partner in the British firm which he had joined, but in 1908 he left to set up his own free-lance consultancy business. He spent the next six years ranging the world and no jet-age president has circled the globe as often as he did by train and boat. By the age of forty he was a multimillionaire. But 'On Monday, 3 August (1914) my engineering career was over forever. I was on the slippery road of public life.'

He was asked by the Wilson government to organise the repatriation of some 120,000 Americans from Europe and he worked as the voluntary head of the American Relief Committee, 1914–15. Then, as director of the Commission for Relief in Belgium, he took on the mammoth task of arranging for the distribution of food supplies to Belgian and French civilians on both sides of the lines. In 1917 he was called home to head the Food Administration. He persuaded the nation to adopt voluntary rationing — to 'Hooverize' — and increased food production in order to be able to allocate food surpluses to Europe.

After the war his international reputation was enhanced when he attended the Versailles peace conference as an economic adviser; and then by his organisation of food shipments to Eastern Europe and Russia. He declared for the Republicans in 1919 and a few votes were cast for him as a presidential nominee in 1920. Under presidents Harding and Coolidge he became a cabinet member and his driving energy turned an office of secondary importance, the department of Commerce, into a model of efficiency between 1921 and 1928.

In 1928, as a man of quite exceptional ability who had proved his talents in several fields, he obtained the Republican presidential nomination on the first ballot. On a programme of 'Prosperity and Prohibition' the 'world's best-known citizen' defeated Alfred E. Smith, the Roman Catholic Governor of New York. In an election which saw the largest total vote ever recorded up to that time he gained more popular votes than any previous candidate and carried forty of the forty-eight states. The presidency was his first elective public office.

In the 1928 campaign he had promised a tariff revision to help the farmers. Unfortunately the advocates of economic nationalism introduced the highly protective Hawley-Smoot Tariff which Hoover signed after fighting for more flexible provisions. This got the administration off on the wrong foot and dimmed the name of Hoover, as did his rejection of farm subsidies in favour of the establishment of a Federal Farm Bureau which was intended to provide price stability and agricultural cooperatives. He was prone to vacillate by appointing numerous fact-finding commissions; and he took what was decried as a 'pussyfooting' stand on a number of public issues, especially Prohibition. (One critic suggested a Hoover Commission to investigate Hoover.)

In 1929 the bubble of 'Coolidge Prosperity' burst in the great Wall Street stock market crash and the rest of Hoover's term was to be spent in the shadow of the Great Depression, when the economy collapsed and unemployment soared to 12 million by 1932. Hoover was essentially an exponent of nineteenth-century *laissez faire* concepts; whilst his advocacy of the traditional American virtue of 'rugged individualism' was a reflection of the self-made man's rise from rags to riches. He believed that there was little that he could, or should, do to correct the economic situation and that massive Federal doles would undermine the nation's moral fibre. The way to recovery was to be by means of 'self-help' and local and state voluntary relief schemes. Labour ought to restrain wage demands, whilst industrialists should retain their workers and farmers should practice crop control. He urged Congress, for its part, to keep the budget balanced, to cut taxes and increase spending on public works.

The crisis was worsened in 1931 by the international situation and called for a totally different approach. Hoover, in an act of great courage and statesmanship, arranged a one-year moratorium on the repayment of reparations and inter-Allied war debts as a way to ease European ills. Then, as the depression deepened, he asked Congress for an unprecedented programme designed to stimulate business recovery, believing, like a true Republican, that all might yet be well if only business confidence could be secured. A Federal Reconstruction Finance Corporation was to aid business; money was to be set aside for remortgages through the Farm Loan Bank and the Federal Home Loan Bank. There were to be banking reforms, loans for states to help feed the unemployed, and millions were to be appropriated for public works schemes. A hostile Congress, following Democratic gains in 1930 and the defection of progressive Republicans, slowly passed only part of these measures, whilst the nation disparaged his leadership and blamed him personally for the ever-worsening situation. Hoover's dispersal of the 'Bonus army' of army veterans in the nation's capital (1932), and the coining of phrases such as 'Hoovervilles' for the tarred paper shacks of the homeless unemployed, and 'Hoover flags' (empty pockets turned inside out) presaged a demand for a change in the national leadership. In the 1932 election Hoover suffered an ignominious defeat at the hands of Franklin D. Roosevelt. With less than 40% of the popular vote, Hoover sustained the worst defeat ever inflicted on a Republican presidential nominee in a two-party race. FDR's was the biggest margin of victory since Lincoln defeated McClellan in 1864. In addition, the Democrats gained their largest majority in the Senate since before the Civil War and the largest majority in the House since 1890. The 'Great Depression' had ended the reign of the Republicans as the nation's majority party and the GOP gained an unwelcome reputation as the party of hard times.

Hoover felt that he had been made a scapegoat: 'The President has increasingly become the repository of all national ills, especially if things go wrong.'

It has become traditional to deride Hoover as a 'do nothing' president; but in fact, unlike Coolidge, within the limits of his own rigid ideology (from which in any case he was prepared to depart as the depression worsened), he was an outright activist. His policies foreshadowed the massive deficit spending relief programme of his successor's 'New Deal' (qv), and without his intermediate steps Roosevelt's task might have been harder. Hoover at least proved that local and state relief was not enough and the need for Federal intervention. As with James Buchanan on the eve of the nation's last major crisis it might be asked if anyone could have done better. And when it is remembered that the political leader of every other major free nation was ruined by the Depression — Ramsay Macdonald in Britain, Laval in France, Brüning in Germany — and that Roosevelt needed eight years, a deficit of twenty billion dollars and the outbreak of the Second World War to conquer it, it is not surprising that Herbert Hoover failed to achieve the impossible.

Foreign policy captured less public attention at this time, but was not unimportant. A delegation was sent to the London Naval Conference (1930) and disarmament was advocated throughout this period. Surprisingly perhaps, for one with his international background, Hoover followed basically a conservative isolationist policy, shying away from the League of Nations and merely denouncing Japanese intervention in Manchuria by means of the Hoover-Stimson non-recognition doctrine. A Hoover visit to South America heralded Roosevelt's 'Good Neighbor' policy, as did his withdrawal of US marines from Nicaragua.

Hoover was to live for another thirty-one years after the completion of his term, the longest-ever such period, and he was to be the only living ex-president from 1933–53. He was to be a powerful critic of Roosevelt's 'New Deal' which he labelled, 'paternalistic, socialistic, collectivistic, fascistic and communistic'. In the following years as prosperity slowly revived so did Hoover's standing, aided perhaps by a sneaking feeling that the American virtues he represented were worthy of respect, but more because of his post-war work. In 1946 President Truman made him chairman of the Famine Emergency Committee to coordinate post-war relief and planning in thirty-eight European countries where he found an adequate outlet for his dedicated humanitarianism. During the Truman and Eisenhower administrations he chaired bipartisan Federal study commissions in 1947 and 1953 aimed at improving the Executive branch of government. When he died in 1964 he had long since ceased to be the bogeyman of the 1930s and the Boulder Dam on the Colorado River had been renamed the Hoover Dam in his honour.

# FRANKLIN D. ROOSEVELT

**Full Name**  Franklin Delano Roosevelt, 1882–1945
**Born**  Hyde Park, NY, 30 January 1882, the only child of his father's second marriage
**Parents**  James Roosevelt (1828–1900), lawyer, financier, railroad executive, and his second wife, Sara Delano Roosevelt (1884–1941). 1 son
**Family lineage**  Dutch and French-Dutch
**College**  Harvard University, Cambridge, Mass, BA 1903, Columbia Law School, New York, NY
**Married**  1905, (Anna) Eleanor Roosevelt Roosevelt (1884–1962), daughter of Elliott Roosevelt, sportsman. 1 daughter, 5 sons
**Occupation**  Lawyer; state senator; Assistant Secretary of the Navy (1913–20); Governor of New York State (1929–33)
**Religious denomination**  Episcopalian
**Notable relationships**  By blood or marriage he could claim relationship to 11 former presidents: Washington, both Adamses, Madison, Van Buren, both Harrisons, Taylor, Grant, Theodore Roosevelt and Taft. F. D. Roosevelt and W. S. Churchill were 7th cousins once removed
**Died**  From cerebral haemorrhage, Warm Springs, Georgia, 12 April 1945, aged 63
**Buried**  Hyde Park, NY

**Party** Democratic **State represented** New York **Terms of office** 4 March 1933 to 12 April 1945 (12 years 39 days) **Age on taking office** 51 **Presidential administrations** 37th, 38th, 39th, 40th **Congresses** 73rd, 74th, 75th, 76th, 77th, 78th, 79th

### PRESIDENTIAL ELECTION STATISTICS 1932–44

| Candidates | Party | Electoral Vote (531) | States Won (48) | Popular Vote | % |
|---|---|---|---|---|---|
| 1932 F. D. Roosevelt | Dem | 472 | 42 | 22,829,501 | 57.3 |
| H. Hoover | Dem | 59 | 6 | 15,760,684 | 39.6 |

| 1936 | F. D. Roosevelt | Dem | 523 | 46 | 27,757,333 | 60.7 |
|------|-----------------|-------|-----|----|------------|------|
|      | A. Landon | Repub | 8 | 2 | 16,864,231 | 36.4 |
| 1940 | F. D. Roosevelt | Dem | 449 | 38 | 27,313,041 | 54.7 |
|      | W. Wilkie | Repub | 82 | 10 | 22,348,480 | 44.8 |
| 1944 | F. D. Roosevelt | Dem | 432 | 36 | 25,612,610 | 52.8 |
|      | T. Dewey | Repub | 99 | 12 | 22,017,617 | 44.5 |

### CONGRESSES

| 1933 | 73rd | Senate | (96) | 59 Dem | 36 Repub | 1 Other |
|------|------|--------|------|--------|----------|---------|
|      |      | House | (435) | 313 Dem | 117 Repub | 5 Others |
| 1935 | 74th | Senate | (96) | 69 Dem | 25 Repub | 2 Others |
|      |      | House | (435) | 322 Dem | 102 Repub | 10 Others |
|      |      |        |      |        |          | 1 Vacancy |
| 1937* | 75th | Senate | (96) | 75 Dem | 17 Repub | 4 Others |
|      |      | House | (435) | 333 Dem | 89 Repub | 12 Others |
|      |      |        |      |        |          | 1 Vacancy |
| 1939 | 76th | Senate | (96) | 69 Dem | 23 Repub | 4 Others |
|      |      | House | (435) | 262 Dem | 170 Repub | 3 Others |
| 1941 | 77th | Senate | (96) | 66 Dem | 28 Repub | 2 Others |
|      |      | House | (435) | 266 Dem | 161 Repub | 5 Others |
|      |      |        |      |        |          | 3 Vacant |
| 1943 | 78th | Senate | (96) | 58 Dem | 37 Repub | 1 Other |
|      |      | House | (435) | 220 Dem | 207 Repub | 4 Others |
|      |      |        |      |        |          | 4 Vacant |

*In 1937 the largest ever majorities were recorded in both the Senate and the House.

### NOTES

1 1940 16th Census: Total population: 131,669,275.
2 Constitutional Amendment: XXI (1933) repealed the XVIII (1919) 'Prohibition' amendment.

### VICE PRESIDENTS

32nd John Nance Garner (Texas), 1868–1967 (the vice president who lived to the most advanced age, 98). Lawyer; member of US House of Representatives, 1903–33; Speaker of the House, 1931–33; vice president, 4 March 1933 to 20 January 1941.

33rd Henry Agard Wallace (Iowa), 1888–1965. Editor; author; geneticist; Secretary of Agriculture, 1933–40; vice president, 20 January 1941 to 20 January 1945; subsequently Secretary of Commerce, 1945–6; presidential candidate, 1948.

34th Harry S. Truman, subsequently 33rd president. Vice president, 20 January 1945 to 12 April 1945 (at 60 he was the oldest vice president to succeed to the presidency).

Franklin Delano Roosevelt, who was to be regarded by some as a little higher than George Washington and by others as a little lower than Caligula, was born in 1882 on his family's estate at Krum Elbow on the Hudson River in New York. He was educated privately and, like his fifth cousin Theodore Roosevelt, by frequent travels abroad, before entering the prestigious Groton School. He graduated from Harvard in three years (instead of four) with a History degree, attended Columbia Law School, and was called to the bar in 1907. He practised law for three years in New York City and then entered politics. A delegate to the New York Democratic Convention in 1910, to everyone's surprise he won election later the same year as State Senator from the up-state, predominantly Republican, 26th District, largely because he campaigned in an automobile. He was re-elected in 1912.

In that year he was a delegate to the Democratic National Convention and supported the nomination of Woodrow Wilson who, in 1913, appointed him as Assistant to Secretary of the Navy Josephus Daniels. He served two terms in this post proving to be a tireless and efficient administrator. During the war of 1917–18, his major contribution was to make improvements to the bases for the fleets, the repair yards, the arsenals and the training stations. In 1914 he ran for the Democratic nomination for US Senator from New York and suffered the only real personal defeat he ever encountered.

In 1920 he supported Alfred E. Smith as presidential nominee and, when Smith failed, wound up on the Democratic ticket as running-mate to James M. Cox. They fought on a League of Nations platform and lost to Harding. In the next year Roosevelt was to be dealt a worse blow. Holidaying on Campobello Island, New Brunswick, he contracted infantile paralysis. At first he was totally paralysed from the waist downwards, but later he recovered enough to be able to walk short distances without crutches. 'I'll beat this thing,' he told his wife.

In 1905 Roosevelt had married a distant cousin, Eleanor Roosevelt, who was given away by her uncle, President Theodore Roosevelt. An enthusiastic sportswoman, she was to become a noted humanitarian, writer, lecturer, and radio speaker; and a devoted mother and wife, who was to be a great asset to her husband's career.

Despite his handicap he continued to be active in politics. In 1924 he made a dramatic appearance on crutches to make one of the

200

greatest nominating speeches in US history on behalf of Smith; and he supported him again in 1928, this time walking in with a pair of canes. In that same year, in which Smith was annihilated by Hoover, Roosevelt was elected Governor of New York by a narrow majority. So popular did he become that in 1930 he was re-elected by the largest majority (725,000) yet recorded in the state. This prodigious victory made him the leading Democratic contender for the presidential nomination; for New York state, with its 47 Electoral College votes, controlled almost one fifth of the 266 necessary for nomination. As governor his policies included (prophetically) unemployment insurance, farm relief, old age pensions, reafforestation and the regulation of public utilities. He gained national recognition for this bold programme which was put forward against great opposition from a Republican-dominated legislature.

On the fourth ballot at the Democratic nominating convention in Chicago in 1932, Roosevelt was chosen to run against Herbert Hoover. In his acceptance speech he offered a programme based on 'Relief, Recovery and Reform'. 'I pledge you, I pledge myself, to a new deal for the American people.' In what was essentially an anti-Hoover election — like McKinley, Harding and others, Roosevelt came to power not because people were intent on electing him, but because they wanted to defeat his opponent — he was swept into office with the largest vote, both popular and electoral, ever recorded up to that time. He won all states except Connecticut, Delaware, Pennsylvania, New Hampshire, Maine and Vermont; but, to adopt a misquoted remark of H. L. Mencken, the Democrats could have beaten Hoover with a Chinaman. In 1933, one month before his inauguration, he narrowly missed death when an assassin fired at him and killed Chicago's Mayor Cermak.

The depression had worsened during Hoover's 'lame duck' period (which the new XXth Amendment would curtail in the future). Industry had continued to decline, unemployment had risen to astronomical heights and, on the day Roosevelt became president, there was not a single bank open anywhere in the land. Despite leg braces and a wheelchair the big (he was six feet tall), exuberant, smiling boss of the Democrats now had the unenviable task of making his 'New Deal' a reality and of instilling a measure of confidence into the shattered nation. 'Let me assert my firm belief', he said in his First Inaugural, 'that the only thing we have to fear is fear itself . . .'

Supported by the 'Brains Trust' of advisers and a distinguished Cabinet which included the first woman, Frances Perkins, as Secretary of Labor, Roosevelt launched into his legendary first '100 days'. He called Congress into special session and put forward a mass of legislation which had all the ingredients of a blitzkrieg. He gave 'fireside chats' over the radio to explain his programme, to calm the public and enlist their support.

Finance and business were buttressed; federal loans were provided for farmers and home owners. The Civilian Conservation Corps (CCC) the first of the 'alphabet agencies', set out to provide work for young men on conservation schemes. The agriculture Adjustment Administration (AAA) provided subsidies to enable farmers to cut production, thus increasing farming prices and incentives. The Tennessee Valley Authority (TVA) was set up to develop the resources of an entire watershed of forty thousand square miles (the area of England is 50,000 square miles), to control floods, promote river navigation, sell electric power and restore hope to a dejected region. Government agencies were established to monitor voluntary codes of business and industrial practice and trades union rights.

Ultimately, as a result of the First and the Second (after 1935) New Deals, the federal government stood committed not only to a conservation programme that Theodore Roosevelt would have envied, but also to temporary work relief for the unemployed, the promotion and protection of trade unionism, and to a permanent reform and social security programme. The New Deal had provided public works, in order to 'pump-prime' the economy, old age pensions, public health reforms, legislation for maximum hours and minimum wages, and even schemes for rural rehabilitation and the promise of federal aid for state school systems. Bank deposits had been insured, the sales of securities regulated, the dollar revalued and the country taken off the gold standard. The depression was by no means solved — unemployment remained consistently high — but the nation had lost many of its fears.

Roosevelt had also gained many critics, for to some he was a dangerous revolutionary and potential dictator, and to others he was too conservative or reactionary. Progress had been made but at a price which, said his opponents, who ranged from Huey Long to Father Coughlin, had endangered 'capitalism' and 'democracy'. The New Deal had certainly altered the balance of power in American government causing a shift from the state governments to the federal and, within the federal government, from Congress to the president, the like of which had not been seen since the Civil War. But the electorate at large ignored any complaints and, contrary to tradition, not only gave the Democrats gains in the 1934 mid-term election, but also re-elected Roosevelt in 1936 with 523 Electoral votes to the 8 of his luckless opponent. (He was the first to be sworn in on 20 January 1937, the new date provided by the XXth Amendment.) Though Roosevelt was never again to attain such dizzy electoral heights — and his opponents were to receive record totals of over twenty-two millions on each occasion — his electoral triumphs in 1940, and again in 1944, were to shatter the two-term tradition and give him an unprecedented (and now unattainable) twelve years in the White House.

After his victory in 1936 Roosevelt joined battle with the Supreme Court (the 'nine old men' in the eyes of rabid New Dealers), which had declared unconstitutional much of the 'alphabet world' of the New Deal, for example the AAA and the NRA (the National Recovery Act). In 1937 F.D.R. brought forward a scheme to add new justices to the Court which was interpreted as an attempt to 'pack' it and undermine the principle of the 'separation of powers'. Although he met his only defeat on this issue the Supreme Court rendered far more favourable decisions thereafter.

By the spring of 1937 the president appeared to be leading the country out of the depression as the nation achieved 1929 levels of production, but in August the economy suddenly slumped. Over the next ten months output fell 33% and support for Roosevelt, already strained over the Supreme Court affair, was seriously tried as unemployment climbed to 9.5 millions. In the 1938 mid-term elections for the 76th Congress there were heavy Republican gains. Attention was also now shifting to foreign affairs and, although 1938 saw additional measures for farm subsidies, minimum wages and child labour, the great spate of New Deal legislation was finally over. Unemployment still stood at 7 millions as late as 1940 and the evils of the depression did not finally abate until the nation mobilised for World War II.

Those critics who believed that the New Deal was part of a communist conspiracy were quick to notice that F.D.R. had already made one major foreign policy shift by granting diplomatic recognition to the Soviet Union in 1933. He had amplified the promise of a 'Good Neighbor' policy, enshrined in his First Inaugural, by instituting a policy of co-operation with Latin American countries in place of direct intervention in their internal affairs.

As a world conflict loomed on the horizon Roosevelt pursued a policy of 'defensive rearmament' against a background of official American neutrality and strong isolationist sentiment. But after the Fall of France and the Battle of Britain, in early 1941 he launched a programme of giving the Allies 'All Aid Short of War'. Following the events at Pearl Harbor, Hawaii, on 7 December 1941 — 'a date that will live in infamy' — the United States became involved in an all-out global effort to defeat the Axis powers of Italy, Germany and Japan.

In January 1941, even before the United States was involved in the conflict, he had already proclaimed as war aims the 'Four Freedoms': of speech and worship, and from want and fear. In August 1941 he had met with British Prime Minister Winston Churchill (a distant relative), off Argentia, Newfoundland, where they had drawn up the Atlantic Charter incorporating these and other war aims.

As war-time Commander-in-Chief F.D.R. delegated responsibility for domestic policy — especially for government control of every aspect of that industrial production that was to make the United States the 'arsenal of democracy' — whilst he concentrated on global strategy and diplomacy. He alone made major decisions — to invade North Africa in 1942; to appoint Gen Dwight D. Eisenhower to command the Normandy landings in 1944 — and he made arduous journeys to meet his allies. The 'Big Three' of F.D.R., Churchill and Stalin, met at Teheran in November 1943 to plan the strategy of unconditional surrender; and at Yalta in February 1945, where deep divisions appeared amongst the allies, to plan for peace, especially through the creation of a United Nations Organisation. In 1943 he had become the first president to travel outside the United States during wartime when he visited American troops in Sicily.

He did not live long enough to witness the final victory. Only weeks before the war ended in Europe he died at his retreat, the Little White House, at Warm Springs in Georgia, whilst posing for an official portrait. He had gone there to prepare an address for an initial meeting of the United Nations Organisation at San Francisco. In a sense he was fortunate in the hour of his death for he did not live long enough to witness that break up of the Grand Alliance that had been foreshadowed by the major disagreements at Yalta.

# HARRY S. TRUMAN

**Full name**  Harry S. Truman, 1884–1972
**Born**  Lamar, Missouri, 8 May 1884, the eldest of 3 children
**Parents**  John Anderson Truman (1851–1914), farmer, livestock salesman, and Martha Ellen Young Truman (1852–1947). 2 sons, 1 daughter
**Family lineage**  English-Scottish-Irish
**College**  None; Kansas City School of Law, Kansas City, Mo, (now, School of Law, University of Missouri at Kansas City), 1923–25. Did not graduate
**Married**  1919, Elizabeth, 'Bess', Virginia Wallace Truman (1885–    ), daughter of David Willock Wallace, farmer. 1 daughter
**Occupation**  Bank clerk, etc; farmer, 1906–17; World War I, Major; haberdasher; county judge, 1922–4; presiding judge, 1926–34 (both administrative positions); Re-Employment Director of Missouri, 1933–4; US Senator, 1935–45; vice president, 1945
**Religious denomination**  Baptist
**Notable relationships**  His grandmother, Ann Drusilla Tyler (d 1887), was descended from the brother of John Tyler, 10th president
**Died**  Kansas City, Missouri, 26 December 1972, aged 88
**Buried**  In the rose garden of the Harry S. Truman Library, Independence, Missouri

**Party** Democratic **State represented** Missouri **Term of office** 12 April 1945 to 20 January 1953 (he served the unexpired term of his predecessor, 3 years, 283 days, and one full term) **Age on taking office** 60 **Presidential administrations** 40th (cont), 41st **Congresses** (79th), 80th, 81st, 82nd

| Candidates | Party | Electoral Vote (531) | States Won (48) | Popular Vote | % |
|---|---|---|---|---|---|
| H. Truman | Dem | 303 | 28 | 24,179,345 | 49.6* |
| T. Dewey | Repub | 189 | 16 | 21,991,291 | 45.1 |
| S. Thurmond | States Rights | 39 | 4 | 1,176,125 | 2.4 |

*Truman did not receive a majority of the popular vote.

## CONGRESS

| 1947 | 80th | Senate (96) | 51 Repub | 45 Dem | |
| | | House (435) | 246 Repub | 188 Dem | 1 Other |

(The Administration lost control of Congress. The Republicans were in control for the first time in 18 years.)

| 1949 | 81st | Senate (96) | 54 Dem | 42 Repub | |
| | | House (435) | 263 Dem | 171 Repub | 1 Other |

(The Administration regained control of Congress.)

| 1951 | 82nd | Senate (96) | 48 Dem | 46 Repub | 2 Others |
| | | House (435) | 228 Dem | 205 Repub | 2 Others |

## NOTES

1 1950 17th Census: Total population: 150,697,361.

2 The Presidential Succession Act 1947: provided for the succession, after the vice president, of the Speaker of the House, the president *pro tempore* of the Senate, and then the heads of the executive departments. This revision (and reversal of the order of 1792 qv) was made so that a popularly chosen figure, rather than an appointed (Senate) official, should stand higher in the chain of succession. This act amended the law of 1886 (qv).

3 Constitutional Amendment: XXII March 1951: Provides that no person shall be *elected* president more than twice; and that no person (vice president) who has served more than two years of his predecessor's term shall thereafter be a candidate more than once. (Technically, therefore, the maximum possible term is now ten years.)

## VICE PRESIDENT

35th Alben William Barkley (Kentucky), 1877–1956. Lawyer; member of US House of Representatives, 1909–27; US Senator, 1927–49; majority leader, 1937–46; vice president, 20 January 1949 to 20 January 1953. He was the last vice president born in the nineteenth century, and, at 71, the oldest to be inaugurated. Subsequently US Senator, 1954–6.

'I felt as though the moon and all the planets and all the stars had fallen upon me,' he said later, of that moment when the devastating news of the death of Franklin Roosevelt was conveyed to him by Mrs Roosevelt. He had been chosen as a compromise running-mate to F.D.R. in 1944, at a time when it was becoming increasingly obvious that Roosevelt was not going to serve out his fourth term. Even so, he had scarcely seen the president since their election. He had not been briefed about deteriorating relations with the Russians and, though he was dimly aware of the existence, he was not aware of the nature of the 'Manhattan Project'. Now to America's oldest-ever accidental president was to fall the unenviable task of concluding the war and of trying to win the peace.

Harry S. Truman (that was his full name, the middle initial did not stand for anything) was born in Lamar, Missouri, but he was to spend the rest of his life in nearby Independence. His father was a farmer. His mother was a staunch Southern Democrat and rabid Confederate until the day of her death at the age of 95. She flatly refused to sleep in Lincoln's bed when she went to stay at the White House. After graduating from high school there was no money for college, so young Harry worked at a variety of jobs before going to help out on the family farm. Here he spent the next twelve years (until he was 33) becoming a knowledgeable and prosperous farmer, the first president since Grant to have engaged in farming as an adult.

During the First World War Capt Harry Truman led Battery D of the 129th Field Artillery during the September 1918 Meuse-Argonne offensive. He left the army as a major and in 1919 married his childhood sweetheart and one-time classmate — they had first met when they were six — Elizabeth 'Bess' Truman. They were to be married for 53 years. He then went into partnership in a haberdashery store in Kansas City with a friend and after it failed in 1922 spent the next 15 years paying off his debts.

Fellow 'Redlegs' (ex-infantry veterans), plus the power wielded by the political machine of 'Boss' Tom Pendergast of Kansas City, elected him as judge (an administrative position) of Jackson County from 1922–4 in which position he earned such a reputation for honesty and efficiency that the Ku-Klux-Klan engineered his defeat. From 1923–5 he studied law at night school, but he quit his studies to serve two four-year terms as presiding judge (another administrative position) of the Jackson County Court from

1926–34. In 1933–4 he also held a New Deal position in the state before, at the age of 50, leaving for Washington as a United States Senator — 'the Senator from Pendergast', as the cynical put it. He was re-elected after a stiff fight in 1940 and in his second term made a name for himself, and learned a great deal about government finance, as the chairman of a Senate 'Special Committee to Investigate the Defence Programme'. (Truman estimated later that this committee had saved fifteen billion dollars.) In 1944, as a border-state Missourian, he was chosen as the vice presidential nominee in preference to candidates supported by either the North and 'left' of the party, or the Southern 'conservatives'.

On 12 April 1945 one question was on everyone's mind: was this anonymous man, who, it was said, looked like a failed haberdasher, whose political experience 'had put the permanent stamp of Jackson County on his personality', capable of guiding the fortunes of the world's most powerful nation through the most complex issues which it had ever faced? His task would have been hard enough without having to follow Roosevelt; for 'Mr Average' it might prove well-nigh impossible. 'Pray for me boys,' he said in his first statement to the press corps, 'I shall need help.'

The press was soon full of attempts to acquaint the nation with their 'unknown' president. He was portrayed as a devoted son, husband and father, a hearty eater and moderate drinker, a gregarious and outgoing man. His favourite relaxation was poker; he was fond of music and could play the piano reasonably well, as he once demonstrated to Churchill and Stalin at Potsdam. He rose early and worked hard. The general picture was of a man of limited accomplishments and homely tastes, but it soon dawned on his close associates that he was by no means an average man. 'I acquired the greatest admiration for the president's capacity to understand complex questions and to *decide*. This is one of the rarest qualities possessed by man,' said Secretary of State Dean Acheson. He ran the cabinet in his own way and made his own policy decisions, taking a strong line with those people, in or out of government, who threatened to challenge the power of the presidency. There was no room for the faint-hearted: 'If you can't stand the heat, stay out of the kitchen' was one of his favourite sayings. A sign on his desk read: 'The Buck Stops Here.'

His first domestic problem was that of converting the economy from war to peace time. Though sympathetic to labour, he met demands from unions anxious to maintain war wages and, at the same time, to secure improved conditions, very forcefully. Striking railroad workers were threatened with the draft and military discipline; they settled. The miners were taken to court and fined $3.5 millions for breach of contract; their leader, the seemingly impregnable John L. Lewis, was fined $10,000 for contempt of court. After these battles Truman was his own man and president in his own right.

In the fall of 1945 he drew up a 21 point programme (the forerunner of the 'Fair Deal' of 1949), which was designed to provide social security, full employment, the protection of minority rights, slum clearance and the like. Unfortunately he could not carry Congress with him for, although there was to be bipartisan support for his foreign policy, his domestic policy was severely attacked by the Republicans (out of office since 1933) and the Southern Democratic opponents of the New Deal. The situation worsened after decisive Republican victories in the 1946 mid-term elections (a certain R. M. Nixon was one of over 50 Republican gains in the House), following which Truman's efforts to control inflation were opposed and his vetoes of labour measures were over-ridden by the new 80th 'Do Nothing' Congress.

So bad was the situation that Truman was written-off long before the 1948 presidential election took place, especially when it was rumoured that Gen Eisenhower would run as a Democrat. But, 'Stuck with Harry', the Democrats reluctantly re-nominated him. Truman fought a brilliant 15-day campaign travelling 32,000 miles: 'I'm going to give 'em hell!' he proclaimed. His eventual narrow victory was largely the result of a brilliant strategem. The Republican's manifesto indicated that they had caught the Democrats bathing and stolen their clothes. 'Give 'em hell Harry' gave them the opportunity to fulfil their campaign pledges *before* their 'victory', by calling Congress into special session in July 1948, and presenting it with an extensive legislative programme culled from Republican sources. When the package was rejected the Republican's naked opportunism stood skilfully revealed. Truman's victory finally established him as the unquestioned successor of F.D.R., though he would still face problems in Congress, despite Democratic gains, because his opponents still controlled the key Congressional committees.

The war in Europe had ended on Truman's birthday in 1945 but that was the only happy augury. At the Potsdam Conference in July and August deep divisions were apparent between the new 'Big

Three' as plans were laid to divide Germany into occupation 'zones' and the war in the Far East was discussed. Whilst the meeting was in progress Truman was handed a cryptic note which told him that the 'Manhattan Project' had produced the world's first atomic explosion at 5.10am on 16 July. As a consequence the 'Potsdam Ultimatum' was issued by Truman, Churchill and Chinese Premier Chiang Kai-shek on 26 July. It called for the unconditional surrender of the Japanese armed forces and threatened Japan with 'prompt and utter destruction'. When the Japanese cabinet replied that they would *mokusatsu* the ultimatum — which can be translated either as 'withhold comment on' or 'ignore' — Truman gave the order to use the Atomic bomb against Japan as soon as possible after 2 August. 'Little Boy' and 'Fat Man' — the only two bombs which had been manufactured — were consequently dropped on Hiroshima and Nagasaki on 6 August and 9 August respectively. (A recent — May 1980 — discovery in the Truman Library in Missouri shows that Truman was far more concerned about the horrible effects of nuclear war than he expressed at the time or even in his memoirs ten years later.)

The boiling cauldron of war now gave way to the 'Cold War'. A Russian threat to Turkey and Greece was met with the enunciation of the 'Truman Doctrine' (March 1947), calling for 'support for free peoples who are resisting attempted subjugation by armed minorities or by outside pressures'. This statement foreshadowed America's policy of the 'containment' of the communist threat by means of collective security alliances and military and economic aid. It was followed by the establishment of the Marshall Plan which poured three billion dollars of American aid into Western Europe between 1947–50. (This had the additional benefit of strengthening the American economy.) Another pre-emptive strike against the forces of communism was promised in Truman's Inaugural Address in 1949, when he called for a 'Point Four' pro-gramme to eliminate poverty in the Third World by means of foreign aid.

The Berlin Blockade (1948–9), following a Russian attempt to deny the allies access to the city deep in the Soviet zone of Germany, was thwarted by the Berlin Airlift which flew an average of 6,000 tons of supplies into the beleagured city every day. It led to the North Atlantic Treaty, which was signed by 12 nations in April 1949, and then to the establishment, under the American nuclear umbrella, of the North Atlantic Treaty Organisation. This 'entangling alliance' constituted a major revolution in American foreign policy.

In 1950, after the withdrawal of American troops from South Korea, the Communist North Koreans poured over the 38th parallel into the South. Taking advantage of Russia's absence from the United Nations Security Council (they were objecting to a refusal to seat the new 'Red' China), a predominantly American, 16-nation United Nations peace-keeping force was organised, the first in the history of the world. Gen MacArthur's brilliant Inchon landings turned the communist's flank, forced them to withdraw from the south, and was followed by an allied advance to within 50 miles of the Chinese border. The appearance of a quarter of a million Communist Chinese troops altered the whole complexion of the war. Truman, anxious to 'contain' communism and not to escalate the situation into a full-scale war against the Chinese, and possibly the Russians, was forced to fire MacArthur, who disagreed with his strategy. He returned to a hero's welcome in the United States, whilst the Korean War ground to an eventual stalemate and Truman's stock fell rapidly.

At home, ever-mounting fear of communism — against the background of a communist coup in Czechoslovakia, the Berlin Blockade, the Soviet Atom bomb (1949), the establishment of Red China and the Korean War — had produced an hysteria which was to provide the scaffolding for the careers of two men in particular, Senator Joseph McCarthy and Richard M. Nixon. The anti-communist McCarran Internal Security Act of 1950, passed over Truman's veto, laid the foundation for a witch hunt, which was to be aided by the discovery of an *actual* communist spy ring in the USA, Canada and Britain. (Klaus Fuchs was arrested in Britain in 1949; Burgess and Maclean fled; Julius and Ethel Rosenberg were executed in the USA in 1953.) Soon it was widely believed that there were 'reds under the beds' and charges of communist infiltration of government departments spared no one, not even Secretary of State Acheson. Richard Nixon first made a name for himself, and earned the undying hatred of Truman, in the case of Alger Hiss (see p 241). Though the Senate Tydings Committee reported that McCarthy's witch-hunting activities were based on 'fraud and sham' he still went from strength to strength as the Democrats became increasingly demoralised.

By the early fifties not only was the feeling beginning to grow that after twenty years of the Democrats it was time for a change,

212

but the 'mess in Washington', as it came to be called, was too palpable to ignore. A network of minor corruption and favouritism was uncovered, spreading out from some of Truman's aides. There were also revelations of widespread dishonesty in the Bureau of Internal Revenue. Truman had begun his political career in the shadow of corruption in Kansas City. Though he was never implicated in either the Pendergast or the Washington scandals, they inevitably tarnished his reputation. In election year national approval of Truman fell to only 23%. Although the terms of the XXIInd Amendment of 1947 (qv), deliberately did not apply to him, he decided to step down. As an elder statesman he threw his weight behind Adlai E. Stevenson, but the Republican ticket of Eisenhower and Nixon proved unstoppable fighting on an 'anti-slogan' of 'K1 C2' — ie Korea, corruption and communism.

There is a famous (debatable) saying about 'Haberdasher Harry' Truman, that he was 'right on all the big things, wrong on all the little ones' — including the loud sports shirts, quick-mouthed remarks and his 'cronyism', all of which detracted from presidential dignity. ('To err is Truman,' as Martha Taft put it.) Few presidents have had a worse relationship with Congress — only Andrew Johnson had more vetoes over-ridden — which contributed to a rather barren record in domestic affairs. Most of his major decisions were either Executive Acts which did not require Congressional approval (like the Berlin Airlift), or by their nature committed Congress to their implementation (like the Truman Doctrine). He divided his party over civil rights in 1948, though no president in at least seventy-five years achieved so much in this area. He intensified the pace of desegregation in the armed forces and ended, by Executive Order, discrimination in Federal employment.) His decision to use the bomb will be debated for evermore.

There is no doubt however that his achievements in foreign policy were monumental. Perhaps the greatest tribute ever paid to Truman, by a man not given to fulsome eulogy — Winston Churchill (in 1952), reflects this. 'The last time you and I met across a conference table was at Potsdam. I must confess, sir, that I loathed you taking the place of Roosevelt. I misjudged you badly. Since that time you, more than any other man, have saved Western civilisation.' Truman, for his part, once remarked that the only accolade he ever desired was: 'He did his damndest.'

# DWIGHT D. EISENHOWER

**Full name**   Dwight David Eisenhower, 1890–1969
**Born**   Denison, Texas, 14 October 1890, the third of 7 sons
**Parents**   David Jacob Eisenhower (1863–1942), mechanic, gas company manager, and Ida Elizabeth Stover Eisenhower (1885–1946). 7 sons
**Family lineage**   Swiss-German
**College**   US Military Academy, West Point, NY, BSc 1915
**Married**   1916, Mamie Geneva Doud Eisenhower (1896–1979), daughter of John Sheldon Doud, meat packer. 2 sons
**Occupation**   Professional soldier. World War I, temporary Lt Colonel (1918); World War II, General of the Army (1944); Supreme Commander, Allied Expeditionary Forces, 1943; Supreme Commander NATO, 1950
**Religious denomination**   Presbyterian
**Notable relationships**   His grandson, Dwight David Eisenhower II, married, 1968, Julie, daughter of Richard M. Nixon, 37th president
**Died**   From heart disease, at Washington, DC, 28 March 1969, aged 78
**Buried**   In the Place of Meditation in the Eisenhower Center, Abilene, Kansas

**Party** Republican **State represented** New York **Term of office** 20 January 1953 to 20 January 1961 **Age on taking office** 62 (his age on leaving office was 70, making him the oldest man to serve as president up to this time) **Presidential administrations** 42nd, 43rd **Congresses** 83rd, 84th, 85th, 86th

### ELECTION STATISTICS

| Candidates | Party | Electoral Vote (531) | States Won (8) | Popular Vote | % |
|---|---|---|---|---|---|
| 1952 D. Eisenhower | Repub | 442 | 39 | 33,936,234 | 55.2 |
| A. Stevenson | Dem | 89 | 9 | 27,314,992 | 44.5 |

```
1956 D. Eisenhower  Repub      457        41      35,590,472  57.4
     A. Stevenson   Dem        73*         7      26,031,322  42.0
          *One elector refused to vote for Stevenson.
```

```
1953   83rd   Senate  (96)      47 Repub  46 Dem     2 Oth 1 Vac
               House  (435)     221 Repub 212 Dem          1 Ind 1 Vac
          (The Administration gained control of both Houses.)

1955   84th   Senate  (96)      49 Dem    47 Repub
               House  (435)     230 Dem   203 Repub         2 Vacant
          (The Administration lost control of both Houses.)

1957   85th   Senate  (96)      49 Dem    47 Repub
               House  (435)     234 Dem   200 Repub         1 Vacant
1959   86th   Senate  (98)      64 Dem    34 Repub
               House  (436)     283 Dem   153 Repub
          (These were the largest majorities since the 75th Congress.)
```

NOTES

1  1960 18th Census: Total population: 179,323,175.
2  New States:  Alaska (49th) 1959 (January)
               Hawaii (50th) 1959 (August).

VICE PRESIDENT

36th Richard Milhous Nixon (California), subsequently 37th
president. Vice president, 20 January 1953 to 20 January 1961.
Nixon was the first vice president born in the twentieth century; the
second youngest (after Breckinridge). Eisenhower and Nixon were
the only Republican team ever re-elected.

---

The man who was to lead the most powerful armies the world has
ever seen, as well as the world's most powerful nation, was born in
1890 on part of what was still left of the American frontier where
Indian warfare still threatened. He grew up in Abilene, Kansas,
whose unmistakable mid-Western stamp he was to bear all his life.
'I come from the very heart of America,' he said at London's Guild
Hall in 1945.

Known as 'Ike' from his earliest days, he was brought up in
genteel poverty by a weak father and an extraordinarily strong
mother on the 'wrong side of the tracks' along with five surviving
brothers. After graduating from Abilene High School he intended

215

to work his way through college but a Kansas Senator arranged for him to sit a state test for entry to both Annapolis (the US Naval Academy), and West Point. He came first in the former test but was rejected because, at 20, he was over age. When the winner of the other test fell out he entered West Point in 1911. As a cadet he marched in Woodrow Wilson's Inaugural Parade in 1913.

At West Point he was an average student in the Class of 1915 — but, since this class is a West Point legend, this was quite an achievement: 59 of its members became generals; two, Eisenhower and Omar Bradley, were to attain five star rank. He graduated with a 'clean sleeve' that is with no rank, following numerous infractions of the rules of conduct and of dress. He had, however, learned to play an excellent hand of poker and he had played a lot of football. A knee injury sustained in tackling the legendary Jim Thorpe ended his footballing career and nearly changed the course of history for, following another accident when riding, the army's doctors were reluctant to recommend him for a commission. On his first tour of duty at Fort Sam Houston in Texas, 2nd Lt Eisenhower first met his future wife Mamie Doud. They were to be married for fifty-two years.

He spent the war of 1917–18 as a training officer at Gettysburg — 'The war passed me by' — rising to the rank of temporary lieutenant colonel. He reverted to captain in 1920 and it took him another sixteen peacetime years to attain his full lieutenant colonelcy. He served in Panama from 1922–4 before graduating first in his class from the Army Staff College in 1926. He then toured France and helped to write a book on the First World War battlefields. The turning point in his career came in 1929–33. First he served in the office of the Assistant Secretary of War and then in that of the Army Chief of Staff, General Douglas MacArthur. He accompanied the latter to the Philippines (1935–40) as Assistant Military Adviser. During this assignment he obtained the only pilot's licence earned by an American president and first came to the attention of the future World War II Chief of Staff, General George C. Marshall. He was to be particularly impressed by Lt-Col Eisenhower's brilliant organisation of the US Army's 'war games' in 1941.

Thereafter Ike's rise — always under Marshall's watchful eye — was without parallel in the annals of the US Army. A lieutenant colonel in March 1941, within twenty-three months he was the holder of the highest post the American Armed Services could then bestow, as Commanding General of the European Theatre (June 1942), and a (temporary) full general. He reached five star rank in December 1944. Eisenhower had overall responsibility for 'Operation Torch', the allied landings in North Africa which destroyed the Axis there by May 1943. This was the first time that he had ever commanded troops in the field (and actual battle operations were entrusted to the British general, Alexander), but he gained a richly deserved reputation and an honorary British GCB. Following the success of his 'Operation Husky' (July 1943), against 'the soft underbelly of Europe' in Sicily, Sardinia and the Italian mainland, Eisenhower was appointed Supreme Commander of 'Operation Overlord' (December 1943), the allied cross-Channel invasion of Hitler's Fortress Europe. On 5 June 1944 he took the decision — the most momentous in the war to date — to launch the invasion on the following day. In September 1944, following the breakout from the beachhead areas, Eisenhower assumed direct command (from General Bernard Montgomery), of all the allied forces. The German surrender took place at Eisenhower's head-quarters in Rheims on 7 May 1945.

Briefly in 1945 Eisenhower commanded the American zone of occupation in Germany before succeeding Marshall as Chief of Staff in Washington (1945–8). He wrote his best-selling *Crusader in Europe* and refused nomination by both political parties. He resigned in 1948 to become President of Columbia University, New York. He was called out of retirement by President Truman to assume command of the forces of the North Atlantic Treaty Organisation. In 1952 he consented to become a Republican presidential candidate and he was nominated on the first ballot. With the slogan 'I like Ike' the GOP won its first presidential election for twenty-four years.

The 10th general to be elected president, Eisenhower, a political greenhorn, brought to the presidency techniques he had learned in the army. He set up a firm chain of command and delegated his responsibilities to trusted subordinates such as Secretary of State John Foster Dulles, Secretary of the Treasury George Humphrey and, especially, his presidential aide, Sherman Adams. As a result his presidency always lacked the firm personal imprint of a Roosevelt or a Truman. 'Leadership,' he said, 'is the ability to decide what is to be done and then to get others to want to do it.' It did not involve concern with the minutiae of government. He also brought an essentially conservative philosophy embodied in a

217

domestic programme which he later labelled 'Dynamic Conservatism' or 'Modern Republicanism'. The Federal budget was to be balanced in three of his eight years — 'fiscal responsibility' was one of his watchwords. Yet this administration was to pass (in 1957) — with Democratic help in the Senate — the first civil rights legislation for eighty-two years — 'There must be no second class citizens in this country.' (Blacks in the South were still discriminated against and the legislation was aimed to bring about equal voting rights. A commission had found that only 1 ½ million of 6 million blacks eligible to vote did so. In Mississippi only 8% of those eligible voted.) The national minimum wage was increased, and unemployment insurance and Social Security were extended to millions of low-income families. Where it could be done, governmental decentralisation was emphasised with the Federal government co-operating with local government and private enterprise to provide, for example, power, schools and inter-state highways. As the desegregation of schools began following the Supreme Court's decision in the case of *Brown* v *Topeka* (1954), Eisenhower was forced to send troops into Little Rock, Arkansas, in 1957 to ensure compliance with the orders of a Federal court. He also ordered the complete desegregation of the armed forces.

But his most pressing problems concerned foreign affairs. He fulfilled a campaign pledge by visiting troops in the Korean front line in December 1952, shortly before an armistice concluded the conflict (1953). Eisenhower was very proud of the fact that thereafter not a single American soldier lost his life in action during the rest of his administration. In 1954 he was instrumental in taking the USA into the anti-Communist South East Asia Treaty Organisation.

Stalin's death in 1953 led to a reduction of tension between East and West and Eisenhower seized the opportunity to try to get agreement on nuclear arms limitations and testing. His proposals to the United Nations for an 'Atoms for Peace' programme, to provide atomic energy in developing countries, led to the creation of the International Atomic Energy Authority.

He met with French, Russian and British heads of state at Geneva in 1955 — the first summit conference since Potsdam — but the 'spirit of Geneva' soon evaporated when the Russians invaded Hungary (1956), and inaugurated the space age with the launching of the first earth satellite (4 October 1957). Eisenhower's response was to establish the National Aeronautics and Space

Administration (1958), and to increase defence spending (though not enough for his critics), and foreign aid.

In 1956 he had joined with Russia and the United Nations in condemning the joint Franco-British-Israeli attack on Egypt. In 1957 he promulgated the 'Eisenhower Doctrine' committing US aid to Middle Eastern countries against communism. The following year saw America stiffening the resistance of Nationalist China against the Chinese Communist's bombardment of the offshore islands of Matsu and Quemoy.

Seeking *détente* by personal diplomacy Eisenhower invited Soviet Premier Nikita Kruschev to tour the USA in 1959. In 1960, following the shooting down of an American U2 reconnaissance aircraft over Russia, Eisenhower's reciprocal visit was cancelled. In the last full year of his presidency grave events cast ominous shadows on three continents: in Laos; in the Congo (Zaire); and in Cuba, with which American diplomatic relations were broken off in January 1961.

Americans meanwhile had responded warmly to their grand-father-figure president who had suffered one heart attack and undergone one operation during his first term. He was re-elected in 1956 (the year of the twin crises in Hungary and Suez) in the most one-sided presidential election since 1936, even breaking into the solid Democratic South. The Republicans, however, were not so popular: they had lost control of Congress in 1954 (as a result of recession and unemployment) and in 1956 Eisenhower became the first president since Zachary Taylor, 108 years previously, to be elected without carrying at least one house for his party.

There was no mandate for Republicanism in 1956. During 'Ike's second recession', there was a slump in 1957–8, his popularity fell sharply and in the 1958 mid-term elections the Republicans suffered further disasters. (Thereafter Ike had no choice but to get along with the Democrats and Senator Lyndon B. Johnson, Democratic majority leader, was known as the second most powerful man in Washington.) In 1958 Sherman Adams was forced to resign over a political scandal; in 1959 John Foster Dulles died — and Ike was deprived of his two most trusted advisers. Three major onslaughts of illness in two years — in 1957 Eisenhower suffered a mild stroke — placed a considerable burden on vice president Nixon (whom Eisenhower had only reluctantly agreed to endorse for a second term). He deputised for the ailing president at home and abroad and he was kept fully apprised of all important policy decisions in both domestic and international affairs.

In a Farewell Address (17 January 1961) Eisenhower warned his audience against 'the acquisition of unwarranted influence, whether sought or unsought, . . . by the (US) military-industrial complex . . .' and of the expansion of communism. He believed, however, that the nation was strong in the face of danger: 'America today is the strongest, the most influential and the most productive nation in the world.'

In 1966, after his retirement, he composed, 'from the top of my head', twenty-three achievements of his administration. These ranged from the statehood of Alaska and Hawaii and the building of the St Lawrence Seaway, to the prevention of Communist efforts to dominate Iran, Guatemala, the Lebanon, Formosa, and Indochina. (In Iran, the Shah was forced to flee the country in 1953 and the CIA prepared and paid for a counter-coup which restored the Shah — and established a partnership upon which US policy in the Middle East was to rest until the late 1970s. In Indochina, it had been Eisenhower's policy, with his 'domino theory', to 'draw the line' to save South East Asia — this later resulted in US involvement in Vietnam.) They ranged from the initiation of a strong ballistic-missile programme to goodwill journeys to more than a score of nations — 'All this with a Congress controlled by the opposition for six years, the other two having only a nominal Republican majority.'

Already, however, the criticism of Eisenhower had begun. It was argued that his streamlining and institutionalising of the presidency, though useful when he was ill, had isolated the president from decision-making; that he had spent too much time on the golf course during 'eight long years of golfing and goofing'. (He became the only president to hole-in-one, in 1968.) His presidency, it has been said, was a disappointment in that Eisenhower failed to give sufficient lead — he was described as 'the bland leading the bland' — in tackling some of the crucial developments of the following decade which first emerged during his administration, including the space race, American involvement in Indo-China, civil rights agitation and *détente*; that he 'benignly ruled' over the 'Great Postponement'. On the other hand it can be argued that he brought to America a sense of calm and rationality after the prolonged crisis years under Roosevelt and Truman and the perilous era of McCarthyism; and, that in the perspective of recent history, he appears a wise and effective leader. Certainly he proved to be a more competent president than his fellow West Pointer, Ulysses S. Grant, the only other Republican ever to serve two full terms.

One of the finest tributes to General Dwight D. Eisenhower is to be found in England, on a brass plaque in the command room at Bushy Park, Teddington, where 'Operation Overlord' was planned. It says simply: 'A great man passed this way in the defence of freedom.'

# JOHN F. KENNEDY

**Full name**  John Fitzgerald Kennedy, 1917–63
**Born**  83 Beals Street, Brookline, Mass, 29 May 1917. The second of 9 children
**Parents**  Joseph Patrick Kennedy (1888–1969), property owner, financier, banker, diplomat, and Rose Fitzgerald Kennedy (1890–    ). 5 daughters, 4 sons
**Family lineage**  Irish
**College**  Princeton University, Princeton, NJ (1935–36); Harvard University, Cambridge, Mass, (1936–40), BSc 1940; Stanford University Graduate School of Business Administration, Palo Alto, California (1940)
**Married**  1953, Jacqueline Lee Bouvier Kennedy (b 1929), daughter of John Vernon Bouvier III, stockbroker. 2 sons, 1 daughter (1 stillborn daughter). Mrs Kennedy remarried subsequently (1968) Aristotle Socrates Onassis
**Occupation**  World War II, Lieutenant, USN; journalist; member of US House of Representatives, 1947–53; US Senator, 1953–60
**Religious denomination**  Roman Catholic
**Notable relationships**  None
**Died**  From assassination by rifle shot, Dallas, Texas, 22 November 1963, aged 46
**Buried**  In the Arlington National Cemetery, Arlington, Virginia

**Party** Democratic **State represented** Massachusetts **Term of office** 20 January 1961 to 22 November 1963 (2 years, 306 days) **Age on taking office** 43 (the youngest man elected to the presidency) **Presidential administration** 44th **Congresses** 87th, 88th

### 1960 ELECTION

| Candidates | Party | Electoral Vote (537) | States Won (50) | Popular Vote | % |
|---|---|---|---|---|---|
| J. Kennedy | Dem | 303 | 22 | 34,227,096 | 49.7* |
| R. Nixon | Repub | 219 | 26 | 34,108,546 | 49.5 |
| H. Byrd | Dem | 15 | 2 | 116,248 | — |

CONGRESS

| 1961 | 87th | Senate (100) | 64 Dem | 36 Repub | |
|------|------|--------------|--------|----------|-----------|
| | | House (437) | 261 Dem | 176 Repub | |
| 1963 | 88th | Senate (100) | 67 Dem | 33 Repub | |
| | | House (435) | 257 Dem | 177 Repub | 1 Vacancy |

NOTE

Constitutional Amendment: XXIII (April 1961): granted the franchise to resident citizens of Washington, DC.

VICE PRESIDENT

37th Lyndon Baines Johnson, subsequently 36th president. Term of office: 20 January 1961 to 22 November 1963.

---

From a blizzard-bound Washington on 20 January 1961 the word went forth '. . . The torch has been passed to a new generation of Americans . . . Let every nation know, whether it wishes us well or ill, that we shall pay any price, bear any burden, meet any hardship, support any friend, oppose any foè to assure the survival and the success of liberty . . . All this will not be finished in the first one hundred days. Nor will it be finished in the first one thousand days, nor in the life of this Administration, nor even perhaps in our lifetime on this planet. But let us begin . . . And so, my fellow Americans, ask not what your country can do for you; ask what you can do for your country . . .' These stirring words were spoken by the first American president to be born in the twentieth century. At 43 he was the youngest man ever to be elected president and, in the context of the world's leaders, he seemed even younger. He succeeded a septuagenarian; Konrad Adenauer of West Germany was 85; Nikita Kruschev and Harold MacMillan both 67; de Gaulle was 71; Nehru 72; and Mao Tse Tung was 68.

The new president was tall, incredibly handsome, exceptionally articulate and photogenic and he — and his beautiful and socially prominent young wife, Jacqueline Bouvier Kennedy — had 'style'. With the Inauguration, it has been said, 'Camelot began' and the White House became the 'Kennedy Court'. Jackie had cried when

223

she had first seen the Eisenhower White House but it had been meticulously refurbished and the State Rooms were soon to be the setting for scenes of grace, culture, *haute cuisine*, high fashion and intellectual stimulation.

John Fitzgerald Kennedy was born in a Boston suburb. Both his grandfathers were the sons of Irish immigrants who had fled from the famine in the 1840s; both had become prominent in Massachusetts politics. P. J. Kennedy, a saloon keeper, had sat in both houses of the legislature; John F. 'Honey Fitz' Fitzgerald had been mayor of Boston.

Young John had grown up in a political atmosphere. His father had been an ardent supporter of F.D.R., who had appointed him chairman of the Securities and Exchange Commission, and then Ambassador to the Court of St James's. He had been reared in a large, closely-knit family in which his mother, a devoted Roman Catholic, had instilled a deep sense of religious obligation. In 1926 the family moved to New York to be near their father's Wall Street headquarters, though they spent their summers at Hyannisport on Cape Cod.

Kennedy spent only one year in a Catholic school before entering the exclusive Choate School at Wallingford, Connecticut. He spent the summer of 1935 at the London School of Economics where he contracted jaundice, a severe recurrence of which, in 1936, ended his career at Princeton University. In 1936 he joined his elder brother Joseph at Harvard where, in his sophomore year, he suffered the spinal injury (at football) that dogged him for the rest of his life. He majored in political science, developing his senior's thesis into his first book, a study of Britain's appeasement of Hitler, *Why England Slept* (1940). He graduated *cum laude* in 1940.

He then spent six months studying business administration before touring South America; and then, but only after extensive medical treatment, he became an Ensign in the Navy. (He was the first of five consecutive naval presidents.) Assigned to a motor torpedo boat squadron as a Lieutenant (jg), his boat, PT 109, was sunk by a Japanese destroyer off the Solomon Islands on 2 August 1943. For his bravery in saving the lives of several crew members during fifteen hours in the water — he towed one man to the safety of a nearby island holding the rope of his life-jacket in his teeth — he was awarded the Purple Heart and the Navy and Marine Corps Medal. Whilst recuperating in hospital the news came that his brother Joe, a Navy flier, had been shot down over the English

Channel. With it came the realisation that he was now left to carry on the Kennedy's political heritage.

He finished the war as an instructor and then went into journalism. As a Hearst employee he attended the opening of the United Nations in San Francisco. He did a tour as a foreign correspondent in Europe for the International News Service where he covered the Potsdam Conference and the British General Election of 1945. Then in 1946, at the age of 28, he was returned to the US House of Representatives as Congressman from the Massachusetts 11th Congressional District; and he was re-elected in 1948 and 1950. In 1952 he ran for the Senate against the incumbent Massachusetts Republican Senator, Henry Cabot Lodge. Although there was a Republican landslide in that year, Kennedy defeated Lodge by over 70,000 votes thanks largely to a whirlwind campaign waged by the Kennedy clan.

In his eight years as a Senator he gained a wealth of experience on a number of major committees including the prestigious Senate Foreign Relations Committee and the Joint Economic Committee. His voting record was that of a moderate liberal whose liberalism had a 'National' vein — though his critics have noted that he joined in the fashionable anti-communist hue-and-cry during the Truman era and that his liberalism became more prominent with his presidential ambitions.

During his second term in the Senate he underwent two critical spinal operations and the last rites were administered to him in October 1954. He used his convalescence to compose *Profiles in Courage*, the short studies of eight morally courageous Senators that won the 1957 Pulitzer Prize.

Kennedy first came to national prominence at the Democratic National Convention in Chicago in 1956 when a sudden groundswell put him into (unsuccessful) contention with Estes Kefauver for the vice-presidential position on the Adlai Stevenson ticket. The Democratic defeat in that year, plus Kennedy's revealed charm and professional flair, meant that he now became the Democrat's bright hope for 1960, and his position was enhanced after his re-election to the Senate in 1958 with a record-breaking 869,000 majority. At the Democratic National Convention in 1960 he was nominated on the first ballot with his chief rival, Senator Lyndon B. Johnson of Texas, as his running-mate. In his acceptance speech he offered Americans a set of challenges, a 'New Frontier' of opportunities — and unknown perils.

Kennedy won the 1960 election by the narrowest-ever popular majority in the closest election since 1888. He polled only some 120,000 popular votes more than his opponent, Richard M. Nixon, out of a total of 69 million. This majority of less than 0.2 of 1% was, however, converted into a respectable majority in the Electoral College. (Later analyses suggested that Kennedy's Catholicism had cost 1.5 million votes; and that if 9,000 voters in Missouri and Illinois, where there were rumours of 'irregularities', had voted for Nixon, Kennedy would have lost.) A vital factor in his victory was probably the first of four nationally televised debates between the candidates, which reached 4 out of 5 voters, revealed Kennedy's telegenic qualities, and made him as well-known as his opponent.

There was to be no 'tail-coat' effect for the Democratic party though, which lost 20 House and two Senate seats; and throughout his Administration the president was to be more popular in the nation at large, and abroad, than he was on Capitol Hill where a coalition of Southern Democrats and Northern Republicans conspired to put a brake on his legislative programme. This was to be master-minded by a cabinet of 'Young Turks' — their average age was 47 — the Kennedy 'whizz kids'. Many, like Robert McNamara of Fords, had been drawn from the top echelons of industry, or, like Arthur Schlesinger Jr, from the universities. The president's 35-year old brother, Robert, was appointed Attorney General.

J.F.K. inherited an economic recession and 7% unemployment. Though a conservative Congress blocked 172 of the Administration's 355 measures in 1961, a great deal of social legislation was passed, in the traditions of the New Deal and the Fair Deal, covering social security, unemployment and minimum wage benefits, and housing. In his '1,000 Days' Kennedy was to bombard Congress with an unprecedented number of legislative requests — 1,054; for he believed that proposals had to be put into the pipe-line if laws were to emerge. His successor was to inherit (and partially untangle), a legislative 'logjam' and Kennedy has been accused of not having pressurised Congress sufficiently over domestic issues.

He achieved a major triumph in 1962 with the Trade Expansion Act which gave the president tariff-cutting powers (to be used as a weapon against the EEC); and in the same year he helped avert a steel strike and a threatened rise in steel prices. He aided industry with a 7% tax credit scheme for plant modernisation and expansion. To get the economy moving he implemented a $10 billion tax cut that, by the end of 1963, had produced 2¾ million new jobs and 16% growth in output.

During the 1962 mid-term elections he campaigned strongly for liberal Democratic candidates and helped to check the traditional anti-Administration swing but not continued domestic legislative failures. The only proposals for major Federal spending that did not meet with opposition were defence and space. Proposals for 'Medicare' for the over-65s were dismissed as 'socialised medicine'.

The major domestic issue was fast-becoming Civil Rights. Arguably, this Administration did more to improve the lot of the blacks than any before but, for many, who forgot that politics is the 'art of the possible', progress was not swift enough. Kennedy expressed the dilemma thus when he said that black rights could be advanced '. . . Only in a way that will maintain a consensus of national opinion.' Blacks were appointed to major diplomatic, administrative and judicial positions. A Commission was established on Equal Employment Opportunities; and the continuing de-segregation of Southern schools was pursued (though there were only 13,000 blacks in white schools in 1963). Robert Kennedy was very active in the Department of Justice on behalf of the black cause. All this took place against a background of mounting tension, of 'freedom riders', of activist leaders, of growing violence; — 2 men died and 375 were injured securing the enrolment of negro James Meredith at the University of Mississippi. In support of Kennedy's (1962) Civil Rights Bill (stalled in Congress), 200,000 marched on Washington in August 1963 and, in a model of non-violent behaviour, listened spell-bound to the 'dreams' of Martin Luther King. 'This policy could cost me the (1964) election but we're not turning back,' said a president whose very name had become anathema in the Deep South.

In foreign affairs, where he had accused the Republicans of losing America's global pre-eminence, the Administration got away to a bad start in April 1961 over the 'Bay of Pigs' affair in Cuba (even though this hare-brained scheme of the CIA was inherited from the previous administration). Unfortunately this disaster was to colour all his subsequent thinking and to lead to over-reaction in future crises. As he himself put it in the summer of 1961, '. . . I think he (sc Kruschev) thought that anyone who was so young and inexperienced as to get into that mess could be taken . . . If he thinks I'm inexperienced and have no guts, until we remove those ideas we won't get anywhere . . .'

In June 1961, only six weeks after the Cuban fiasco, J.F.K. and Kruschev met at the Vienna summit. Kennedy felt that he was negotiating from a position of weakness both in a psychological and a physical sense. He had been horrified to discover in 1961 that the US was militarily naked, with only 11 combat-ready divisions, and already he had begun that build-up of conventional forces that would lengthen the fuse of conventional warfare. The American 'credibility gap' had apparently been widened by the 'space gap' in April 1961 when the Russian Yuri Gagarin in *Vostock I* had become the first man in space. Ignoring both the greater number and the greater sophistication of US satellites and rocketry Kennedy had asked Congress, in May, for $24 billion to fund 'Project Apollo' with the object of putting an American on the moon before the end of the decade.

At Vienna Kruschev dropped a bomb-shell over Berlin (or merely set out to test Kennedy), by demanding the legal recognition of divided Germany, the internationalisation of Berlin and East German (DDR) control of access to it. The alternative would be a separate Russian peace treaty with the DDR whose existence the US did not even recognise. To emphasise the point, on 13 August a concrete and barbed-wire 'wall' was first erected between East and West Berlin. Though the 'crisis' was to peter out, this was not before Kennedy had called up the reservists — and begun the greatest arms race in history which, by October 1962, had already given the US a 3:1 superiority in ballistic missiles.

In that same month the installation of Soviet missiles in Cuba, only 90 miles from the soft underbelly of America, was revealed by U2 reconnaissance aircraft. For several days in October the two super powers stood eyeball to eyeball and the world held its breath. Kennedy ordered a naval quarantine of Cuba to keep out further Russian cargoes and on 22 October warned Kruschev that any missile attacks anywhere in the Western hemisphere would be followed by a 'full retaliatory response' upon the Soviet Union. On 24 October Russian ships halted in mid-ocean; on 28 October it was announced that the missiles were to be removed — a task that was completed by 19 November. In December Kruschev remarked wryly that the 'American paper tiger . . . had atomic teeth'.

Thereafter a 'thaw' set in in the 'cold war'. A partial Nuclear Test Ban Treaty was ratified by Russia, Great Britain and the USA in September 1963 banning nuclear tests in the atmosphere, under water and in space. A 'hot line' — a direct communications line — was established between Moscow and Washington, via London, Stockholm and Helsinki, for at the height of the October 1962 crisis it had taken four hours for messages to be exchanged. In October 1963 the US agreed to sell Russia $250 million of surplus wheat. Lest his actions should be misinterpreted, Kennedy took the opportunity during a visit to West Berlin in 1963 to demonstrate his identification with the people of West Berlin when he proclaimed, 'Ich bin ein Berliner.'

In his relations with the rest of the world Kennedy continued to struggle for peace and against communism. He failed to persuade Congress to increase spending on foreign aid, but did succeed in obtaining $30 million to establish the Peace Corps (1961). By 1964 10,000 young American volunteers were working in 46 countries on projects ranging from agriculture to literacy. The 1961 proposals for an 'Alliance for Progress' between the US and Latin American countries, though well-intentioned, eventually collapsed in an atmosphere of 'gringo' imperialism. In Black Africa, Kennedy supported the United Nations in the Congo operation that was designed to prevent the secession of Moishe Tshombe's Katanga province, a possible Russian base in the heart of Africa. His relations with his European allies proved to be as fraught as any other. He failed to get agreement on a multilateral European nuclear force — France preferring its independent 'force de frappe' — and had to settle instead for the Nassau Agreement (1962) with British premier Harold Macmillan (who once twitted Kennedy about the threat of 'annihilation without representation'), by which American Polaris missiles with British warheads were to become part of NATO's nuclear force. Kennedy's grandiose scheme for a federated states of Western Europe, his 'Grand Design', which involved British entry into the Common Market, was blocked by de Gaulle (1963) who regarded Britain as an American Trojan horse.

In South East Asia Kennedy was determined to 'hold the line', the unofficial Eisenhower 'line' against communism which had never been given Congressional sanction, or support, or issued as an Executive Order. 'We have a problem in trying to make our power credible and Vietnam looks like the place,' he said. By October 1962 15,000 US 'advisers' were supporting the corrupt, aristocratic, Catholic, landlord régime of President Ngo Dinh

Diem in Saigon against the threat from Hanoi. The alternative, argued the president, was that '. . . we pull back our defenses to San Francisco'. He was receiving warnings that Vietnam might yet prove a quagmire, but this was at a time (1963) when the grand total of US combat deaths there stood at seventy.

In the autumn of 1963 the pre-election campaign took Kennedy to Texas to do some Democratic fence-mending. His tour took him to Dallas, a city with a strong, rightwing, extremist tradition. As the presidential motorcade passed the Texas School Book Depository, Kennedy was shot in the head. He was pronounced dead shortly afterwards at 1pm on 22 November 1963. Within an hour Lee Harvey Oswald was arrested. He was a 24-year-old ex-marine marksman and self-styled anarchist, who had defected to Russia, where he had lived for three years and married a Russian girl. Later he was shot by a Dallas nightclub owner, Jack Ruby, in front of TV cameras in Dallas jail.

A massive investigation — hurried and flawed, say its critics, because of the need to complete it before the 1964 election — headed by Chief Justice Earl Warren, announced that John F. Kennedy had been killed by a single assassin. Ever since that date 'conspiracy' theories have abounded linking Oswald, or 'persons unknown', with the Cubans, or the KGB, or the Mafia, or even the CIA. Ballistic, and other 'evidence', has also been put forward to suggest that more than one gunman was involved.

'The world's loss', said Theodore Sorensen, 'is the loss of what might have been,' as the youngest president to die was laid to rest in Arlington National Cemetry between a still-born daughter (1956) and his son Patrick (died 1963).

The secular beatification that followed in the emotion generated by Dallas has helped to contribute to the fact that the 'Kennedy legend' has been surprisingly little tarnished since 1963. The rich playboy patrician who, it has been argued, symbolises the days before the Fall, has emerged relatively unscathed from character-assassination attempts. No direct evidence has linked him to the 'bugging' of political opponents on the grand scale; or to wild CIA schemes to kill Fidel Castro of Cuba; or to the assassination of President Ngo Dinh Diem of Saigon. Not even supported evidence of his womanising has produced any major criticism of J.F.K. (Indeed, to date, criticism has appeared to be almost sacrilegious.) However, in the wake of some events in the presidencies of Johnson and Nixon, the knives are being sharpened behind the scenes and doubts are beginning to be cast on some of the claims that have been made on his behalf by less than disinterested biographers.

# LYNDON B. JOHNSON

**Full name** Lyndon Baines Johnson, 1908–73
**Born** Near Stonewall, Gillespie County, Texas, 27 August 1908, the eldest of 5 children
**Parents** Sam Ealy Johnson (1877–1937), farmer, trader, railroad inspector, member of Texas State Legislature, and Rebekah Baines Johnson (1881–1958). 3 daughters, 2 sons
**Family lineage** English
**College** Southwest Texas State Teachers College, San Marcos, Texas, BSc 1930. Georgetown University Law School, Washington, DC 1934–5
**Married** 1934, Claudia 'Lady Bird' Alta Taylor Johnson (b 1912) daughter of Thomas Jefferson Taylor, storekeeper, rancher. 2 daughters
**Occupation** Teacher; political secretary; Texas Director of National Youth Administration, 1935–7; member of US House of Representatives, 1937–49; World War II, Lt Commander, USN (1942); US Senator, 1949–61; vice president, 1961–3
**Religious denomination** Disciples of Christ
**Notable relationships** His paternal grandmother was the niece of J. W. Bunton, signatory of the Texas Declaration of Independence and Constitution, a hero of the Battle of San Jacinto, 1836
**Died** From a heart attack, San Antonio, Texas, 22 January 1973, aged 64
**Buried** On the L.B.J. Ranch, Stonewall, Texas

**Party** Democratic **State represented** Texas **Term of office** 22 November 1963 to 20 January 1969 (he served the unexpired portion of his predecessor and one full term) **Age on taking office** 55 **Presidential administrations** 44th (cont), 45th **Congresses** (88th), 89th, 90th

| Candidates | Party | Electoral Vote (538) | States Won (50)* | Popular Vote | % |
|---|---|---|---|---|---|
| L. Johnson | Dem | 486 | 44* | 43,167,895 | 61.1 |
| B. Goldwater | Repub | 52 | 6 | 27,146,969 | 38.5 |

*Plus Washington DC

## CONGRESS

| 1965 | 89th | Senate (100) | 68 Dem | 32 Repub |
|---|---|---|---|---|
| | | House (435) | 295 Dem | 140 Repub |
| 1967 | 90th | Senate (100) | 64 Dem | 36 Repub |
| | | House (435) | 248 Dem | 187 Repub |

## NOTES

1 Constitutional Amendment: XXIV (February 1964) banned the Poll Tax as a voting requirement in Federal elections.

2 Constitutional Amendment: XXV (February 1967) rationalised the procedures in relation to 'the removal of the president from office or of his death or resignation'; made provision for the period of a president's disability; and made provision for the appointment of a new vice president. (For the 17th time there was no vice president between 1963–5. If Johnson had died in office, under the existing constitutional provisions he would have been succeeded by the House Speaker, who was 72, and then the President of the Senate, who was 86. The new procedures first went into operation in 1973 and 1974.)

## VICE PRESIDENT

38th Hubert Horatio Humphrey (Minnesota), 1911–78; state politician; mayor of Minneapolis, 1945, 1947; US Senator, 1948–65; vice president, 20 January 1965 to 20 January 1969; subsequently college professor, 1969–70; US Senator, 1970–8.

---

The presidential oath was administered aboard the presidential jet *Air Force One* at Love Field, Dallas, Texas, on the afternoon of 22 November 1963 by Sarah T. Hughes, US District Judge for the Northern District of Texas. At the same time a 'be alert' signal was flashed to every American base round the world. The Signal Corps 'bagman' with his nuclear trigger codes was moved close to the new president. 'Let's get this plane back to Washington,' he said. The nation was stunned by the fourth presidential assassination in its history but it was not paralysed. Lyndon Baines Johnson had been an active vice president, he had enjoyed good relations with President Kennedy, and, unlike Truman, he was exceptionally well-informed when a 'heart-beat' no longer separated him from the presidency.

Johnson was America's first genuinely Southern president since Andrew Jackson. He had been born on his father's farm in South West Texas but raised in nearby Johnson City (pop 600), which had been founded by his paternal grandfather, a Confederate veteran. He graduated from the local high school in 1924 and then did various jobs in California and Texas for some three years. He entered South West Texas State Teachers College in 1927, paying his way by working part-time, before graduating in 1930. He taught briefly and then entered politics.

He campaigned for Texas Congressman R. M. Kleberg who then took him to Washington as his secretary. Here he became a protegé of his father's old friend, Sam Rayburn, the House Majority Leader, who was rising fast to the Speaker's Chair, and of President Roosevelt himself — 'He was a daddy to me,' Johnson would say later. In September 1934 he met Claudia Taylor, the daughter of a well-to-do Texan, and they were married in November. He attended law school briefly but did not graduate.

Johnson then became the Texas director of the New Deal's National Youth Administration in 1935 and over the next two years developed what was regarded as a model programme. He entered the House in 1937, picking up an unexpired term, having campaigned on a New Deal platform. Re-elected in 1938 he was to serve for the next five terms with a short break for war service. Johnson was the first member of the House to volunteer for active service. He rose to the rank of Lt Commander, served as a special presidential emissary to Australia and New Zealand, and gained a Silver Star following a hazardous flying operation over New Guinea. He was then recalled to Washington in 1942 with all other Congressmen, who were now forbidden to serve in the armed forces.

In 1949 he entered the Senate and served on the prestigious Armed Services and Appropriations Committee. He became majority whip in 1951 (the youngest ever), Senate Minority Leader in 1953 and then, in 1955, Democratic floor leader, that is Majority leader, the youngest man ever to hold this influential position in either party. He suffered a severe heart attack in July 1955 but appeared to make an excellent recovery.

He soon earned the reputation for getting things done. Even his opponents were impressed by this powerful legal craftsman who seemed to stir up the minimum of controversy. He avoided doctrinaire positions and worked with the Eisenhower Republican Administration in the national interest, co-operating to secure the passage of national security measures and important Civil Rights legislation. 'If you're in an airplane flying somewhere you don't run up to the cockpit and attack the pilot,' he said. 'Mr. Eisenhower is the only President we've got.' Defeated for the presidential nomination in 1960, he accepted the vice presidential rôle on the Kennedy ticket. He campaigned strenuously in the South where Kennedy was weakest and made a signal contribution to the ticket's narrow victory.

A little over one thousand days later Johnson stood before the American people as their 36th president. 'I will do my best. That is all I can do. I ask for your help — and God's.' Addressing Congress he recalled his predecessor's dreams for the nation: '. . . All my fellow Americans, let us continue.' Johnson was clearly not a Kennedy; though only ten years older than J.F.K., they were worlds apart. The tall (at 6ft 3in the second tallest president), powerful, self-made man, with his drawling Texan 'hog-calling' oratory of the 'howdy, you-all', type, with an earthiness in speech and demeanour, who went in for old-fashioned baby-kissing and 'pressing the flesh', was a far cry from the 'Ivy League' grace and sophistication of the Kennedys. Many found him patronising, too emotional, too 'corny'. But the man was what he was; a provincial American who had known the pinch of rural poverty; a populist New Dealer who understood ordinary people both white and black.

He 'continued' with a vengeance. Capitalising upon the nation's grief he brought his considerable legislative skills to bear on Congress. In a whirlwind of White House activity which invites comparison with F.D.R.'s '100 days', 'Mr Manoeuvre' coaxed, flattered, wheedled, prodded and arm-twisted, and called-in political debts of long-standing, in order to ensure the passage of an impressive number of Kennedy initiatives that had been bottled up for months. He 'Johnsonised' or 'Texanised' his inherited régime and burned the L.B.J. brand on it — too much so for some people who complained about the 'one man rodeo'. So impressive was his initial constructive leadership (and so extreme the right-wards lurch of the 'GOP' and Goldwater), that eleven months later he was elected in his own right — 'All the way with L.B.J.' — with the largest plurality in American history, which was accompanied by the largest Democratic majorities since 1937. Moreover, many new Congressmen were liberal Democrats and the days of the Southern Democrat-conservative Republican coalition were numbered. This election also allowed Johnson to shrug off the Kennedy mantle: Bobby Kennedy was rejected as vice president in 1964 in favour of Senator Hubert Humphrey of Minnesota. He was now his own man.

With the country united behind him — he had managed to win over a large part of the Republican business community — even Henry Ford voted for him — this 'consensuscrat' could begin to implement that programme at which he had hinted in his acceptance speech; 'This nation, this generation, this hour has man's first chance to build a great society where the meaning of man's life matches the marvels of man's labor.' The 'Great Society' objectives were outlined in January 1965. They included aid to education, urban renewal, the 'beautification' of the United States, regional development, attacks on crime and delinquency and the removal of every obstacle to the right to vote, as well as war on poverty.

There followed a rush of legislation such as America had not seen since the 1930s. Massive tax cuts marked the beginning of an attempt to relieve poverty by blanket stimulation of the economy. Then Congress was asked for $1 billion for an anti-poverty programme on behalf of America's 'forgotten fifth' living on less than $5,000 per year. (By 1968 Federal spending on aid to the poor had risen three-fold compared to 1960.) The 'Head Start' and 'Upward Bound' schemes offered pre-school and college courses for poor children. A domestic version of the Peace Corps, Volunteers for Service in America, was set up. An Education Act (1965) was the first general Federal aid to education law in American history. Johnson succeeded where Kennedy had failed with the Medical Care Act (1965), which offered 'medicare' for the aged and 'medicaid' for the poor though, increasingly, both sets of patients were referred to America's understaffed and underfinanced 'public' hospitals.

Much was done to beautify America. Federal funds were provided for recreational centres, slum clearance and the development of 'model' cities. 11 Conservation Bills went through Congress in 1968, including one to set up the Redwood National Park. Federal funds, and controls, were applied to traffic safety, food and drug labelling and credit operations, *inter alia*.

Johnson signed the 1965 Voting Rights Act in the President's Room in the Capitol where Lincoln had signed the bill freeing slaves in the Confederate forces. (Some spectacular results followed: Mississippi with 6% of its voting-age blacks registered in 1964 had a 60% registration by the spring of 1968.) The choice of venue was a tacit admission that this act, like the omnibus Civil Rights Act of 1964 which Johnson had also championed, was merely part of the too-long-delayed enabling legislation to implement the 13th, 14th and 15th Amendments of the post-civil-war era.

Johnson was to argue that, when he left office, 12.5 million had been lifted out of the 'poverty trap'. Unemployment had fallen to 3.3% and the average annual income had risen by $535. All this was true; but as early as June 1966 Gallup Polls showed that L.B.J.'s popularity stood at only 46% (the lowest since Truman), and in the mid-term elections there were significant Democratic losses. This opposition reflected not only (as with the New Deal), fears of 'socialist' legislation, but also the simple fact that, by this point, more money and energy was increasingly being spent on Vietnam than on the alleviation of domestic poverty, and that, clearly, there was a 'Law and Order' issue. The honeymoon was over long before Johnson virtually 'resigned' on 31 March 1968 when, he told an astonished TV audience: 'I shall not seek, and I will not accept, the nomination of my party for a second term as your President.' What should have gone down in American history as one of the most constructive Administrations of the twentieth century was being ruined by enormous problems at home and abroad: by race riots at home and by the escalation of the war in South East Asia.

It was ironic that an Administration that had done so much for the blacks should be torn apart by 'five long hot summers'. But, as the question of negro 'equal rights' was increasingly tackled, it was being overtaken by the issue of 'equal opportunities', an area where there was much covert discrimination and mounting frustration. The problem was now no longer one of seats in restaurants and on buses but of 'who gets the money?' Leadership of the black movement — the word 'black' replaced the ethnic term 'negro' in the mid-sixties because it carried an air of cultural and political militancy and rejection of the white man — increasingly passed out of the hands of moderates, like Martin Luther King, who favoured racial integration and still talked in terms of civil rights, into those of extremists. Men like Stokeley Carmichael, and later Rap Brown, of the 'Black Power' movement, favoured separatism. Others included Malcolm X (who was later to be killed by blacks), of the 'Black Muslims', and the 'Black Panthers' who believed in armed revolution.

Riots in Harlem, New York in July 1964, marked the start of violence; but the first massive riots occurred in the Watts district of Los Angeles in August 1965. These caused $45 million worth of damage and the loss of 34 lives. 1966 saw 7 killed in 42 cities; and in 1967, 46 died in Newark and Detroit as violence erupted in 128 cities. Following the assassination of Nobel Peace Prize Winner, Martin Luther King, in the spring of 1968, trouble in 168 cities caused $30 million worth of damage and 39 died. It reached three blocks from the White House and smoke from the negro ghetto hung over Capitol Hill. That summer, as 19 died in Cleveland, the unrest began to die down as leaderless and exhausted black communities began to count the cost of the self-inflicted damage. It was left to two black American athletes to raise their black-gloved fists in a near-final gesture of defiance at the 1968 Mexico Olympic Games. There was little, however, that Johnson could do about all this as the question of 'law and order' came home to roost on his Administration, for law enforcement was a state issue. But people who had grown used to the 'big Federalism' of the 'Great Society' found this difficult to accept.

Lyndon Baines Johnson has been vilified as the 'Vietnam President'. His two predecessors had committed the US to involvement in that area since 1954 though, by January 1964, there were only 23,000 American 'advisers' in South Vietnam. In August 1964 the US destroyers *Maddox* and *Turner Joy* were allegedly fired on by North Vietnamese torpedo boats in international waters in the Gulf of Tonkin. Congress produced the 'Tonkin Gulf Resolution' which declared that the United States was prepared 'to use force to help defend the freedom of South Vietnam'. Johnson, a non-elected president could not, in an election year, be the president 'who saw South East Asia go the way China went'. More than disturbed by the revelation of Communist China's nuclear capability in 1964, he firmly believed (like Kennedy), that unless America held the line '. . . All of South East Asia would fall like the proverbial Eisenhower row of dominoes.' In January 1965 'Operation Rolling Thunder' inaugurated a sustained programme of bombing in North Vietnam; and in March 3,500 US Marines were deployed under the command of General Westmoreland. The United States was now part of an (undeclared) Asian land war.

The next four years demonstrated that the US could neither force a settlement on North Vietnam nor, apparently, withdraw. It was tempting to attempt a 'firepower' solution by bombing the North back into the Stone Age — and the North was subjected to more bombing than Germany and Japan in World War II — but it had no major industrial centres to cripple. Not even a massive troop concentration — by 1968 there were 550,000 American ground troops in Vietnam — could achieve the desired effect. As the cost of the war soared to $60 million a day, as the casualty lists mounted — 'Hey! Hey! L.B.J.! How many kids did you kill today?' — as the news of draft (and race) riots shared the headlines with napalm, defoliation and CS gas — Johnson's America, his Great Consensus Society, fell apart. The scene was set for the dramatic announcement of 31 March 1968: firstly, to halt the bombing; secondly, not to run for another term.

He had fought an unwinnable war in Vietnam and he bears the responsibility for the first military defeat in American history. Moreover, America had been more divided over this war than over any other development since the Civil War. He had tried to fight the war without imposing the necessary taxation to pay for it and thus started that inflation which has debilitated the American economy ever since. Already he, who might have been seen as a second F. D. Roosevelt, is being written off as the 'worst president in American post-war history'.

239

# RICHARD M. NIXON

**Full name**   Richard Milhous Nixon (b 1913)
**Born**   Yorba Linda, California, 9 January 1913, the second of 5 sons
**Parents**   Frank Anthony Nixon (1878–1956) handyman, grocer, gas station operator, and Hannah Milhous Nixon (1885–1967). 5 sons
**Family lineage**   English-Scottish-Irish and English-Scottish-Irish-Welsh
**College**   Whittier College, Whittier, California, BA 1934, Duke University Law School, Durham, North Carolina, LLB 1937
**Married**   1940, Thelma Catherine 'Pat' Ryan Nixon (b 1912), daughter of William Ryan, miner, truck operator. 2 daughters
**Occupation**   Lawyer; World War II, Lt-Commander USN; member of US House of Representatives, 1947–51; US Senator, 1951–3; vice president, 1953–61
**Religious denomination**   Society of Friends
**Notable relationships**   Richard M. Nixon is 20th in descent from Edward III, King of England. He is distantly related to Presidents Taft and Hoover

**Party** Republican **State represented** New York **Term of office** 20 January 1969 to 9 August 1974 (resigned, the only president to do so) **Age on taking office** 56 **Presidential administrations** 46th, 47th **Congresses** 91st, 92nd, 93rd

ELECTION STATISTICS

| Candidates | Party | Electoral Vote (538) | States Won (50)* | Popular Vote | % |
|---|---|---|---|---|---|
| 1968 R. Nixon | Repub | 310 | 32 | 31,765,480 | 43.4 |
| H. Humphrey | Dem | 191 | 13* | 31,275,165 | 42.7 |
| G. Wallace | Am Ind | 46 | 5 | 9,906,473 | 13.5 |
| 1972 R. Nixon | Repub | 520 | 49 | 47,169,911 | 60.7 |
| G. McGovern | Dem | 17 | 1* | 29,170,383 | 37.5 |

*Plus Washington DC. In 1972 one electoral vote was cast for Hospers, 'Libertarian'. McGovern won Massachusetts.

| 1969 | 91st | Senate (100) | 57 Dem | 43 Repub | |
|------|------|--------------|--------|----------|--|
| | | House (435) | 244 Dem | 191 Repub | |
| 1971 | 92nd | Senate (100) | 54 Dem | 44 Repub | 2 Others |
| | | House (435) | 255 Dem | 179 Repub | 1 Vacant |
| 1973 | 93rd | Senate (100) | 57 Dem | 43 Repub | |
| | | House (435) | 242 Dem | 192 Repub | 1 Vacant |

(The opposition controlled Congress throughout.)

## NOTES

1 1970 19th Census. Total population: 204,765,770.

2 Constitutional Amendment: XXVI (June 1971) granted the vote to 18–21 year olds.

## VICE PRESIDENT

39th Spiro Theodore Agnew (Maryland), b 1918. Lawyer; teacher; politician; Governor of Maryland, 1967–9; vice president, 20 January 1969 to 10 October 1973 (resigned).

40th Gerald Rudolph Ford, subsequently 38th president. Nominated by President Nixon under the terms of the 25th Amendment (1967), Ford's appointment as the first non-elected vice president was confirmed by Congress (in the Senate by 92 votes to 3, and by 387 to 35 in the House) in December. He was sworn in on 6 December 1973.

---

Richard Nixon was born in 1913 into a poor, Quaker family in Yorba Linda, California, but he was raised in nearby Whittier from whose Union High School he graduated in 1930. He then graduated second in his class from Whittier College before going on to law school. He practised law in Whittier and in 1940 married Pat Ryan. When the war came, out of respect for his mother's pacifism and his own Quaker upbringing, he first took an administrative job in Washington. Then he slipped quietly into the Navy.

After the war he thought of returning to the law, but in 1946 he ran for Congress and defeated a popular local Democrat. Nixon attributed his victory to a series of public debates with his opponent. 1947 was a good time for an aspiring young Republican to enter Congress after '20 years of Democrat treason', and soon a watershed arose in Nixon's career in the case of Alger Hiss. Hiss, a former State Department official, was accused of being a communist spy. Nixon, in the House Un-American Activities

241

Committee, turned the case into a personal crusade which chimed in perfectly with national feelings of xenophobia and anti-communism. In 1950 he won a Senate seat with a large majority.

In 1952, as a sop to the right-wing Republicans, Senator Nixon was chosen to be the running mate of Dwight David Eisenhower. The issue was never in doubt and the GOP romped home. The only sour note concerned the campaign of Richard Nixon. It was revealed that he had been subsidised from a secret fund established by Californian millionaires but such was his standing that 'Tricky Dicky' was able to shrug off any charges in his famous 'Checkers' speech during a dramatic TV appearance.

Through eight years as vice president Nixon held his own with considerable skill. He was energetic, efficient and loyal. He improved his technique as a speaker. He showed tenacity and courage. In Latin America in 1958 he was stoned in Peru and mobbed in Venezuela. In 1959 he had an impromptu slanging match with Nikita Kruschev in the kitchen of a Moscow hotel.

He was sent out to head the election campaigns of 1954, 1956 and 1958. Apart from Ike's crushing defeat of Adlai Stevenson in 1956 the Republican record was a disastrous one and possibly left Richard Nixon with an abiding insecurity about his ability to win elections.

He was the natural choice as Ike's successor in 1960. Initially neither of the candidates aroused much enthusiasm. Nixon ran ahead in the polls until a series of four nationally televised debates in September and October left him outpointed by Kennedy and defeated for the first time in his political career. (He refused to pursue alleged vote frauds: 'The President couldn't govern not knowing whether he was really President.')

Nixon's decision to run for the governorship of California in 1962 was a shock to his friends who thought the post a political graveyard. His ignominious defeat was made more embarrassing by a famous press conference: 'You won't have Nixon to kick around any more because this is my last press conference.' Six years later, almost to the day, Richard Nixon was elected President of the United States.

He tried to build a new legal career, and possibly a new power base, in the East, in New York. He was a very good lawyer — he argued an historic right of privacy case involving *Life* magazine before the Supreme Court in 1965 — but things did not work out for him amongst the Eastern establishment and, in any case, the law was less challenging than public life. He had lost the 1960 election by only the narrowest of margins. After the Republican annihilation in 1964, old friends began to tell him that perhaps he could make it again, in 1968.

It was as a private citizen that he led the Republican's climb out of the abyss. In the 1966 congressional elections he campaigned tirelessly on behalf of others and received much of the credit when the Republicans won 4 Senate seats, 47 seats in the House, 8 governorships and 540 state legislative seats. This performance projected Richard Nixon into the presidential politics of 1968.

In that year the Democrats were shattered by the withdrawal of Lyndon Johnson and the murder of Robert Kennedy. America was deeply divided by Vietnam, racial violence and student militancy (which was also taking place in Tokyo, Berlin, Prague, London (LSE) and, especially, Paris) — student demonstrators had virtually sealed up President Johnson in the White House. The Democratic National Convention in Chicago was marred by violent clashes between Mayor Daley's Chicago police and anti-Vietnam war demonstrators. In this, for Republicans, auspicious year, Nixon had sufficient claims on his party to get the Republican nomination with Governor Spiro Agnew as the vice presidential nominee. 'Spiro Who?' a man noted for racial slurs and chauvinistic invective was certain to rally Democratic defectors — as was the most formidable Third Party in American politics in a generation, headed by Governor George Wallace of Alabama.

Haunted by the shades of J.F.K., Nixon refused to debate with his main opponent, Senator Hubert Humphrey, and he stopped campaigning before he tired himself out. His winning margin was a very slender 0.7 of a percentage point in the popular vote, and he had the smallest victor's share of the poll since 1912, though he had a respectable majority in the Electoral College. The Vietnam War and social dislocation had cost the Democrats dearly. In four years their 16 million vote majority of 1964 had evaporated, and for the first time a party that had won a landslide victory in one election had failed to carry the White House at the next. In a very real sense 1968 was a defeat for the Democrats rather than a Republican victory, though not since 1848 had a president been elected without having a majority of his party in control of either House or Congress.

'The next President', said Richard Nixon during the 1968 campaign, 'must unite America'. Against a background of war, riots, assassinations and chaos, he offered leadership and calm. Instead the 'Nixon years' were to be years of continuing crisis. There were crises at home and abroad; crises in energy, in pollution and in the economy. These were to be the years of the Manson murders, the Mylai massacres, sky-jackings, Kent State, 'hardhats', campus 'bums', Chappaquidick creek; of 'Middle America', the 'silent majority', drugs, Woodstock and the counter-culture; of the Wallace shooting, the 'Pentagon Papers', and Lt Calley's trial; of Gay-Lib and hard-core pornography; of inflation and devaluation of the dollar; of political corruption; of, above all, 'Watergate' and 'I am not a crook'.

Domestically he set out to create a new Republican party purged of its liberals and dissenters. Its foundations were to be the old GOP conservatives and moderates, and perhaps former Southern Democrats, as well as blue collar and 'ethnic' voters, who were to be won over by appeals to law and order and all the other main concerns of 'Middle Americans'. His 'New Federalism' also promised to bring the vast government bureaucracy into line and return decision-making, and a greater share of Federal funds, to the states and local communities (though this was at variance with his own concepts of the powers of the Executive).

'Everybody is saying that Mr Nixon is doing better than they expected,' was an initial comment on policies which were based on flexibility and pragmatism (possibly in view of the need to reach an accommodation with the Democrat-dominated Congress). There was increased spending on health and education, and social security benefits went up 50%. 'War' was declared on crime and narcotics. Economic policy, however, against a background of a balance of payments deficit, high inflation and unemployment, met with only moderate success. Here mandatory controls on wages, prices and rents (the first in US peace-time history), and devaluation of the dollar (for the first time in forty years), left the Administration vulnerable, though unemployment was down to 5.5 million by mid-1972 and inflation fell to 3.2%.

'Law and Order' was *the* issue facing this Administration and here there was some success though unrest was by no means ended. The black protest was declining in the ghettos. Though 1970 was yet to see the culmination of student rioting, at Kent State, the student movement was long on protest and short on solutions; and, unlike its counterpart in France, for example, there was no dangerous solidarity between students, workers and trade unionists. The gradual downturn in the draft and the conversion of the armed forces into 'volunteer only' forces contributed to the dampening down of a movement that was already being undermined by marijuana and rock music. Nixon, in an effort to tighten up on the legal system, obtained the appointment of the conservative Warren Burger as Chief Justice of the US Supreme Court.

Nixon once said that a president was only needed to run foreign policy, a competent Cabinet could do the rest. In this sphere the general problem was to continue the adjustment of America's role in the world in order to match her economic resources, and the particular problem was Vietnam. Backed by his National Security Adviser Henry Kissinger, Nixon made an historic journey to Communist China in February 1972 to establish the first high-level contact between the two nations. Later in the same year he visited Russia (and he went again in 1974) where, in a spirit of *détente*, he signed a treaty to limit nuclear weapons (SALT I) and discussed co-operation in outer space, trade and international affairs.

The Nixon, or Guam, Doctrine of 1969 committed the United States to the 'Asianisation' or the 'Vietnamisation' of the conflict in South-East Asia, and US forces were gradually reduced, from 475,000 in 1969 to 23,000 by January 1973. The attempt to effect a dignified retreat was threatened by enemy offensives which produced US incursions against their strongholds in Cambodia and Laos. (The 'secret' bombing of Cambodia produced riots at Kent State Unversity, Ohio, in 1970 in which 4 students were killed.) Heavy bombing of North Vietnam (against the background of the Sino-American and Russo-American *détente*) eventually produced peace talks in Paris which finally succeeded in securing the disengagement of American forces in Vietnam. In January 1973, three days before he died, Lyndon Johnson was informed by Richard Nixon that America's involvement in Vietnam had ended.

In the November 1972 presidential election Richard Nixon obtained a landslide. His percentage of the popular vote came to within a few points of Johnson's record 61.1%. He carried an unprecedented 49 states. His Electoral College vote was the highest for any Republican and comparable to that of F.D.R. in 1936. He also made history as the first president to face two terms with a Congress dominated by the opposition. As his second term got under way it became increasingly clear that the Administration was about to veer sharply to the right and to assert the traditional American virtues of 'rugged individualism' and 'self-help' — but the greatest political scandal in American history was about to subsume all else.

'Watergate' has become a generic term to describe a whole range of questionable activities which were indulged in by Cabinet members, key aides and campaign advisers, but at the heart of the affair was the 'cover-up' of a break-in at the Watergate, in Washington DC. This fashionable, ultra-modern hotel, office and appartment complex stands next to the John F. Kennedy Center on the Potomac. Here, on 17 June 1972, five men were caught in the act of burgling the offices of the Democratic National Committee. (Exactly what they were doing there has never been satisfactorily established.) Within days reporters on the *Washington Post* had established a connection between CREEP (the Committee to Re-elect the President) and the burglars. That committee (and Nixon himself on June 22) issued categorical denials of any White House involvement in what was dismissed as a 'third rate burglary', which was 'not on our behalf or with our consent'.

The Chairman of the Democratic National Committee, however, entered a one million dollar suit against CREEP, in what was considered to be an election ploy (though in fact the development of the whole affair appears to have had no effect at all on the election campaign). But when *Time*, the *New York Times* and the *Washington Post* — the latter with access to an anonymous White House source, 'Deep Throat' — started to suggest that responsibility for the break-in went very high up in the White House, 'Watergate' began to assume very menacing proportions.

The trial and conviction of the 'Watergate five' in January 1973 before Federal Court Judge 'Maximum John' Sirica, not only cast considerable doubt on the defendant's version of events — the 'cover-up' story — but also led to the establishment, under the fearless chairmanship of Senator Sam Ervin, of the Senate Select Committee on Presidential Campaign Activities. Under relentless probings during televised hearings conspirators cracked and, as the inquiry moved ever-closer to the White House, presidential aides began to resign, including the Presidential Counsel, John Dean, the White House Chief of Staff, Bob Haldeman, and the President's Assistant for Domestic Affairs, John Ehrlichman.

Ironically, this same 'Watergate' period was to see major achievements in foreign policy. The last US troops were withdrawn from Vietnam. In the wake of the 'Yom Kippur' Arab-Israeli War, in October 1973, an American-Egyptian *détente* was achieved, and

246

as late as July 1974 Richard Nixon could make a triumphal tour of the Middle East.

In a separate matter vice president Spiro Agnew resigned in October 1973 after pleading 'no contest' to tax frauds when Governor of Maryland. The untried procedures of the recent 25th Amendment were utilised to secure the nomination, and the confirmation, of Gerald R. Ford as vice president of the United States.

One of the major discoveries made by the Ervin Committee was the existence of a tape-recording system in the White House — part of a plan to make the Nixon Administration the most fully-documented in American history. This proved to be the turning point in the whole affair. Nixon spent nearly a year — during which he barely governed — trying to hold on to the tapes. But, ultimately, in one of the gravest crises in American constitutional history, the Supreme Court unanimously overruled the president's assertion of 'executive privilege' and ordered him to produce all tapes and other documents relevant to the Watergate hearings. When these were made public as the 'White House Transcripts' (May 1974), complete with 'gaps' at critical points — one lasting for 18½ minutes — and 'expletives deleted', 'Honks for Impeachment' began to resound along Pennsylvania Avenue. Late in July the House Judiciary Committee debated on television the charges against the president in preparation for full impeachment. Three articles were finally recommended: obstruction of justice; abuse of power; and contempt of Congress.

On 5 August 1974 Nixon finally surrendered three transcripts of conversations which had taken place within days of the Watergate break-in. They indicated clearly his involvement in the 'cover-up' operation at a very early stage. At that point his last remaining support vanished and he decided to resign (8 August), and accept what he termed 'voluntary impeachment'. In so doing he spared the United States six months of impeachment proceedings during which the nation would have been unable to exercise any influence in the world.

Nixon is on record as saying: 'People should not forget that twenty years ahead American historians may judge the throwing out of office of a great statesman quite differently from the way it is seen now.' What would have been the estimate of Richard Nixon as 37th president of the United States if Watergate had not intervened? Certainly he would (and still might) go down as one of the greatest foreign-policy presidents of the United States. He built a bridge with the People's Republic of China and steered the country out of an era of dangerous confrontation with Russia. The SALT Agreement was the first major arms agreement of the nuclear age. He ended US involvement in Vietnam. He improved relations with the Arabs without alienating the Israelis. At home, it could be argued, he laid the basis for a progressive ideology for the Republican party with his 'New Federalism':

But by indulging in abuses of power which obliged him to resign in August 1974 . . . he helped weaken that very strength and the search for world peace about which he felt so deeply. Some of that strength comes from the belief of Americans in the rightness of their cause, the integrity of their system and the basic justice of their actions . . . America's faith in herself had been undermined by Watergate. (*Truman to Carter: A Post-War History of the United States of America* [1979] by Peter J. Mooney and Colin Brown).

# GERALD R. FORD

**Full name** Gerald Rudolph Ford (though he was born Leslie Lynch King; legally adopted by his step-father, his name was changed in 1916)

**Born** Omaha, Nebraska, 14 July 1913, the only son of his mother's first marriage

**Parents** Leslie Lynch King (1882–1941) wool, lumber merchant, and real estate agent, and Dorothy A. Gardner (1892–1967), who married, secondly, in 1916, Gerald Rudolph Ford (1890–1962)

**Family lineage** English

**College** Michigan State University, AB 1936; Yale University Law School, LLB 1941

**Married** 1948, Elizabeth 'Betty' Bloomer Warren Ford (b 1918), the divorced wife of W. G. Warren, daughter of W. S. Bloomer. 3 sons, 1 daughter

**Occupation** Assistant football coach, Yale University, 1935–41; lawyer; World War II, Lt Commander, USNR; member of US House of Representatives, 1949–73; vice president 1973–74

**Religious denomination** Episcopalian

Gerald Rudolph Ford succeeded to the presidency on 9 August 1977 following the resignation of Richard M. Nixon.

**Party** Republican **State represented** Michigan **Term of office** 9 August 1974 to 20 January 1977 (he served the unexpired portion of his predecessor's term) **Age on taking office** 61 **Presidential administration** 47th (cont) **Congresses** 93rd (cont) 94th

| | CONGRESS | | | |
|------|------|------|------|------|
| 1975 | 94th | Senate (100) | 61 Dem | 38 Repub | 1 Ind |
| | | House (435) | 290 Dem | 145 Repub | |

VICE PRESIDENT

41st Nelson Aldrich Rockefeller (New York), 1908–79. Banker;

Governor of New York, 1958–73; vice president, 20 August 1974 to 20 January 1977. He was the second nominated, non-elected vice president under the terms of the XXV Amendment.

---

On the day after Richard Nixon resigned Gerald Ford succeeded to the presidency, the first man to become chief executive by the appointment route. 'Our long nightmare is over. Our Constitution works. Our great Republic is a government of laws and not of men . . . I am acutely aware that you have not elected me as your President by your ballots . . . as I begin this very difficult job.'

He began with a large reservoir of good-will which it is traditional for an accidental president to have when he takes over the White House. In normal times the prospect of a President Ford might have given rise to the bleakest pessimism. His long service in Congress had generated a reputation for integrity, but not notably for intellect or wisdom. The tired gags attributed to the late president, Lyndon B. Johnson, that Mr Ford, a one-time star lineman at Michigan had 'played too much football without a helmet' and that Ford 'could not walk and chew gum at the same time', had become ready clichés about him. But Congressman Jerry Ford, House Minority Leader for nearly a decade, and lately vice president — in which position he had acquitted himself with prudence and restraint — had support both in Congress and among the electorate. Untainted by Watergate himself, he was as well-positioned as any Republican to pick up the pieces of Nixon's shattered administration. The American people looked to Mr Ford's integrity rather than to his intellectual leadership or inspiration and there was a widespread hope that the office would bring out the very best in the man.

How would the new president stand up to the rigours of the loneliest job in the world? He was a 'regular guy', strong, athletic and aggressively healthy — he had never had a headache in his life. Star player in Michigan University's national championship football teams of 1932–3, he had been the very model of the crew-cut, 'All-American' young man of the 1930s and he had posed for photographs in *Look* magazine. Instead of becoming a pro footballer he had gone on to Yale and combined coaching with Yale Law School where, if entrance was not as competitive as it is today, the standards have never been in doubt and he got good grades. Yale also took him away for the first time from his Mid-Western background.

He was born in Omaha, Nebraska, but raised from the age of one in Grand Rapids, Michigan. Yale introduced Ford to the greater sophistication of the East Coasters and this was increased by his service in the Navy from 1942. He rose to the rank of Lt Commander on board the aircraft carrier *Monterey* which saw action in the Pacific.

He left the navy aged 32 and still unmarried, in 1946, but soon he married a former Martha Graham dancer and divorcée, Betty Bloomer. He practiced law in Grand Rapids from 1946–9 and then entered politics. He had had political ambitions from an early age — his stepfather was very active in the local Republican party — and in 1948 he was elected to the House of Representatives from the Michigan Fifth District. He was returned every two years after that with little or no difficulty.

Ford once described himself as a 'moderate in domestic issues, a conservative in fiscal affairs and a died-in-the-wool internationalist in foreign affairs'. His record, however, suggested that he stood well to the right of the Republican party. In his twenty-five years in the House he had an impressive voting record, attending over 90% of the roll calls and declaring his position 99% of the time. Almost invariably he voted with the conservatives.

On domestic issues he was more Nixonian than his friend Nixon. In 1948 he voted against Public Housing and a Minimum Wages Bill; later against Federal-funded public works programmes, 'medicare' and the entire Johnson anti-poverty programme. He opposed Johnson's 'Great Society' from the start; 'The great society of Lyndon Johnson,' he said, 'has become a runaway loco-motive with a wild-eyed engineer at the controls!' These views, and this record, could hardly be described as those of a domestic moderate.

In foreign affairs, whilst supporting the Nixon-Kissinger policy of *détente*, he was still something of a cold-war warrior. An unregenerate 'hawk' over Vietnam, he advocated the bombing of North Vietnam. In 1971 he supported the American-backed South Vietnamese invasion of Laos. 'I really feel,' he told the Senate during his vice-presidential confirmation hearings, 'that the number one priority today is the adequate funding of our national defence.'

He had risen slowly in Congress and it was not until after the Goldwater fiasco in 1964 that he achieved some prominence, being elected Republican leader in the House in 1965 with the task of helping to rebuild the party along less extreme lines. In 1968 he was Chairman of the Republican Convention and he helped Richard Nixon to secure the nomination. Thereafter his loyalty to Nixon was almost total; and following the Agnew disaster he was Nixon's choice (his fourth choice) for vice president. A very thorough investigation by Congress and the FBI revealed that Ford was honest, incorruptible and worth a quarter of a million dollars.

In this role he had an unenviable task. He could not be disloyal to Nixon and yet, as Watergate was unravelled, he had to remain aloof. Not a party to the proceedings he maintained the innocency of his chief until shortly before Nixon's resignation, whereupon he found himself America's first-non-elected president — with America's second-non-elected vice president.

One of his first important actions dissipated the good-will with which he had begun. On 8 September 1974 he announced a 'full, free and absolute pardon' for Richard Nixon — which he had every constitutional right to confer — for all federal crimes he 'committed, or may have committed, or taken part in', while in the White House. During his confirmation hearings for the vice presidency when asked whether he would consider such action, Mr Ford had replied: 'I don't think the public would stand for it.' Now he clearly took the view that there was nothing further to be gained by hounding the ex-president who could have faced a sentence of more than 30 years in jail as well as a fine of some $50,000. The agony and disgrace was punishment enough. With the passage of time the gesture has come to appear both magnanimous and sensible in the circumstances — though it certainly contributed to Ford's very narrow defeat in 1976. In October 1974 President Ford became only the third president to testify before a Congressional Committee when he appeared before a House of Representatives Sub-Committee to answer questions about the pardon. He denied that any 'deal' had been made.

In many respects President Ford's administration closely resembled that of his predecessor. In foreign affairs he relied on the new Secretary of State, Henry Kissinger (the first naturalised US citizen to attain such a high post) and, despite the lessons of Vietnam, contemplated intervention in the civil war in Angola. In domestic matters he was as reactionary as his own past record indicated and less-imaginative than Nixon. During a period of high unemployment (6–9%), and double figure inflation (14%), his administration persisted with hackneyed policies, and Ford vetoed legislation providing for public housing, federal aid to education, health care and other social reforms. He had a conservative's doctrinaire belief in the values of private enterprise, telling industrialists that he wanted Washington, 'out of your business, out of your lives, out of your pockets, and out of your hair'.

Early in 1976 a poll found that the majority of Americans thought that Jerry Ford was a 'nice' guy but not 'very smart' about the issues the country was facing. America's hopes for a second Truman had apparently not been realised, and no one summed up his performance better than the president himself when he quipped: 'I am a Ford not a Lincoln.'

Then he went back on a 1973 pledge 'not to run in 76' and began to seek his party's presidential nomination. Even though he was the incumbent he could not take this for granted, for right-wing Republicans were supporting Ronald Reagan, one-time Governor of California and ex-second-feature film star. Reagan, who has been described as the spiritual heir of Barry Goldwater, prepared to temper his views and, with his presence and photogenic air, proved to be a strong contender. Ford had to go all the way to the party Convention before he won the nomination by a very narrow majority.

Initially Ford trailed well behind his Democratic opponent, former Governor of Georgia, Jimmy Carter; but gradually the Democratic campaign began to lose momentum. When the election came Ford had all but won back a huge popularity deficit and he actually carried more states than his opponent.

Narrowly defeated in 1976 Gerald Ford went out of office having restored respect for the office of president and he was living proof that Richard Nixon had not damaged the institution irremediably. A grateful House of Representatives passed a resolution commending President Ford's 'openness and honesty that have done much to restore confidence in our government'. The prestigious British *Economist* wrote that, 'To be sure nothing of a material nature got done, but a process of healing took place and Mr Ford gets the credit for it.'

President Ford retired into private life to play golf (execrably), and to write his autobiography, *A Time to Heal* (1979). He made a dramatic political come-back at the Republican National Convention in Detroit in July 1980 when, briefly, it appeared that he was about to become the first former president to be nominated as vice president, before that position on the Reagan ticket went to George Bush.

# JAMES E. CARTER

**Full name**   James Earl Carter Jr (b 1924)
**Born**   Plains, Georgia, 1 October 1924, the eldest of 4 children
**Parents**   James Earl Carter (1894–1953), farmer, storekeeper, and Lillian Gordy Carter (b 1898). 2 sons, 2 daughters
**Family lineage**   English
**College**   Georgia Institute of Technology, Atlanta, Georgia, 1942–43; US Naval Academy, Annapolis, Maryland. BSc 1946; graduate student Union College, Schenectady, NY, 1952
**Married**   1946, Rosalyn Smith Carter (b 1927) daughter of Edgar Smith, garage mechanic. 3 sons, 1 daughter
**Occupation**   Officer in the US Navy, 1946–53 (retired); farmer, since 1953; Georgia state senator, 1963–7; Governor of Georgia, 1971–5
**Religious denomination**   Southern Baptist

**Party** Democratic **State represented** Georgia **Term of office** 20 January 1977 to 20 January 1981 **Age on taking office** 52 **Presidential administration** 48th **Congresses** 95th, 96th

### 1976 ELECTION

| Candidates | Party | Electoral Vote (538) | States Won (50)* | Popular Vote | % |
|---|---|---|---|---|---|
| J. Carter | Dem | 297 | 23* | 40,249,963 | 50.4 |
| G. Ford | Repub | 240 | 27 | 38,498,496 | 48.3 |

*Plus Washington DC; one Republican Elector voted for Ronald Reagan.

### CONGRESS

| | | | | | |
|---|---|---|---|---|---|
| 1977 | 95th | Senate (100) | 62 Dem | 38 Repub | |
| | | House (435) | 290 Dem | 145 Repub | |
| 1979 | 96th | Senate (100) | 59 Dem | 41 Repub | |
| | | House (435) | 273 Dem | 159 Repub | 3 Vacant |

### VICE PRESIDENT

42nd Walter Fritz Mondale (Minnesota), b 1928. Lawyer; Attorney

General of Minnesota, 1960–4; US Senator, 1964–76; vice president, 20 January 1977 to 20 January 1981.

NOTE
1980 20th Census. Total population, 226,504,825 (11% higher than the 1970 figure, the new total reveals a massive population shift from older eastern and central cities to the warmer towns of the South and West. This will mean the re-allocation of 17 seats in the House of Representatives and of millions of dollars of federal funds.)

---

America's first deep South president since Zachary Taylor in 1848 was born in Plains, Georgia, but raised in nearby Archery. He grew up on a farm in the Great Depression. His autobiography (1975) tells of how he lived in a house with no modern conveniences, rose at 4am to help with the chores, helped his father on the farm and in the store, and sold boiled peanuts on the streets. Inspired by his sturdy, independent mother, and his school teacher, he did well at high school and graduated in 1941. He then spent a year at 'Georgia Tech' brushing up on his maths before entering the US Naval Academy at Annapolis. He graduated 59th out of 820 in 1946 and got married shortly afterwards.

His naval career spanned the years 1946 to 1953, and he served on both the East and West coasts and as far as Hawaii and the Far East. He spent two years on board experimental radar and gunnery vessels before converting to submarines. Then he was chosen by the legendary Admiral (then Captain) Hyman G. Rickover to join America's nuclear submarine programme. (Later Carter used Rickover's personal motto, *Why Not the Best?* as the title of his own autobiography). He served aboard the nuclear submarine USS *Sea Wolf* before doing postgraduate work in nuclear physics and reactor technology at Union College, Schenectady, NY, in 1952. The death of his father led to the resignation of Lt Carter from the US navy and he returned home to take charge of the family's peanut producing and processing business.

Such was his business acumen that within a few years he had converted the ailing business into a prosperous concern and, on paper, he became a dollar millionaire. In the family tradition — his father had been a state representative — he also became very active in civic affairs. The successful agribusinessman became a state senator after a very tough legal battle to get a recount in a state Democratic primary election which, initially, he had 'lost'. In the state senate he gained a reputation as a moderate and, in 1966, he passed up the chance of a seat in the US House of Representatives in order to run for Governor. He was beaten into third place by 20,000 votes. 'I didn't intend to lose again. Show me a good loser and I'll show you a loser,' he said, as he spent the next four years running for the single four-year term allowed by Georgia law. It was in this period also that the religious faith of this long-time Baptist churchman was deepened to the extent that he was 'born again' as he accepted Jesus Christ as the most important influence in his life. After victory in 1970 he struck a high note in his Inaugural Address when he said, 'I say to you now quite frankly that the time for racial discrimination is over.' Blacks were advanced to high positions in the Georgia government as Governor Carter reorganised the sprawling state bureaucracy, instituted prison reform, modernised budgeting — and developed a taste for political power to the extent that he decided to run for president of the United States.

A turning point in his career came in 1974 when he was chosen to co-ordinate the Democratic National Campaign and in this position he had an opportunity to travel all over the nation meeting Democratic leaders. From early 1975 he began to be regarded as a presidential nominee. Before 1972 he would not have been nominated. But in that year, under the chairmanship of George McGovern, the Democratic party had rewritten the party's rules in order to 'open up' the nominating process and prevent the imposition by party 'bosses' (as with the case of Hubert Humphrey in 1968), of a nominee who had not entered a single primary election. There was now to be proportional representation of delegates at the nominating Convention — 30% of primary votes would result in 30% of the delegate votes, for example — so that there was now every incentive for unknown candidates to compete in the primaries. (An important part of the 'opening up' of the process of presidential selection has been the increasing number of primary elections: in 1968 there were 17; in 1972, 23; in 1976, 30. In 1980 there were 35 state primaries plus 2 others in Washington DC and Puerto Rico.) This change opened the way for 'Jimmy Who?' the unknown ex-Governor of Georgia (as Governor in 1973 he had appeared on 'What's My Line' as the celebrity — and defeated the panel), to run in 1976.

Political experts regarded his cause as hopeless in 1976 when he was one of the 250 who registered with the Federal Election Commission as seekers of the presidency. (In the event there were to be 13 candidates plus miscellaneous independents.) But when the primary season opened he was well-prepared, for he had spent two years drafting policies and strategy and gathering around himself a corps of bright, young, Georgia political experts.

He set off on a long, lonely journey of persuasion, first to Iowa where his campaign style — 'My name's Jimmy Carter and I'm running for President' — struck a welcome note in the wake of recent abuses of power. When he won pluralities in the Iowa caucuses he suddenly became recognised as a national contender. His victory in the first primary in New Hampshire catapulted him to a fame which was increased when he defeated the previously formidable Governor George Wallace of Alabama (now confined to a wheel chair after an unsuccessful assassination attempt), in Florida. A crowded Democratic field on the left of the party cancelled each other out in the race for the blue-collar vote and, by the time Jimmy Carter defeated Senator Henry 'Scoop' Jackson in the Pennsylvania primary, the nomination was as good as his.

Carter's presidential campaign was based on the fact that he was an 'outsider', a fresh face with no connections in Washington. He generated self-confidence from behind a broad grin and he made a startling promise: 'I will never lie to you.' He built up a network of adherents in the key states and fought an exceptionally shrewd campaign against a Republican incumbent hobbled by the worst economic slump since the 1930s and his pardon of Richard Nixon. With a lead of more than 30 points in the opinion polls in July 1976 the Carter ticket looked a safe bet, but it was not to be that easy. Carter's small-town campaign style did not translate smoothly to the broad national stage. By November his big lead had evaporated, partly because of a series of mishaps, such as his indiscretion in giving a frank interview to *Playboy* magazine, and partly because President Ford attacked Carter for being 'fuzzy' on volatile issues such as abortion, where he had revealed a penchant for trying to please both sides. Carter was also seen to be thin-skinned when under constant press scrutiny and daily campaign pressures. Ford however made bad blunders of his own especially when, in a televised debate with Carter, he made the astonishing assertion that 'There is no Soviet domination of Eastern Europe.'

The vote which elected Carter was narrow. He won by a slim 1.75

million popular votes out of a total of 80 million, with a shade over 2% more than Ford. The margin of victory in the Electoral College was the narrowest since 1916. But he won — with the support of his native South and the traditionally Democratic East, whilst scoring heavily amongst blacks and labour voters.

Begotten by Vietnam out of Watergate, Jimmy Carter, evangelist and engineer, came to the capital pledged to restore old-time values. The first thing he changed was the style of leadership. He walked back to the White House from the Capitol after his inauguration, and he set out to 'de-imperialise' the presidency by dropping 'Hail to the Chief' (it had to be restored later when it was discovered that most people wanted 'majesty' in the office), and dispensing with numerous presidential cars and helicopters, and hard liquor at receptions. His appeal lasted for about a six-month honeymoon period and then he began his long slide down the public opinion polls.

The problem was that he had no roots in Washington. His governmental experience had been entirely on the state level, as had that of many of his aides, and his performance was affected from the start by a disdain for that political wheeling and dealing at which his Democratic predecessor, L. B. Johnson, had been so adept. The situation was made worse by the tendency of the White House to develop an insularity — the 'Fortress Georgia syndrome' its critics called it — and for the president to surround himself with his Georgia *mafiosi*. Not surprisingly the administration experienced highly publicised failures in its relations with Congress, and it developed an aura of amateurism that it found hard to shake off. There were numerous examples of crossed signals, with one official saying one thing about economic policy and others the opposite. Carter himself produced a string of contradictions, such as his claim that he was in favour of a 'Palestinian homeland', that had to be 'clarified' by the White House.

Strongly insulated in the White House, the president relied for counsel on delicate issues on his wife Rosalyn — the 'Steel Magnolia' to her enemies — who was reckoned to be one of the most influential and powerful First Ladies in memory, and on his Georgia political advisers. His trust was sometimes misplaced and an erosion of his popular support in the polls, in September 1977, followed the enforced resignation of his friend and Office of Management and Budget director, Burt Lance. Later, the over-extension of his loyalty to his brother, Billy — whose financial relations with the Libyan government in the so-called 'Billygate' affair were investigated by a Senate Committee — meant that he now appeared 'just like all the other politicians'.

This is not to say that the administration was devoid of major achievements. On the domestic front there was a new energy programme; new Departments of Energy and Education; civil service reforms; rising farm prosperity; budget restraint in the federal government; jobs and training for the unemployed; declining unemployment and new social security funding.

In foreign affairs there were significant developments. Carter broke a Turkish arms embargo; won an arms package for Saudi Arabia and Israel; pushed through a new Panama Canal treaty, and personally negotiated a Middle East peace agreement at Camp David between Egypt and Israel — both of which were major achievements that had eluded his predecessors. He completed the second Strategic Arms Limitation Treaty (SALT II) with the Soviet Union; increased defence spending; and, though he cancelled the B1 bomber and a fifth nuclear aircraft carrier on the grounds that they were too expensive and not needed, he began a new MX missile system and gave his blessing to a new form of 'stealth' technology. In addition, he normalised relations with the People's Republic of China; gave a lead in enlarging and revitalising NATO; made 'human rights' a global crusade; as well as increasing American influence in the Third World by supporting the principle of black majority rule in Zimbabwe-Rhodesia.

But all this was not enough. Domestic inflation had grown since 1977 from 4.5% to over 13% (1980). 8 million new jobs by 1977 still left a further 8 millions out of work in November 1980. And the answer to the question posed by Ronald Reagan with disarming simplicity during the election campaign of 1980 — 'Are you better off now than you were four years ago?' — was clearly in the negative for many right across the social spectrum. Whilst Jimmy Carter was making his 'human rights' declarations, the Soviets were subverting the government of Afghanistan prior to the invasion of December 1979, and interfering in Ethiopia; 40,000 Cuban troops were rampaging through Central Africa, and Iran was being fragmented.

An August 1979 Gallup poll found that only 20% or so of Americans thought that their president was 'doing a good job', and only 27% were satisfied that he was displaying 'strong leadership qualities' — though 80% still regarded him as a man of high moral principles and a religious person', and 50% thought that he was 'bright and likeable' and a man who 'says what he believes even if it is unpopular'. That was before the fateful day, of 4 November 1979, when Iranian students seized 64 US hostages at the American Embassy in Tehran, an event which triggered off a foreign policy crisis, focussed a spotlight on Jimmy Carter's abilities and contributed to his defeat exactly one year to the day later.

The immediate impact for the president was wholly good. As is usual in times of crisis, the nation rallied behind him. His ratings soared to a healthy 61%, and he overtook Senator Edward Kennedy as the first choice of 48% of Democrats in the developing presidential campaign. Because of the Iranian crisis Carter waged a low-key campaign, from the White House 'Rose Garden', said his critics, whose voices began to be heard again as the situation in the Middle East deteriorated. In late December 1979 the Russians invaded Afghanistan. Against a background of apparent American powerlessness, Ronald Reagan led the chorus of protests when he said that the Carter foreign policy reminded him of 'the sorry tapping of Neville Chamberlain's umbrella on the cobblestones of Munich'. A commando mission designed to rescue the hostages from the American embassy in Tehran, on 25 April 1980, ended in failure and tragedy in a remote desert area some 200 miles from the capital.

Rightly or wrongly such an aura of omnipotence has come to be associated with the modern American presidency that, as Herbert Hoover — the last incumbent to be defeated — pointed out, the occupant of the office will get all the blame when things go wrong. Jimmy Carter 'failed' to solve America's energy problems, and American inflation; and he had to bear the odium of a nation which gradually awoke to the realisation that they must see themselves as others see them, garbed in the 20th century version of the 'Emperor's new clothes'. The cynical will say that with Carter, as with the Cheshire cat, there was nothing there really, except the smile. It is too early (1981) to pronounce judgement on the Carter administration. Incompetent in certain areas and vacillating in others he might well have been, but he also fell victim to an 'expectation gap' both at home and abroad. In his Farewell Address in January 1981 Carter summed up the situation when he spoke of the presidency as 'at once the most powerful office in the world, and among the most severely constrained by law and custom'.

# RONALD W. REAGAN

**Full name**  Ronald Wilson Reagan (b 1911)
**Born**  Main Street, Tampico, Illinois, 6 February 1911, the younger of 2 sons
**Parents**  John Edward Reagan (1883–1941), shoe salesman, and Nellie Wilson Reagan (1883–1962)
**Family lineage**  Irish-Scots
**College**  Eureka College, Eureka, Illinois, BA 1932
**Married**  (1) 1940, Jane Wyman (born Sarah Jane Faulks, 1914), divorced wife of Myron Futterman, daughter of Richard Faulks, mayor of Minneapolis. 1 daughter, 1 adopted son. Divorced 1948 (2) 1952, Nancy Davis, (b 1923) daughter of Kenneth Robbins, gentleman-farmer, car salesman, by his 2nd wife, Edith; adopted daughter of her mother's 2nd husband, Dr Loyal Edward Davis, neurosurgeon. 1 daughter, 1 son
**Occupation**  Sports announcer, 1932–7; motion picture and TV actor, 1937–64; World War II, Capt USAAF, 1942–6; President of the Screen Actors Guild, 1947–53, 1959–60; 33rd Governor of California, 1967–75; businessman; rancher
**Religious denomination**  Christian Church

**Party** Republican **State represented** California **Term of office** from 20 January 1981 **Age on taking office** 69 (the oldest president to be inaugurated) **Presidential administration** 49th **Congress** 97th (1981–3)

1980 ELECTION

| Candidates | Party | Electoral Vote (538) | States Won (50)* | Popular Vote | % |
|---|---|---|---|---|---|
| R. Reagan | Repub | 489 | 44 | 42,951,145 | 51 |
| J. Carter | Dem | 49 | 6* | 34,663,037 | 41 |

*Plus Washington DC. (Based on unofficial returns compiled by the News Election Service, 8 November 1980.)

CONGRESS

| 1981 | 97th | Senate (100) | 53 Repub | 46 Dem | 1 Ind |
|---|---|---|---|---|---|
| | | House (435) | 243 Dem | 192 Repub | |

261

43rd George Herbert Walker Bush (Texas), b 1924. Public official and former oil industry executive; member of United States House of Representatives, 1967–71; Ambassador to the United Nations, 1971–3; chairman of the Republican National Committee, 1973–4; head of the US liaison office in Peking, 1974–5; Director of the Central Intelligence Agency, 1976–7; vice president 1981–

---

Only one other president had previously lost his party's nomination twice and then gone on to win both the nomination and the presidency — James Buchanan who won at the third attempt in 1856. For nearly one hundred and forty years William Henry Harrison was the oldest man — at 68 — ever to be inaugurated as president. But when in January 1981 Ronald Wilson Reagan was sworn in as the 40th president of the United States he was within a few days of his 70th birthday, and within four months he took from Eisenhower the title of America's oldest-ever president.

Ronald Reagan grew up in modest surroundings in several small farm and factory towns to the west of Chicago in rural northern Illinois. He was the younger of the two sons of an alcoholic Irish-American, Roman Catholic father, and a Protestant mother of Scottish descent who loved the theatre. His father was a shoe salesman whose career was ruined by the Depression. Both his parents were staunch Democrats. At the age of nine Ronald settled with his parents in Dixon, Illinois, and he did his first acting there in Dixon's North High School.

After graduating from a small, Christian Church, liberal arts college where he majored in (pre-Keynesian) economics and sociology, he got a job as an announcer for Station WOC (World of Chiropractic), an Ohio radio station. 'Dutch' Reagan did football and baseball play-by-play broadcasts throughout the Mid-West. He developed a national reputation and became *the* sports voice of the day when he moved on to another station which became part of the NBC network.

A big break came in 1937 when he was signed up by Warner Brothers and he made his film debut in *Love Is In The Air* in which he played the part of a radio announcer. This marked the beginning of a film acting career that was to produce 54 films and 8 'shorts' between his 27th and 54th years. He became established as the 'good guy' who always 'got the girl' in the end. In *Brother Rat* the girl he got was Jane Wyman who became his first wife.

He was a very good, very professional and very competent actor, but few of his films received much attention and even fewer won much acclaim. His best-known roles were as George Gipp, legendary Notre Dame football player, in *Knute Rockne, All American*; and in 1942 he reached what was to prove to be the peak of his career in *King's Row*. He played the part of a small-town playboy, Drake McHugh who, waking to find that both his legs had been amputated by a sadistic surgeon, cried out 'Where's the rest of me?' He would probably prefer to forget some parts in other films such as *Bedtime for Bonzo* (1951), where he played opposite a chimp (though this was a big hit), and the 1964 film *The Killers*, in which he was totally miscast in his only villainous role and where his film career burned itself out.

During World War II — having entered as a 2nd Lt in the US Cavalry Reserve — he spent four boring years as an Air Corps officer (he is the only president to have served with the air force), making training films. When he came back from the war he found that the tenuous hand-hold on stardom provided by *King's Row* had vanished and he had been virtually forgotten. From now on he was given increasingly mediocre parts; but more and more his career became involved with the 'political' aspects of his profession.

In 1947 he was elected President of the Screen Actors Guild, one of the major unions representing Hollywood talent, and he was to serve five one-year terms and then a sixth in 1959–60. In the McCarthy era he and SAG earned a certain notoriety by co-operating in the purge of suspected communists from the movies and for supporting the blacklisting of Hollywood writers and critics thought to have 'communist' affiliations, though they did oppose unofficial blacklists. In 1947 he appeared before the infamous House Un-American Activities Committee, as a 'friendly witness' (along with Robert Taylor and Gary Cooper) in its investigations of 'reds' in Hollywood. In this period also his eight-year-old marriage to Jane Wyman began to founder. She claimed that Reagan was becoming too deeply involved in politics. Certainly in 1948 he was asked to run for Congress and in 1950 for the state legislature, but he turned down both invitations.

He had grown up in the family tradition as a Democrat. In his autobiography (1965) he describes himself in the late 1940s as a '. . . near-hopeless haemophiliac, I bled for causes'. He supported Harry S. Truman in 1948, campaigned against Richard Nixon's 1950 Senate campaign, and in 1952 and 1956 was still a Democrat, though he worked *for* the Eisenhower presidential effort. Not until two years after he had given his support to Richard Nixon in 1960, did he register as a Republican.

By the mid 1950s he had remarried — he married a young MGM contract actress, Nancy Davis in 1952 — and he had all but abandoned his fading movie career. He broke with Warner Brothers to go freelance and to make a fresh start in television. Between 1954 and 1962 Reagan was the host on the General Electric Company's 'Theater of the Air' show, a TV anthology programme which also involved him in speaking tours which took him to factories and Chambers of Commerce lunches throughout America. The programme won 'Emmy' awards and swept the ratings for its half hour of prime time on Sundays. It also gave Reagan a political platform and enabled him to crusade for right-wing causes, in line with his strong anti-communist attitude, and to inveigh against 'big' government, high taxation, creeping socialism and communism both at home and abroad.

As the programme became controversial in tone it was finally dropped by its sponsors (ironically in favour of one of Reagan's own favourite programmes, 'Bonanza'), and he went on to do two seasons in a syndicated Western series called 'Death Valley Days', before he finally hung up his make-up after his last film in 1964.

Ronald Reagan now prepared to transfer his not inconsiderable gifts as a media politician to the Republican party. He arrived on the national political scene as the result of a single electrifying speech which he delivered on nationwide television in 1964 on behalf of Senator Barry Goldwater's presidential aspirations. In this he articulated all that conservatism which by now had become a part of him. America, he said, had come to 'a time for choosing' between free enterprise and big government, between individual liberty and totalitarianism. 'We stand here on the only island of freedom left in the whole world . . . We defend freedom here or it is gone . . . You and I have a rendezvous with destiny. We can preserve for our children this, the last best hope on earth, or we can sentence them to take the first step into a thousand years of darkness.' Another rousing speech at the Republican Convention in that year established him as Goldwater's heir among conservatives. In 1964 he was approached by a trio of conservative, wealthy, southern Californian businessmen who saw him as a future Governor of California and a possible President.

He was finally persuaded to run for state governor and he

prepared to make the transition from TV personality, and star of the American lecture circuit, to that of credible political figure. In 1966 he defeated a moderate ex-mayor of San Francisco by a two-to-one margin in the GOP primary. Then it was as a 'citizen politician', making a virtue of his amateurism, that he went on to defeat Democratic Governor Pat Brown (who had vanquished Richard Nixon in 1962) by nearly a million votes, with the largest plurality since 1950. (Four years later he was to be re-elected by nearly a half a million vote majority.) He had won the biggest and meatiest part in his 55 years to date. But, without any previous governmental or political experience, he now had the task of running the nation's largest state.

He had waged a hard-line campaign against high taxes, waste, bureaucracy, crime, welfare scroungers and 'communist-inspired' student unrest. But his actions as governor, which have been the subject of endless analyses, proved to be far more moderate than his campaign rhetoric; so much so that one veteran Californian journalist was to sum him up as a 'pragmatic compromiser'. He discovered, the hard way, that politics *is* the art of the possible. Intending to slash taxes and curb the welfare programme, he found that an inherited deficit of nearly $200 million and the opposition of the state legislature, whether Democratic (as it was for all but two years of his term) or Republican, meant that there were no quick solutions. 'There's no way you can wave a magic wand and change things. It's like pouring water on sand.' State spending doubled during his term to $10.2 billion per annum; taxes rose 50% faster than in any other state in the same period.

What Reagan was able to achieve was a gradual lowering of the expectations which people had of government, as he vetoed 993 bills from a legislature which was forced to curb its liberal appetites. The price that Reagan had to pay for this eight-year education in what cannot be done was that he had to learn to compromise with his principles. What he discovered was the necessity, and finally the craft, of making government work; and there is a general consensus that the State of California was administered most competently during his two terms as governor.

He ran the state as the chairman of a board rather than as a chief executive. He gradually assembled a competent team around him which used to meet for three mornings a week for a wide-ranging debate of major issues. Instead of lengthy bureaucratic reports he had one-page memos produced. At his 'cabinet' meetings argument

265

was promoted — as the governor handed round his jar of jelly-beans — but there were no votes. 'Reagan decided,' said one of his staff. 'He delegated everything except his vision of governance and the big decisions as to how it might best be realised,' — usually before he finished for the day at around six.

In this same period he was also assuming national political stature as the governor of the state with the largest Electoral College vote. He made his first appearance in the presidential stakes, in 1968, at the Republican Convention in Miami Beach when he collected 182 delegate votes: 'Son,' said the veteran Republican Senator Strom Thurmond, 'you'll be President one day but this isn't your year.' In 1976 he mounted the most serious challenge to a sitting Republican president since 1912; and he fell only a handful of votes short of becoming the first candidate since 1884 to wrest the nomination from an incumbent.

When Gerald Ford announced in October 1979 that he would not be an active candidate in 1980, Ronald Reagan's status as the undisputed GOP front-runner seemed assured; but he had to beat off a very strong initial challenge from ex-CIA director George Bush — whom he later chose as his running mate — before he finally, comfortably, secured the nomination at Detroit, and set out to make his third bid for the presidency.

After a lacklustre campaign, during which personalities tended to take precedence over political issues and Reagan promised massive tax cuts, a balanced budget and an enormous increase in defence spending, he and Jimmy Carter came to the eve of the election neck and neck. At least they did so according to the pollsters who proved to have produced the most inaccurate prognosis since 1948. For Reagan and the Republicans won a landslide victory.

The lowest poll since 1948 (52.9%), gave the Republicans the sort of victory they had not achieved since 1952. Republicans plus 25% of Democrats and 52% of Independents combined to give Reagan some 43 million popular votes though, like Jimmy Carter in 1976, this meant that he received the votes of only some 26% of those eligible to vote. He won 44 states and a ten to one majority in the Electoral College. He carried organised labour, other blue-collar workers, Catholics, Jews and Protestants alike, his native West, Carter's native South, the rural Mid-West, the industrial North East and most of the traditionally liberal East Coast.

Totally unexpected — and possibly of even greater significance in the long term than the change in the White House — was the change in Congress. The Republicans gained control of the Senate for the first time since 1952–4, and control of all the key Senate Committee chairmanships. They made a nett gain of 33 seats in the House of Representatives, to halve the previous Democratic majority, and to record the largest number of gains made by a party out of office for fifty years.

With their control of the Senate in particular the Republicans were now well-placed to effect a revolution in American foreign and military policy and in American trade relations, as well as in the planning and in the shaping of domestic legislation. Of the 53 Republican Senators 35 stood well to the right of the party and were likely to be supported by some 20 'conservative' Democrats in a body where, traditionally, 'party' loyalties count for less than political philosophies. The Senate Judiciary Committee, which handles judicial nominations, had it in its power to effect a transformation in the make-up of the United States Supreme Court that could last well on towards 2000 AD, for five of the nine justices were older than 70 in 1980.

That Americans did not just vote against Jimmy Carter in 1980 was well-evidenced by the results in the states. The Republicans won four governorships and control of four legislative chambers — as well as tying three others — to give them gubernatorial control in 21 states (compared to 12 in 1977), and the veto power — a vitally important factor this in the constitutional amending procedure — in a total of 32 of the 50 states. Twelve million dollars were spent on the most lavish inaugural in the nation's history as the Republicans marked their return to political power after a generation in the wilderness. Following the first swearing-in ceremony to take place outside the west front of the Capitol, President Reagan in his Inaugural Address offered the American people a 'New Beginning'. Half an hour later (following days of continuous negotiations by President Carter) aircraft took off from Iran carrying the remaining fifty-two American hostages whose plight had bedevilled US foreign policy for a year. President Reagan's hands were thus freed to cope with the immense burden he had inherited.

A president runs a 10:1 risk of being assassinated and a 5:1 chance of being shot at. President Reagan became the first president to be wounded in office when he was shot outside a Washington hotel on 30 March 1981. John W. Hinkley Jr was charged with the attack.

267

# 1980 PRESIDENTIAL ELECTION RESULTS

BASED ON NEARLY COMPLETE, UNOFFICIAL RETURNS COMPILED BY THE NEWS ELECTION SERVICE*

(270 Electoral Votes Needed to Win)

| State | POPULAR VOTE | | | ELECTORAL VOTE | | PERCENTAGE | | |
|---|---|---|---|---|---|---|---|---|
| | Carter | Reagan | Anderson | Carter | Reagan | Carter | Reagan | Anderson |
| Alabama | 626,934 | 640,621 | 15,844 | | 9 | 48 | 50 | 1 |
| Alaska | 31,408 | 66,874 | 8,091 | | 3 | 26 | 55 | 7 |
| Arizona | 243,498 | 523,124 | 75,805 | | 6 | 28 | 61 | 9 |
| Arkansas | 397,919 | 402,946 | 21,057 | | 6 | 48 | 48 | 3 |
| California | 3,040,600 | 4,447,266 | 727,871 | | 45 | 36 | 53 | 8 |
| Colorado | 368,906 | 650,749 | 130,580 | | 7 | 31 | 55 | 11 |
| Connecticut | 537,407 | 672,648 | 168,260 | | 8 | 39 | 48 | 12 |
| Delaware | 106,650 | 111,631 | 16,344 | | 3 | 45 | 47 | 7 |
| District of Columbia | 124,376 | 21,765 | 14,971 | 3 | | 76 | 13 | 9 |
| Florida | 1,366,365 | 1,937,269 | 178,011 | | 17 | 39 | 55 | 5 |
| Georgia | 870,483 | 631,470 | 33,842 | 12 | | 56 | 41 | 2 |
| Hawaii | 135,879 | 130,112 | 32,021 | 4 | | 45 | 43 | 11 |
| Idaho | 109,410 | 290,087 | 27,096 | | 4 | 25 | 67 | 6 |
| Illinois | 1,949,985 | 2,342,450 | 344,807 | | 26 | 42 | 50 | 7 |
| Indiana | 835,541 | 1,231,295 | 107,090 | | 13 | 38 | 56 | 5 |
| Iowa | 508,735 | 676,556 | 114,589 | | 8 | 39 | 51 | 9 |
| Kansas | 324,974 | 562,848 | 67,535 | | 7 | 34 | 58 | 7 |
| Kentucky | 609,687 | 625,820 | 29,843 | | 9 | 48 | 49 | 2 |
| Louisiana | 707,981 | 796,240 | 26,198 | | 10 | 46 | 52 | 2 |
| Maine | 220,387 | 238,156 | 53,450 | | 4 | 42 | 46 | 10 |
| Maryland | 706,327 | 656,255 | 113,452 | 10 | | 47 | 44 | 8 |
| Massachusetts | 1,048,391 | 1,054,390 | 382,044 | | 14 | 42 | 42 | 15 |
| Michigan | 1,519,474 | 1,808,832 | 258,924 | | 21 | 42 | 50 | 7 |
| Minnesota | 897,882 | 824,007 | 166,066 | 10 | | 47 | 43 | 9 |
| Mississippi | 428,948 | 439,843 | 11,828 | | 7† | 48 | 50 | 1 |
| Missouri | 917,663 | 1,055,355 | 76,488 | | 12 | 44 | 51 | 4 |
| Montana | 109,940 | 191,208 | 27,492 | | 4 | 33 | 56 | 8 |

| State | Carter | Reagan | Anderson | Carter | Reagan | Carter | Reagan | Anderson |
|---|---|---|---|---|---|---|---|---|
| Nebraska | 164,270 | 413,338 | 44,024 | | 5 | 26 | 66 | 7 |
| Nevada | 66,468 | 154,570 | 17,580 | | 3 | 27 | 64 | 7 |
| New Hampshire | 109,080 | 221,771 | 49,295 | | 4 | 28 | 58 | 13 |
| New Jersey | 1,119,576 | 1,506,437 | 224,173 | | 17 | 39 | 52 | 8 |
| New Mexico | 164,794 | 245,191 | 28,400 | | 4 | 37 | 55 | 6 |
| New York | 2,627,959 | 2,790,498 | 441,863 | | 41 | 44 | 47 | 7 |
| North Carolina | 875,947 | 913,949 | 52,375 | | 13 | 47 | 49 | 3 |
| North Dakota | 71,544 | 173,825 | 21,749 | | 3 | 27 | 64 | 8 |
| Ohio | 1,744,226 | 2,202,212 | 255,555 | | 25 | 41 | 52 | 6 |
| Oklahoma | 399,292 | 683,807 | 38,051 | | 8 | 35 | 60 | 3 |
| Oregon | 445,352 | 555,859 | 109,363 | | 6 | 39 | 48 | 10 |
| Pennsylvania | 1,932,392 | 2,251,058 | 285,094 | | 27 | 43 | 50 | 6 |
| Rhode Island | 185,319 | 145,576 | 56,213 | 4 | | 48 | 37 | 14 |
| South Carolina | 422,029 | 445,414 | 14,877 | | 8† | 48 | 50 | 2 |
| South Dakota | 103,909 | 198,102 | 21,342 | | 4 | 32 | 61 | 6 |
| Tennessee | 781,464 | 787,156 | 35,927 | | 10 | 49 | 49 | 2 |
| Texas | 1,779,025 | 2,433,290 | 103,431 | | 26 | 41 | 56 | 2 |
| Utah | 123,447 | 435,839 | 30,191 | | 4 | 21 | 73 | 5 |
| Vermont | 81,409 | 93,443 | 31,670 | | 3 | 39 | 44 | 15 |
| Virginia | 745,600 | 979,871 | 92,769 | | 12 | 40 | 53 | 5 |
| Washington | 583,299 | 763,631 | 165,368 | | 9 | 38 | 49 | 11 |
| West Virginia | 353,508 | 326,645 | 30,499 | 6 | | 49 | 46 | 4 |
| Wisconsin | 988,255 | 1,089,750 | 159,793 | | 11 | 44 | 48 | 7 |
| Wyoming | 49,123 | 110,096 | 12,350 | | 3 | 28 | 62 | 7 |
| Total | 34,663,037 | 42,951,145 | 5,551,551 | 49 | 489 | 41 | 51 | 7 |

*Returns for third party candidates and write-ins were scattered. Total reported for Ed Clark (Libertarian) was 876,557 (1%); for Barry Commoner (Citizens), 220,769.

†Candidates for electors listed separately on state ballots, and late returns may show some Carter electors winning.

(This table is reproduced by permission of Congressional Quarterly Inc.)

# FURTHER NOTES:
# PEOPLE, PLACES AND TERMS

**Anti-slavery and Abolitionist**
Anti-slavery groups were opposed to the further extension of the area of slavery; Abolitionists wanted to do away with the South's 'peculiar institution', either by Constitutional amendment or, in the case of a radical minority, by force.

**Bay of Pigs**
In April 1961, the Bay of Pigs was the scene of an ill-fated invasion of Cuba by Cuban exiles supported, trained and equipped by the US State Department and the Central Intelligence Agency.

**Bunker Hill, Battle of**
On 17 June 1775, Gen William Howe, at the third attempt, succeeded in dislodging 1,600 Americans from the heights above Boston harbour. The British sustained over 1,000 casualties, including 92 officers, out of a total force of 2,400. The Americans lost 400, but gained the respect of the British.

**Boston Massacre**
This was a fracas, on 5 March 1770, between British redcoats and Bostonians. Five of the leaders were killed or mortally wounded (Crispus Attucks, Samuel Gray, Samuel Maverick, James Caldwell and Patrick Carr).

**Civil Rights Act 1964**
This Act passed the House with bipartisan support by 290 to 130 votes and the Senate by 73 to 27 after seventy-four days of Southern 'filibustering'. It provided, among other things, that six years of schooling was proof of literacy, assured access to public facilities, blocked federal funds to programmes involving discrimination and required that most companies and unions provide equal employment opportunities.

**Constitutional Amendments**
These are alterations made to the world's oldest written constitution. Although over 2,500 changes have been proposed over two centuries only twenty-six have been adopted by Congress and ratified by the necessary three-quarters of the states, thanks largely to the tortuous amending process devised by the Founding Fathers.

**Continental Congresses (First and Second)**
These two Congresses, which met in September 1774 and May 1775

respectively, arose out of colonial grievances against British policy and became 'The Congress' which for nearly six years directed the war against England. It was superseded by the permanent Congress in 1789.

## 'Continental System' and the Orders in Council
Napoleon hoped by means of a 'Continental System' of blockades to bankrupt the 'nation of shopkeepers'; any country under his control was forbidden to trade with Britain or accept any vessel which had called at a British port. With the Orders in Council Britain claimed the right to seize neutral shipping bound for French-controlled ports.

## 'Copperheads'
Those Northerners during the Civil War, mostly Democrats, who turned against their own people to support the South, were labelled 'Copperheads' after the Copperhead snake, which strikes without warning.

## Coughlin, Father
Father Charles E. Coughlin the 'Radio Priest', pastor of the Shrine of the Little Flower near Detroit, Michigan, began a series of contentious broadcasts in 1930. In these, and through the medium of his National Union for Social Justice, he spoke out for inflation and isolationism, and against labour, Communists, international financiers, Jews and, above all, President Roosevelt. He was ultimately silenced by his superiors.

## Crédit Mobilier
In 1867 a construction company, known as Crédit Mobilier, was formed by leaders of the Union Pacific Railroad. The promoters managed to divert $20,000,000 into their own pockets. In the hope of preventing a Congressional inquiry large blocks of shares were diverted 'where they would do most good'. In 1872, the New York *Sun* published the names of those involved and a number of prominent politicians were disgraced. Representative James A. Garfield of Ohio never satisfactorily explained his connection with the affair.

## Davis, Jefferson
Jefferson Finis Davis, the first and only President of the Confederate States of America, was born 3 June 1808 at Fairview, Christian (now Todd) County, Kentucky. He was the 10th and youngest child of Samuel Emory Davis and Jane Cook. His mother was of Scottish–Irish descent and reputed to be the niece of Gen Nathaniel Greene of Revolutionary War fame. The family were Baptists. Davis was educated at Transylvania University, Lexington, Kentucky, and West Point Academy from which he graduated as a 2nd Lt in 1828. He spent the next seven years on the frontier, resigning in 1835 to marry the second daughter of Col Zachary Taylor, later 12th President of the United States. From 1835–45 he was a planter in Mississippi before entering the US House of Representatives as Congressman from that state, 1845–6 (resigned).

He was a volunteer Colonel in the Mexican War and became known as 'the hero of Buena Vista'. Elected to the US Senate in 1847, he served until

1851 when he retired. From 1853–7 he served as Secretary of War in the Cabinet of President Franklin Pierce and then, in 1857, he returned to the Senate where he became a champion of slavery and states' rights and an advocate of secession. He resigned in 1861 and became the President of the Confederate States, to which position he was inaugurated (for a six year term) on 22 February 1862. As president he was never able to resolve the essential paradox of the Confederacy: namely, how to reconcile the conflicting demands of the individual states which had seceded from one Union, with the urgent need to transform those same states into a coherent unit. At the end of the war he was imprisoned in Fort Monroe, Virginia, 1865–7. He was indicted for treason, though the charges were dropped in 1869. He died at New Orleans on 6 December 1889 and was buried in Hollywood Cemetery, Richmond, Virginia.

## Democratic Republicans

The Democratic Republican party grew out of the 'anti-Federalists' when George Washington was converted to the Federalists. Adherents believed in individual liberty and an agrarian-based society. They were pro-France and the French Revolution, and anti-British and federal power. The party won the presidential election of 1800 (qv) and controlled Congress from 1801 to 1825. Loyalties became divided between two factions — radical and conservative — and, following the radical victory in 1828 headed by Andrew Jackson, the name was fixed as Democratic.

It won the support of farmers, mechanics and small businessmen. Except for the elections of 1840 and 1848 (qv), it dominated politics until 1860. By that year the party had clearly split into its Northern and Southern wings. During the Civil War most 'War Democrats' supported Lincoln; those who did not were called 'Copperheads' (qv). The Republican association with Reconstruction in the South (1865–77) created a South which was solidly Democratic and the prime source of the party's strength for decades. The development of the agrarian West, with its demands for a lower tariff, urban unrest and dissatisfaction with the Republicans' long reign, put Grover Cleveland into the White House in 1885 (and again in 1893) as the only Democrat between 1861 and 1913. A Republican split led to the election of Woodrow Wilson in 1913; whilst Roosevelt's victory in 1932, the 'New Deal' measures, and World War II, kept the presidency in Democratic hands until 1952. The party continued to dominate Congress during the Republican presidencies of Eisenhower and Nixon and the Democratic hold was not broken until the election of 1980.

## Federalists

Led by the ardently pro-British Alexander Hamilton, the Federalists comprised mainly those who favoured strong federal government — merchants, property owners and industrialists. The party became increasingly led by New Englanders who contemplated secession. It finally expired during the so-called 'Era of Good Feelings'.

## 'filibuster'

A 'filibuster' is the deliberate obstruction of a bill by delaying tactics, especially in the Senate where almost unlimited debate is allowed and the 'closure', bringing debate to an end, is rarely invoked.

### Fort Sumter
The bombardment of this federal fortress, in the harbour of Charleston, South Carolina, at 4.20am on 12 April 1861 is generally held to mark the start of the American Civil War. Brigadier General P. G. T. Beauregard was in command of the attacking Provisional Forces of the Confederate States.

### 'freedom riders'
In 1961, groups of blacks and whites known as 'freedom riders' rode through the Deep South in chartered buses challenging segregation laws on public transport and in restaurants.

### French and Indian War
Usually referred to as the Seven Years' War (1756–63) in English text books, this is the war by which England gained Canada, *inter alia*, from France by the Treaty of Paris (1763).

### Hague Tribunal
The Tribunal was establised in 1899 but, after the creation of the League of Nations, lost its power to the League's Permanent Court of International Justice, known popularly as the World Court, which also sat at the Hague. An American jurist was always a member of the Court though the US was never a member.

### Hamilton, Alexander
The West Indian born Hamilton (1755–1804) served as secretary and *aide de camp* to George Washington. As Secretary of the Treasury, 1789–95, he was the author of several brilliant state papers on national finance and the economic structure. He became leader of America's first political party, the Federalists (qv). His death on 11 July 1804 followed a duel with Aaron Burr (qv).

### Kennedy, Robert, murder of
Robert Francis Kennedy (1925–68), one of the youngest men ever to hold the post of US Attorney General, announced his candidacy for the Democratic presidential nomination in March 1968. In the early hours of 6 June, shortly after it had become clear that he had won the primary in California (and also in South Dakota), he was shot as he walked through the kitchen passageway at the Ambassador Hotel in Los Angeles. His assassin was Sirhan Bishara Sirhan, a 24-year-old Jordanian-born resident of Southern California, who resented Kennedy's support of Israel. Kennedy died later that morning. He was buried near his brother in Arlington National Cemetery, Virginia.

### 'lame-duck' presidency
This name is given to the period during a presidency, originally from November to March, now from November to 20 January, during which an outgoing president still exercises power.

**Lexington and Concord**
On 19 April 1775 Lexington and Concord were the sites of the first bloodshed in what became the War of Independence. Paul Revere, amongst others, roused the Massachusetts countryside against Gen Thomas Gage who was approaching from Boston. British casualties were 273, American 73.

**'logrolled'** see **'pork barrel'**

**Long, Huey**
Known as the 'Louisiana Kingfish', Huey Pierce Long, as governor (1928–31) and then Senator (1931–5), built up a ruthless regime in that state. He achieved much-needed reforms but by methods that invited comparison with contemporary European fascist dictators. He was aiming at the presidency when he was assassinated on 8 September 1935 by Dr Carl A. Weiss.

**Mason-Dixon Line, The**
The line marks the boundaries of the present states of Pennsylvania (north) and Delaware, Maryland and West Virginia (south) and was surveyed in the 1760s by English astronomers Charles Mason and Jeremiah Dixon. Popularly the line designated the boundary between the 'slave' and the 'free' states (though legally after 1820 this was the 'Missouri line') and it is still used to distinguish between North and South.

**Meuse-Argonne offensive**
Lasting for forty days (26 September — 11 November 1918) this was the greatest battle in which American forces had ever been engaged. It involved every available American division, with their English and French allies, and led to a breach of the Hindenburg line and the armistice.

**'Muckraking movement'**
The term was first used by President Theodore Roosevelt in 1906 (alluding to a character in *Pilgrim's Progress*), though the movement of protest and exposure in the US had been inaugurated in 1881. It attracted many brilliant critics of American life and contributed much to the success of the Progressive Movement.

**'Mugwumps'**
The word 'Mugwump' now means any independent voter, but originally referred to those Republicans who refused to support Blaine in the 1884 campaign, bolted the party and voted for Cleveland.

**popular vote**
There is no official tabulation of the popular vote and every source tells a slightly different story. The reason is that the popular votes are cast for Presidential Electors *who do not necessarily receive the same number of votes*. For example in the 1940 Presidential election there were 47 Democratic Electors in New York. Some received 3,251,918 votes whilst others received fewer, eg 3,251,915. Multiply these discrepancies by several hundred (being the number of Democratic Electors throughout the states),

and it becomes possible to see why the popular vote ascribed to F. D. Roosevelt in the 1940 Presidential Election ranges from 27,243,466 in one source, to 27,307,819 in another and to 27,313,041 in a third. All the figures for the popular vote (to 1968) in this book have been culled from a single source: *The Book of Presidents*, Tim Taylor (New York, 1972).

### 'pork barrel'
This term, derived from the practice of setting aside a pork barrel for slaves, embraces the provision of Federal funds for special local projects that benefit only the districts of those who sponsor the bills. Such legislation is usually enacted by '*logrolling*', ie by obtaining reciprocal political help.

### presidential primary elections
Primaries allow voters in certain states to express a choice of party candidate either by a preferential vote or by the election of delegates to a party's National Nominating Convention. Few citizens usually bother to vote but the earliest primaries have an enormous propaganda value and can either eliminate a candidate or enhance his chances.

### President pro tempore of the Senate
This is the presiding officer of the Senate, often the most junior, who officiates at meetings which are not chaired by the vice president.

### Republican Party
The party grew out of an amalgam of disgruntled Democrats and Whigs who opposed the Kansas–Nebraska Act, 1854. The name was chosen to revive memories of the defunct Democratic Republican party of Thomas Jefferson. From the Civil War to 1932 it enjoyed almost uninterrupted political success as the party of 'sound money', a protective tariff and the expansion of industry. It then suffered five successive defeats, 1932–48, before Gen Eisenhower in what were essentially personal victories, carried 'the GOP' — the Grand Old Party — back into the White House (qv).

### 'Square Deal'
President Theodore Roosevelt applied the label 'Square Deal' to those policies which aimed at 'a more substantial equality of opportunity and reward'.

### 'Stalwarts'
During the presidency of Hayes (1877–81) the professional Republican politicians, such as Roscoe Conkling, went under the name of 'Stalwarts'. They sought a third term for Grant in 1880.

### Stamp Act 1765
Imposed by Britain to raise revenue for colonial defence, the Stamp Act of 1765 produced united opposition and the slogan 'No taxation without representation'. It was repealed in 1766 following a boycott of British trade.

### tariff in US history
Apart from the revenue tariff of 1789 tariffs have been aimed at protecting

industry from foreign competition. The tariff of 1828, the 'tariff of abominations', produced threats of secession, leading to the enactment of the Compromise Tariff of 1833 and biennial reductions over the next decade. An upward (Whig) revision in 1842 was followed by (Democratic) modifications in 1846 and these more moderate rates were extended by the tariff of 1857 which virtually made the US a free-trade country. The Morrill Tariff Act of 1861 set the US on the course of protectionism which it followed into the 1930s. The tariff became a political football in the 1880s, with the Democratic party, pledged to reduction, facing the high-tariff Republicans. The tariff rose and fell, but protectionism was the main theme throughout. After the World War I, tariff barriers were also symptomatic of US isolationism. The Trade Agreements Act (1934), allowing the president freedom from specific Congressional action, helped to reduce the political significance of the tariff in twentieth-century politics.

### 'trusts'
'Trusts' were large-scale business combinations, eg in the oil, railroad, whisky and sugar industries. Anti-trust laws were passed after 1890.

### 'Underground Railroad'
Abolitionists in the North and South, some 3,000 all told, established 'stations' along a secret and shifting network of routes to help escaped slaves flee to the 'free' states and to Canada. The 'Underground Railway' spirited away only about 1,000 a year after 1850 but enraged the slave owners.

### Valley Forge
Some 22 miles north-west of Philadelphia, Valley Forge was the scene of Washington's winter quarters from December 1777 to June 1778. It is now a national shrine.

### Voting Rights Act 1965
This Act empowered the Attorney General to appoint federal inspectors to supervise voter registration in states where either some form of literary test existed, or where less than 50% of those of voting age had cast ballots in the 1964 presidential election.

### 'Whisky Ring'
In 1875 a group of distillers and revenue officials in St Louis, Missouri, who became known as the 'Whisky Ring', systematically defrauded the government of millions of dollars of taxes with the connivance of Treasury officials and President Grant's secretary, General Orville Babcock.

### Yorktown
A peninsula in Virginia, Yorktown was the scene of Cornwallis' surrender on 19 October 1781 after the British had been cut off on the seaward side by the French West Indies fleet under Admiral de Grasse.

# FURTHER READING

### The history of the United States

The best one-volume introductory history, with very full bibliographies, is:
Morison, Commager and Leuchtenberg, *A Concise History of the American Republic* (New York, 1977)

### The presidency

Corwin, Edwin S., *The President: Office and Powers, 1787–1957* (New York, 1972)
Cunliffe, Marcus, *American Presidents and the Presidency* (London, 1969)
Hughes, Emmet J., *The Living Presidency* (New York, 1973)
Rossiter, Clinton, *The American Presidency* (London, revised ed 1960)
Schlesinger, Arthur M. Jr, *The Imperial Presidency* (London, 1974)
Hodgson, Godfrey, *All Things to all Men — The False Promise of the Modern American Presidency* (New York, 1980)

### American politics

A concise introduction to the American political scene is:
Nicholas, H. G., *The Nature of American Politics* (Oxford, 1980)

### Biographical and other details of the presidents

*Concise Dictionary of American Biography* (several editions, New York)
Ferris, R. G. (ed), *The National Survey of Historic Sites and Buildings vol XX: The Presidents* (Washington DC, 1977)
Taylor, T., *The Book of Presidents* (New York, 1972)
Freidel, Frank, *Our Country's Presidents* (Washington DC, 1966)
Klapthor, Margaret B., *The First Ladies* (Washington DC, 1979)
*Burke's Presidential Families of the United States of America* (London, 2nd ed 1981)

## Foreign Affairs

Bailey, Thomas A., *The Pugnacious Presidents: White House Warriors on Parade* (London, 1980)

## Presidential elections

Petersen, S., *A Statistical History of American Presidential Elections* (New York, 1963)

## The presidents

*George Washington*

Flexner, James T., *Washington: The Indispensable Man* (London, 1976)

Freeman, Douglas S., *George Washington: A Biography* 7 vols (Fairfield, NJ, 1975); 1 vol abridgement, (ed) R. Harwell London, 1970)

Cunliffe, Marcus, *George Washington: Man and Monument* (London, 1959)

*John Adams*

Smith, Page, *John Adams* 2 vols (Westport, Conn, 1962)

*Thomas Jefferson*

Malone, Dumas, *Jefferson and His Times* 5 vols (Boston, 1948–74)

Schacner, Nathan, *Thomas Jefferson: A Biography* (Cranbury, NJ, 1951)

*James Madison*

Brant, Irving, *The Fourth President: The Life of James Madison* (Indianapolis, 1956)

*James Monroe*

Cresson, William P., *James Monroe* (Conn, 1971)

*John Quincy Adams*

Nevins, Allan (ed), *The Diary of John Quincy Adams* (New York, 1969)

Bemis, Samuel F., *John Quincy Adams and the Union* (New York, 1956)

*Andrew Jackson*

Schlesinger, Arthur M. Jr, *The Age of Jackson* (Boston, 1945)

Van Deusen, G., *The Jacksonian Era* (New York, 1959)

*Martin Van Buren*
Remini, R. V., *Martin Van Buren and the Making of the Democratic Party* (New York, 1959)

*William H. Harrison*
Freeman, Cleaves, *Old Tippecanoe* (New York, 1969)

*John Tyler*
Chitwood, Oliver P., *John Tyler: Champion of the Old South* (New York, 1964)
Seamer, Robert, *And Tyler Too* (New York, 1963)

*James K. Polk*
Gerson, Noel B., *The Slender Reed* (New York, 1965)

*Zachary Taylor*
Hoyt, Edwin P., *Zachary Taylor* (Chicago, 1966)

*Millard Fillmore*
Rayback, Robert J., *Millard Fillmore: Biography of a President* (New York, 1959)

*Franklin Pierce*
Nichols, Roy F., *Franklin Pierce, Young Hickory of the Granite Hills* (Penn, 1964)

*James Buchanan*
Klein, Philip S., *President James Buchanan: A Biography* (Penn, 1962)

*Abraham Lincoln*
Sandburg, Carl, *Abraham Lincoln: The Prairie Years and the War Years* (New York, 1954)
Thomas, Benjamin P., *Abraham Lincoln* (New York, 1952)
Oates, Stephen B., *With Malice Toward None* (London, 1978)

*Andrew Johnson*
McKitrick, Eric I. (ed), *Andrew Johnson: A Profile* (New York, 1969)
Andrew, Robert W., *Andrew Johnson: Plebian and Patriot* (New York, 1970)

*Ulysses S. Grant*
Catton, Bruce, *U S Grant and the American Military Tradition* (Boston, 1954)

Heseltine, William B., *Ulysses S. Grant: Politician* (New York, 1954)

Mc Feely, T., *Grant: A Biography* (New York, 1981)

*Rutherford B. Hayes*
Bernard, Harry, *Rutherford B. Hayes and His America* (New York, 1954)

*James A. Garfield*
Severn, Bill, *Teacher, Soldier, President: The Life of James A. Garfield* (New York, 1964)

*Chester A. Arthur*
Howe, George Frederick, *Chester A. Arthur: A Quarter Century of Machine Politics* (New York, 1934)

*Grover Cleveland*
Nevins, Allan, *Grover Cleveland: A Study in Courage* (New York, 1932)

—— (ed), *Letters of Grover Cleveland* (New York, 1933)

*Benjamin Harrison*
Sievers, Harry J., *Benjamin Harrison: Hoosier Warrior, Statesman, President* (2nd ed, New York, 1960)

*William McKinley*
Leach, Margaret, *In the Days of McKinley* (New York, 1959)

*Theodore Roosevelt*
*Autobiography* (2nd ed, New York, 1926)
Mowry, George E., *The Era of Theodore Roosevelt, 1900–1912* (New York, 1958)
Morris, Edmund, *The Rise of Theodore Roosevelt* (London, 1979)

*William H. Taft*
Pringle, Henry F., *The Life and Times of William Howard Taft* 2 vols (New York, 1939)

*Woodrow Wilson*
*Memoirs of Mrs Woodrow Wilson* (London, 1939)
Link, Arthur S., *Woodrow Wilson and the Progressive Era* (New York, 1954)
Hoover, Herbert, *The Ordeal of Woodrow Wilson* (New York, 1958)
Smith, Gene, *When the Cheering Stopped* (London, 1964)

*Warren G. Harding*
Russell, Francis, *The Shadow of Blooming Grove: Warren G. Harding in His Times* (New York, 1968; pub London, 1969, as *President Harding: His Life and Times 1865–1923*)

*Calvin Coolidge*
*Autobiography* (London, 1929)
White, William H., *A Puritan in Babylon: The Story of Calvin Coolidge* (New York, 1938)
Fuess, Claude M., *Calvin Coolidge, The Man from Vermont* (Westport, Conn, 1977)

*Herbert Hoover*
*Memoirs* 3 vols (London, 1951–5)
Warren, Harris G., *Herbert Hoover and the Great Depression* (New York, 1967)

*Franklin D. Roosevelt*
Burns, James MacGregor, *Roosevelt: The Lion and the Fox* (New York, 1956)
—— *Roosevelt: The Soldier of Freedom* (New York, 1970)
Gunther, John, *Roosevelt in Retrospect* (New York, 1950)
Schlesinger, Arthur M. Jr, *The Age of Roosevelt* 2 vols (Boston, 1957, 1960)
Woods, John A., *Roosevelt and Modern America* (EUP, 1970)

*Harry S. Truman*
*Memoirs* 2 vols (New York, 1955, 1956)
Phillips, Cabell, *The Truman Presidency* (New York, 1966)
Miller, Merle, *Plain Speaking: Conversations with Harry S. Truman* (New York, 1974)

*Dwight D. Eisenhower*
*Memoirs* 2 vols (New York, 1963, 1965)
Childs, Marquis, *Eisenhower: Captive Hero* (London, 1959)

John F. Kennedy
Schlesinger, Arthur M. Jr, *A Thousand Days: John F. Kennedy In The White House* (Boston, 1965)
Sorensen, Theodore C., *Kennedy* (New York, 1965)
Longford, Lord, *Kennedy* (London, 1976)

*Lyndon B. Johnson*
Kearns, Doris, *Lyndon Johnson and the American Dream* (New York, 1976)

Miller, Merle, *Lyndon: An Oral Biography* (New York, 1980)

*Richard M. Nixon*
*RN: The Memoirs of Richard Nixon* (New York, 1978)
Nixon, Richard M., *Six Crises* (New York, 1962)
White, Theodore, *Breach of Faith: The Fall of Richard Nixon* (New York, 1975)
Longford, Lord, *Nixon: A Study in Extremes of Fortune* (London, 1980)

*Gerald R. Ford*
*A Time to Heal: The Autobiography of Gerald R. Ford* (London, 1979)
Ter Horst, Jerald F., *Gerald Ford: Past . . . Present . . . Future* (New York, 1974)

*Jimmy Carter*
Carter, Jimmy, *Why Not The Best?* (New York, 1975)
Glad, Betty, *Jimmy Carter: From Plains to the White House* (New York, 1978; pub London, 1980, as *Jimmy Carter in Search of the Great White House*)

*Ronald Reagan*
Reagan, Ronald, *Where's the Rest of Me?* (New York, 1965; pub London, 1981, as *My Early Life or Where's the Rest of Me?*)
Boyarsky, Bill, *The Rise of Ronald Reagan* (New York, 1968)
Brown, Edmund G. Sr, *Reagan and Reality: The Two Californias* (New York, 1970)
Hobbs, Charles D., *Ronald Reagan's Call to Action: Realistic Democracy* (New York, 1976)
Von Damm, Helene, *Sincerely, Ronald Reagan* (Ottawa, Ill, 1976)
Smith *et al, Reagan the Man, the President* (Oxford, 1981)

# ACKNOWLEDGEMENTS

I am indebted to the then Warden, Sir William Hayter, and the Fellows of New College, Oxford, for electing me to a Schoolmaster Fellowship in 1976 which provided me with the necessary leisure and intellectual stimulation required to begin contemplating this book.

I have received enormous help from patient librarians at Rhodes House, in Oxford, the Embassy of the United States of America, in London, and the Library of Congress in Washington DC.

Mr C. P. Hill read the book in manuscript and corrected many errors both of fact and interpretation. Those which remain are my responsibility. I am deeply grateful to my good friend and colleague Peter Greed for his companionship during a visit to Washington DC, at Easter 1980; to Miss M. Millard and Mrs Julia Davis who typed the manuscript; and to my long-suffering family to whom I dedicate this volume.

D.V.C.
Baydon
*February 1981*

# INDEX

*Note:* In this index, *n* indicates a reference in the Further Notes

137-41; Tariff A. (1883), 141;
Presidential Succession A. (1886),
144; Electoral Count A. (1887), 144;
Inter-state Commerce A. (1887),
146; Disability Pension A. (1890),
151; Sherman Anti-Trust A. (1890),
151; McKinley Tariff A. (1890), 151,
158; Sherman Silver Purchase A.
(1890), 151; Wilson-Gorman Tariff
A. (1894), 154; Meat Inspection A.
(1906), 167; Pure Food and Drugs
A. (1906), 167; Underwood Tariff
A. (1914), 178; Federal Reserve A.
(1914), 178; Farm Loan A. (1916),
178; Presidential Succession A.
(1947), 207; Trade Expansion A.
(1962), 226; Education A. (1965),
236; Medical Care A. (1965), 236;
Voting Rights A. (1965), 237; Civil
Rights A. (1964), 237, *n*
Congress, United States, Library of, 36-7
Constitution, United States, 7, 40, 62;
Amendments, *n*; Amendments I-X,
19, 41; Amendment V, 31; Amendment XI, 24; Amendment XII, 31, 76;
Amendment XIII, 114, 117, 119, 237;
Amendment XIV, 117, 120, 175, 237;
Amendment XV, 123, 237; Amend-
ment XVIII, 175; Amendment XX,
193, 201; Amendment XXI, 199;
Amendment XXII, 207, 213; Amend-
ment XXIV, 233; Amendment XXV,
77, 233, 250; Federalist Papers, 41;
George Washington and, 20-1; new
C., 33, 40-1
Conventions, 10-11
Coolidge, John Calvin, 182, 187-91;
aims, 190; character, 191; early life,
188; election (1924), 187-8; foreign
policy, 191; method of leadership,
190; non-activity of, 189, 190
Coughlin, Father Charles E., *n*
Crédit Mobilier, *n*
Cuba, 95, 99, 165, 219, 227-8

Davis, Jefferson, *n*
Declaration of Independence, 25, 32
Democratic Party, 66, 69, 256; 'Barnburners', 70; convention (1932), 201;
convention (1956), 225; election
(1840), 72, 73; election (1852), 103-4;
election (1912), 176-7; election (1968),
243; 'Expansionism', 83; F. Pierce
and, 97, 100; 'Jacksonian Democracy',
54, 62; J.K. Polk and, 83, 85; North/
South wings, 105; slavery and, 88

Democratic Republicans, 34, *n*
Douglas, Stephen A., 10, 91, 94, 100,
105, 110, 111

Economy, 47, 68, 104, 154, 159: *see also*
under individual presidents' domestic
policy
Eisenhower, David Dwight, 214;
achievements, 220; army career,
216-17; criticism of, 220; domestic
policy, 218; early life, 215-16; election
(1952), 214-15; election (1956), 219;
Farewell Address, 220; foreign
policy, 218-19; method of government, 217-18; retirement, 220; tribute
to, 221
Electoral College, 8-10, 61, 201, 243,
245
Executive Mansion, *see* White House

Federalist Party, 26, 27, 28, 29, 34, 35,
41, 46, 52, *n*
Fillmore, Millard, 92-5; compromise
measures, 94; early life, 93; foreign
policy, 95; later career, 95; reputation,
94; vice president, 88, 93; White
House, 95
Ford, Gerald R., 10, 11, 110, 241, 247,
249-53; character, 250; domestic
policy, 252-3; early life, 250-1; election
(1976), 25; foreign policy, 252;
pardons Nixon, 252; vice president,
252; wife, 251
Foreign Policy, 14; of G. Washington,
21; of J. Adams, 27; of T. Jefferson,
35-6; of J. Madison, 42-3; of J.
Monroe, 48-9, 53; of J.Q. Adams,
54; of A. Jackson, 63; of M. Van
Buren, 69; of J. Tyler, 78; of J.K.
Polk, 84-5; of M. Fillmore, 95; of A.
Johnson, 120-1; of U. Grant, 128; of
R. Hayes, 134; of A. Garfield, 142; of
B. Harrison, 151; of G. Cleveland,
154; of W. McKinley, 159-60; of T.
Roosevelt, 167; of W. Wilson, 178; of
C. Coolidge, 191; of H. Hoover, 197;
of F.D. Roosevelt, 203-4; of H.S.
Truman, 210-12; of D.D. Eisenhower,
218-19; of J.F. Kennedy, 227-30; of
R.M. Nixon, 245, 246-7; of G.R.
Ford, 252; of J.E. Carter, 259
Fort Sumter, *n*
Founding Fathers, 7, 8, 14, 33, 41, 76
France, 27, 28, 33, 35, 42, 63
Franklin, Benjamin, 20, 25, 33

288